CUBA

CUBA

A CULTURAL HISTORY

Alan West-Durán

REAKTION BOOKS

For Ester, always

Published by Reaktion Books Ltd
Unit 32, Waterside
44–48 Wharf Road
London N1 7UX, UK
www.reaktionbooks.co.uk

First published 2017
Copyright © Alan West-Durán 2017

Printed and bound in Great Britain
by TJ International, Padstow, Cornwall

A catalogue record for this book is available from the British Library

ISBN 978 1 78023 839 5

Contents

Contents

Introduction

Cuba is a rare and fascinating place. In a world where revolutionary socialism seems an almost quaint reminder of the Cold War thirty years ago, the island remains one of the few nations on the planet guided by a Communist party, still committed to fighting imperialism, opposed to the injustices of globalization and wedded to the dream of one day building a classless society, albeit in a distant future. But Cuba is more than a struggling socialist country; it is a nation with a complex and turbulent history and a rich and varied culture. This book is an exploration of Cuban culture as a way to tell the story of Cuba's history. It is neither a timeline narrative of Cuban history, nor is it a traditional history of Cuban culture going genre by genre; instead, I invite the reader to enter Cuban history from the perspective of the island's uniquely creative cultural forms. Imagine as well that Cuba's flowing and overlapping culture and history is like the Yoruba's description of their culture, as a 'river that never rests'. This book will trace that restless river as it ebbs and flows with the power, beauty and longings of its culture and history.

Cuba's history has been lived under the shadow of three superpowers: Spain (for four centuries, Cuba being Spain's last colony in the region), the u.s. (for sixty years) and the ussr (for thirty years). One could argue that there is a fourth superpower – from below: Cuba's African heritage, a rich cultural legacy devalued by a history of enslavement and offering wellsprings for resistance, which has profoundly affected its music, religious practices and social mores. Because of these power struggles, Cubans have long historical memories. During its colonial period (1490s to 1898) Cuba went from being a strategic military outpost because of its geographic location, to a somewhat forgotten backwater to a great sugar producer, taking the role that Haiti had previously occupied and lost after the Haitian Revolution (1791–1804). During the nineteenth century Cuba became one of the largest importers of slaves in history, and this influx of almost a million Africans would indelibly change the country's culture. Even as a Spanish colony, the island's relationship with the U.S. was strong; and before the U.S. intervention in the Spanish-American-Cuban War (1898) the U.S. was the island's largest trading partner and had made several attempts to purchase the island from Spain or annex it through military adventurers known as *filibusteros*. During the nineteenth century Cuba was viewed as a ripe fruit ready to drop into the hands of a benevolent imperial overlord, then as a woman (needing rescue from Spanish colonialism), then in the first decades of the twentieth century as a child learning to ride a bicycle, then junior partner in the Caribbean and Latin America (1930s to '50s), and finally, implacable adversary and Communist menace after 1959. And beyond these metaphors U.S. views and desires have often been imposed by force.

The post-1959 period has been fraught with considerable drama: nationalizations, the Bay of Pigs invasion, nuclear showdown, international commitments to socialist, decolonization and anti-apartheid movements that put Cuba at odds with the West, harsh exchanges at the UN and often bitter rhetoric. However, since the fall of the Soviet Union, Cuba's adversarial role has been diminished. Compared to, say, 1989, we can point to the following: the USSR no longer exists and Cuba's military presence in the Third World is almost non-existent compared to thirty years ago; there are no guerrilla insurgencies in the Americas that would cause friction (as happened in the 1980s under Reagan with Central America), and it has been more than twenty years since the last major crisis related to immigration (1994).

In fact, Cuba's new travel rules, effective since January 2013, allow Cubans to travel for up to two years before returning home, eliminating red tape in obtaining permission to travel. There are many areas where Cuba and the U.S. are either cooperating or could improve on what is already being done: science, health, education, sports, climate change, disaster response, weather-storm data and cultural exchange.

Since President Obama's policy statement of 17 December 2014 and his visit to Havana in March 2016, many of the barriers to relations between the two countries are gradually being dismantled (by the lifting of travel restrictions, banking and financial obstacles, removal of Cuba from lists of countries that support terrorism, educational exchanges and so on). There had been significant changes in Cuba before Obama's new policy of 2014. It had been years since Fidel Castro stepped down from daily governance of the island (in 2006, and definitively since 2008, when he officially stepped down), and recently Raúl Castro announced his intention to relinquish the presidency in 2018, arguing that in the future Cuban presidents should only serve for two consecutive terms. There has been a loosening of travel restrictions for Cubans, a greater willingness to introduce market incentives allowing small businesses to function, as well as the ability for Cubans to privately sell their cars and residences. Scholars and interested observers have been speaking about a Cuban transition from a command economy to one under less state control, often drawing on examples from the former Soviet bloc but, more significantly, the recent historical experiences of China and Vietnam.

What do these changes say about the fate of Cuban socialism? Is Cuba still tied to the discarded notions of twentieth-century state socialism? How does Cuba both reflect and differ from that model? Is Cuba still a viable alternative to neo-liberalism? When I use the term state socialism I refer to the twentieth-century model pioneered by the USSR and used by other countries as well: those of Eastern Europe which became part of the Soviet bloc, in addition to China, Vietnam and North Korea, as well as some African countries for a short period of time. I find the term state socialism more useful than terms like the Soviet model or Soviet-style socialism, because each country that used the model adapted it in a different way, and did not merely blindly copy the Soviet experience. Hence we find different types of socialist states like the USSR, China, Yugoslavia, Vietnam and Cuba, which, despite their many commonalities, did create different paths towards building socialism. Just as capitalism is not monolithic in its history, so different in England, the U.S., France and more recently Brazil, Mexico, South Korea, Saudi Arabia and so on, neither is socialism, nor societies run by Communist parties. This being said, there are aspects to twentieth-century socialist experiments that do share common features: (1) state control over the economy (instead of social control, as argued for by Marx); (2) a one-party state with lack of political pluralism, with a reduced presence of civil society; (3) because of points 1 and 2 a blurring of the distinction between party, state and, often, the leader of the party; (4) a lack of worker or intellectual self-management in their respective workplaces; (5) state control of media, education and science, with a strong ideological slant; (6) centralized economic planning along non-market lines as an alternative to 'the anarchy of the market' and the economic domination of the many by the few. These features define what I call state socialism. Cuba is a country that fits this definition in many ways, but because of its pre-1959 history and culture it offers unique elements as a Caribbean society that is strongly African-influenced – what Che Guevara himself described as 'socialism with pachanga', a lively, infectiously danceable Cuban musical style bringing together son montuno and merengue, often with mischievous lyrics.

In interpreting Cuba, and keeping in mind its legacy related to state socialism, it is important to remember the words of Alexei Yurchak, a Russian scholar, speaking about what he calls the binaries of Soviet socialism. This structured terminology comes with a series of assumptions that can be troublesome, if not reductive:

> oppression and resistance, repression and freedom, the state
> and the people, official economy and second economy, official

culture and counterculture, totalitarian language and counter-language, public self and private self, truth and lie, reality and dissimulation, morality and corruption, and so on.[1]

First of all, some of these binaries can be used to describe capitalist societies as well. In a society like Cuba, these binaries function in a continuum, with many grey areas that Cubans negotiate with enormous skill and ingenuity. In any society, binaries serve a function of control, be it social, ideological or political; by doing so, these binaries obscure nuance, something valuable in understanding Cuba. Cubans love to subvert binaries, and do so with considerable wit and irreverence. Cubans are called bad Catholics because they often fail to adhere to the strict moral code of the Church, particularly regarding sexuality. Cubans are also said to be bad socialists, since the socialist code of ethics can also be rather strict. (As a famously erotic Spanish love song that equates physical and divine bliss says, 'You don't need to die to go to heaven.') Does this mean that Cubans are morally lax and socially irresponsible, as a colonizing Catholic Church implied before 1959? No, it just means that they live their belief systems, spirituality and ideology cognizant of the complexities of life, aware that noble aspirations need to be reshaped by daily struggles.

Over the next few chapters we will see how Cuba adheres to or differs from this state socialist model, and how its culture both modifies and coincides with these parameters. Culturally speaking, Cuba is a country with a significant literary tradition, world-renowned music, a world-class national ballet company, a powerful and vibrant legacy in the visual arts and a modest but important film industry. It is also home to syncretic Afro-Cuban religions that are an enduring legacy making its culture unique. Cuba may not have a Nobel laureate in literature, but writers such as José Martí, José Lezama Lima, Nicolás Guillén, Alejo Carpentier, Virgilio Piñera, Reinaldo Arenas and Severo Sarduy are the equal of any authors anywhere. Musically speaking, the country has been blessed with composer-musicians like Ignacio Cervantes, Ernesto Lecuona, Miguel Matamoros, Ignacio

Piñeiro, Amadeo Roldán, Leo Brouwer, Israel 'Cachao' López, Juan Formell and Chucho Valdés; this is a very short list of what could go on for pages. Artists like Wifredo Lam, Mario Carreño, Amelia Peláez, Carlos Enríquez, Ana Mendieta, José Bedia, Tania Bruguera and Luis Cruz Azaceta are in major collections and museums around the world. Film-makers like Santiago Alvarez, Tomás Gutiérrez Alea and Fernando Pérez have exhibited their work in major festivals, delighting both audiences and critics. Essayists and thinkers like Félix Varela, Martí, Enrique José Varona, Jorge Mañach, Fernando Ortiz, Walterio Carbonell, Cintio Vitier, Lezama, Lydia Cabrera and Juan Marinello have offered great insights into Cuban society, history and culture.

The intricate layers of Cuban culture have taken centuries to create and the island's culture was forged under colonialism and slavery (under Spain), under dependent capitalism heavily tied to the U.S., and Marxian socialism, first under Soviet tutelage, and later under post-Cold War conditions after the collapse of the USSR in 1991. Added to this are the profound West and Central African influences that underlie many aspects of Cuban society. Many of these strands of Cuban culture preceded the Cuban Revolution of 1959 and still shape Cuba, although not unchanged, of course.

Cuba is widely renowned for its creative arts and, consistent with its idea of itself as a major actor on the world stage, Cuban music, literature, film and dance have been influential and recognized far beyond the borders of the island. Not only do the arts reflect the crossroads of cultural encounters over the course of the island's history, they themselves become a way of representing and transforming these struggles through creative forms – what ethnographer Fernando Ortiz termed 'transculturation', a process that emerges in historical contexts and strives to address/negotiate/resolve them. In a previous book, *Tropics of History: Cuba Imagined*, I took the work of several emblematic Cuban authors (Lezama, Carpentier, Piñera, Sarduy, Morejón Loynaz) and examined certain tropes or images they used to define Cuba. Five major areas were identified: 'history

(Cuban and otherwise), religious or mystical thought, ideology and politics (Marxism), literature (both Cuban and world); and landscape'.[2] I used the tropes and metaphors not only as representation but also as a generative matrix that expresses important aspects of collective reality; that is, tropes are not just the ingenious expression of an artist but a trans-subjective experience tied to a collective reality and a shared history.

In *Cuba: A Cultural History*, the focus on creative arts as a means of representing Cuban history is more expansive, since it covers not only more writers and thinkers, but also includes music, the plastic arts, film, performance art and photography, as well as the importance of Afro-Cuban religions on these genres. However, the emphasis will be on Cuban writers, artists and thinkers and how they help us understand the island's history and culture, whether they live there or abroad. By examining those generative matrices from the twentieth and twenty-first centuries, a complex portrait emerges of the 'Cuban adventure', one that Carlos Franqui defines as 'without fear of the unexpected, the magical, the impossible, of the unknown'.[3]

In the conclusion, I discuss some of the issues still facing Cuban culture in the wake of the Obama visit in March 2016 and the future course of Cuban society. Is Cuba still an alternative to neo-liberal paradigms of development? Will Cuba perhaps come up with a socialist model that is different from China or Vietnam? What role will Cuban culture play in this future?

ONE

Building a New Cultural Foundation (1898–1930)

Freedom? In the clouds. Equality? Underground.
Fraternity? Nowhere to be found.

Enrique José Varona, 1927

In 1900, Cuba was in a unique and ambiguous situation. The island had been Spain's last colony in Latin America, its independence coming some eight decades after Mexico's. It had just concluded a second war of independence (1895–8) only to see the U.S. step in and deal the final military blow to Spain, then militarily occupy the island for four years before turning the country over to a civilian administration and its first president, Tomás Estrada Palma, sworn in on 20 May 1902. The war had devastated Cuba: it lost some 300,000 people, though not all on the battlefield – many perished due to disease and starvation; 100,000 small farms were destroyed, as well as three thousand livestock ranches and seven hundred coffee *fincas*. The number of sugar mills had decreased by 80 per cent, coffee production was down by four-fifths of 1894 levels, and 90 per cent of the island's cattle and livestock had been lost. Half the schools had closed down, illiteracy was at 60 per cent and only 1 per cent had a higher education. Overall, over 50 per cent of whites could read, but for people of colour the figure was 28 per cent. Slavery had ended in 1886, less than twenty years before independence.[1]

Cuba was faced with the daunting task of rebuilding its economy, creating a new political system and repairing its fractured society. Unlike other Latin American countries, Cuba received enormous help from the u.s. and the Spanish population of the island, who did not leave when colonial rule ended. In fact, Spanish immigration to Cuba was constant and significant: some 300,000 between 1880 and 1910 and more than 400,000 between 1914 and 1930. This immigration not only formed part of Spain's colonial policy before 1898; it was also the desire of Cuban elites to whiten the country. The Spanish dominated in the areas of small commerce and the u.s. began to take control of large sugar estates, infrastructure, banking and communications.

One of the key elements of the new relationship with the u.s. was the Platt Amendment (1901) and other treaties (1903) that permitted the u.s. to lease Guantánamo, where a naval base was built; it is still currently under control of the u.s. The Platt Amendment was an amendment included in the Cuban constitution that allowed the u.s. to intervene – including militarily – if its interests were threatened. The u.s. did intervene on several occasions until the Platt Amendment was abrogated in 1934.

Cuba began its new life as a republic with great aspirations of fulfilling its hopes as an independent nation, wanting to build a society that Antonio Maceo, Carlos Manuel de Céspedes, Máximo Gómez and other pro-independence patriots had dreamed about. One of those patriots, who had spent many years in exile, was a gifted poet, José Martí.

José Martí: Myth and Messiah

Cuba lost its two greatest poets before the turn of the twentieth century – José Martí in battle, Julián del Casal to tuberculosis. Martí was 41, Casal thirty. Cuba's other great poet of the nineteenth century, José María Heredia, died at 36. Martí (1853–1895) is probably the best-known figure of Cuba's history, a poet, journalist, polymath, fiery orator, political activist, revolutionary and one of the great fighters for Cuban independence. Despite having Spanish parents, at a very young age Martí grew to abhor slavery and the colonial regime that shackled Cuba's freedom. Imprisoned for his political beliefs at sixteen, he was deported to Spain where he studied, while keenly following the events of the Ten Years War (1868–78); then he went to Mexico and Guatemala before returning to Cuba in 1878. His political activities landed him in prison the following year and he was again deported to Spain. He escaped, and finally made his way to New York (1880). Martí did not return to Cuba until 1895, as political head of the Cuban independence forces, and tragically died in his first battle, only a month after returning from many years in exile. His first book of poems, *Ismaelillo* (1882), written in Caracas, is one of the first books of the *modernista* movement, not to be confused with European-U.S. modernism. Latin American *modernismo* was a cosmopolitan, highly aesthetic, deeply musical (especially the poetry) movement that lasted roughly from 1880 to 1918. The *modernistas*, almost all from Latin America, renovated the Spanish language and gave Latin American literature an ascendancy in Spanish-language letters which persists until today. Among its exemplary writers were Rubén Darío (Nicaragua), Manuel Gutiérrez Najera (Mexico), Amado Nervo (Mexico), José Asunción Silva (Colombia) and Martí's compatriot Julián del Casal.

Martí wrote tirelessly for newspapers, the bulk of his work being for this medium, but his language was a rich, highly metaphorical cultural journalism that is rarely practised today. From his exile in New York he sought to unite all the forces to bring about Cuban independence. Wherever there were Cubans, be it New York, Tampa, Mexico, New Orleans, Caracas or Costa Rica, Martí spoke to them and helped fundraise for the liberation of Cuba. By 1892 he had created the Cuban Revolutionary Party (CRP) as the political instrument to lead the independence struggle. Martí, along with veteran generals from the Ten Years War such as Antonio Maceo and Máximo Gómez, launched a new war of independence, which began in February 1895. Martí arrived in April and was killed in his first skirmish on 19 May 1895.

When Martí died, he was not well known in Cuba, having been in exile for the last fifteen years, with virtually all his publications printed outside Cuba. His reputation grew after his death and continues to do so. His mythic stature began to spread quickly and a Cuban song from the early 1900s poses one of the great what-ifs of Cuban history: what if Martí had not died in 1895? The core lyrics state the case forcefully:

> *Martí no debió morir*
> *Ay de morir*
> *Si fuera maestro del día*
> *Otro gallo cantaría*
> *La patria se salvaría*
> *Y Cuba sería feliz*

> Martí shouldn't have died
> Oh! Not have died
> If he were in charge now
> It would be a different tune
> The fatherland would be saved
> Cuba would be happy.[2]

There is no doubt that Martí should not have died so young – his literary and political talents were desperately needed by the young republic – but what about the 'what if'? If he had lived, would Cuba's fate had been radically different? Would the fatherland have been saved? Would Cuba be happy? Cuba was a society fractured along lines of class, race and gender. Would Martí have been able to resolve those divisions? What about the military and economic presence of the U.S. in Cuba? Could that presence be willed away by Martí and his followers? Cuba was a mono-product economy with the sugar industry in the hands of large landowners, many of them foreign: would Martí have curtailed their influence or nationalized them?

As Lillian Guerra has pointed out, the Martí myth has created a sacrament for Cuban society, a civic religion if you will, depicting Martí as mystic, messiah and mediator. His mysticism is that of patriotic duty and a vision of a free country, messiah because he is a selfless leader who will deliver Cubans to a better future, and mediator because he unites all Cubans, which he stated famously in a speech as 'with all and for all'. Martí's comments were made with Cuba's racial history in mind, something that had caused divisions within the separatist movement and ultimately defeat in previous failed efforts. Martí's appeal to all Cubans still holds, and Fidel Castro and his bitterest enemies all rally to the Martí banner.

There are many different Martís according to political orientation. There is a liberal Martí who is a pluralist, seen to be above class and race, pragmatic, nationalist and secular (believing in the separation of Church and State), perhaps leaning towards social democracy. Some *martianos* are more centrist-conservative, saying that Martí was protective of social hierarchies, defended private property (and small business owners), was pro-capitalist, respected religious belief and was also a nationalist. Then there is a liberal revolutionary Martí who is resolutely anti-imperialist, nationalist, identified with the people ('con los pobres de la tierra quiero mi suerte echar'; I cast my lot with the poor, as he said in his 'simple verses'), but not necessarily socialist or Communist, with a strong social democratic component. Finally, there is a revolutionary Martí with all the previous revolutionary traits, but further radicalized in support of a utopian classless society, with little private property, a powerful state and a highly unified political system, who has been greatly popularized since 1959.

Throughout the twentieth century, when social observers, politicians and activists – whether in government or in opposition – wanted to lament the island's economic, social and political problems, they usually evoked Martí, claiming those they were criticizing, whether oligarchs, politicians, journalists or ideologues, were betraying

Martí's ideals. Those claims were made from the different political orientations described previously, but usually centred around issues of sovereignty, which under the Platt Amendment was a constant refrain in Cuban discourse for over three decades.

Julián del Casal and Art as Transfiguration

There are few statues – if any – of Casal (1863–1893) in Cuba, and certainly not one in every school, as is the case with Martí. Casal died younger than Martí and not in battle but due to illness. His mother died when he was five, his father when he was 22. Some say he never recovered from his mother's death, and death is a recurrent theme in his poetry. He was sickly and reclusive as a child, adolescent and adult: poetry, art and beauty became his only refuge and salvation. Considered 'queer' in the current meaning of the word, Casal was an introvert and given to gloomy, nihilistic observation; his work does not revel in nature, patriotism or political struggle, but focuses on art and beauty, and also suffering, loneliness, the bewitching and dark elements of desire, dreams and the lure of faraway places. Because of his health (tuberculosis), he could ill afford the demands of political activism, much less the rigours of armed combat.

It is tempting – and easy – to set up Martí and Casal as polar opposites, and many have done so. If Martí lived in exile, Casal lived as an internal exile; if Martí was a public intellectual and a political figure, Casal was a private aesthete. One could continue this set of differences: Martí was a political activist, exhibited traditional virility and was heterosexual; Casal was more private, 'feminized' and queer. Martí believed in transparency, worshipped nature and transcended the literary, becoming a national hero: Casal was oblique, loved masks, treasured art over nature, was a poet *maudit* and totally embraced the literary and artifice. Martí eagerly sought sacrifice (in the patriotic sense), duty and health; Casal was enthralled by sensuality, pleasure, and was sick most of his life. Martí had a family, is almost always depicted as serious, and is popular; Casal was an orphan, cultivated frivolity and was seen as somewhat elitist.

While this binary schema simplifies matters, it does offer a rough outline of how Cuban cultural life has emerged from the tension of these binaries over more than a century along the lines of ethics versus aesthetics, politics versus art (or the nature of political art), national expression versus personal authenticity, public discourse versus individual creativity. These threads, or obsessions, crop up again and again in Cuban society. From the perspective of queer studies and their reading of Casal, one can establish an entire genealogy that begins with Casal and continues with the likes of Emilio Ballagas, Mercedes Matamoros, Hernández Catá, Carlos Montenegro, Ofelia Rodríguez Castro, Lezama Lima, Virgilio Piñera, José Rodríguez Feo, Lorenzo García Vega, Antón Arrufat, Severo Sarduy, Reinaldo Arenas and more recently writers like Abilio Estévez, Ena Lucía Portela, Norge Espinosa, Elías Miguel Muñoz and Achy Obejas, among others. This queer perspective (on Casal and others) has been joined by alternative analytic approaches (race, women/gender, youth subcultures, Cubans abroad) as the island delves into more inclusive and complex attempts at defining *cubanía* (the epitome of Cuban-ness), nationhood and culture.

One of Casal's most cited poems contains the following quatrain:

> Love, fatherland, family, glory, status
> Dreams of flaming fantasy
> Like open white lotuses in the mud
> You dwelled in my soul only for a day.[3]

These verses could never have been penned by Martí, and the poem, appropriately enough, is titled 'Nihilism'. If Martí exalted in the simplicity and charm of nature – in an Emersonian sort of rapture – Casal spoke of the city, beautiful clothing, preferring the glitter of diamonds to the light of the stars ('I have the impure love of the cities').[4] Casal's work expresses the unambiguous notion of the autonomy of art, a love of the artifice (and artificiality) of human creativity as embodied by the artist, and it is linked to pleasure, sensuality and the dark side of the psyche. His poetic mentors were Baudelaire, Huysmans, Verlaine, Rimbaud and Lautréamont. He carried on a correspondence with Gustave Moreau (1828–1898) and the French painter's lush, symbolic style, laden with mythological references, appealed to the young Cuban's imagination. His second (and last) book published while he was alive, *Nieve* (Snow; 1892), includes a cycle of ten poems called 'My Ideal Museum', all based on paintings by Moreau, mostly works of the 1860s based on mythological figures (Prometheus, Galatea, Hercules, Venus, Jupiter and so on).

Casal used two different pseudonyms, Hernani and Alceste, for his prose work, which he published in different periodicals. The first is a character from a Victor Hugo play, first staged in 1830, and subsequently made into an opera by Verdi, *Ernani* (1844). Alceste was a Greek princess, and also the subject of several operas, the most notable by Glück (1767) and Lully (1674). Hernani, a male character, was a bandit, Alceste a woman who is willing to sacrifice herself for her husband. Both Hernani and Alceste are willing to die for love (Hernani actually does), but what is important in the case of Casal is that Hernani is a social outlaw, albeit with noble intentions towards Doña Sol, the woman he loves; as for choosing the name of a woman (Alceste), it makes Casal a gender outlaw, so to speak.

Many scholars have written about the unequivocal erotic references in Casal's work. Lezama said the following: 'Sexuality in Casal is urgent and decisive.'[5] Some critics have pointed out that Casal's erotic poetry contains few references to women, and seems to have an ambiguity, as well as a 'twisted' fascination with transgression and 'aberrant' behaviour (homosexuality, masochism, asceticism). Still others have talked about Casal's sense of guilt, his 'neurotic-ness', his talk of 'open secrets', which, combined with his illness and pessimism, shape his sexuality as fluid. There is nothing in his work (poetry, prose, letters) that makes direct reference to his being gay or bisexual, but all of the elements justify a 'queer reading' of his work.[6] This queering of Casal helps us understand some of the cultural complexities of Cuba and how certain voices have been either silenced or not given their true place within the cultural mainstream of the island.

Decades later, Virgilio Piñera (1912–1979) would join the fray (Martí versus Casal) and insist that Casal was the better poet, one with a project (aesthetic, obviously, since Martí had a political project), who concentrated on the crafting of poetry. Piñera was not dismissing Martí as a poet – on the contrary – but he argues in favour of Casal for the autonomy of art, which less generous critics mistook for a defence of art for art's sake. Piñera's essay, from 1960, reprises what others have defined as the differences between the ethical *modernista* (Martí, Rodó, González Prada) and the aesthetic *modernista* (Darío, Asunción Silva, Casal). A year after Piñera's essay, the ideological undercurrents of these positions would shape the meeting between Fidel Castro and a group of Cuban intellectuals in June 1961. As for Piñera, his queerness and resolute defence of the autonomy of art – even if his own work was socially mordant – was to bring him difficulties with the revolutionary cultural bureaucracy.

The ethical–aesthetic divide can be a useful yet simplistic opposition with regard to Cuba. In the case of Martí, many argue that he was the perfect synthesis of these two tendencies, but his canonical status as Cuba's literary star of the nineteenth century is due more to extra-literary factors such as his speeches, essays, activism and ultimate sacrifice for the liberation of Cuba. Casal did not go to jail for his political beliefs, nor was he forced into exile, nor did he negotiate with the great rebel generals like Maceo and Gómez, nor was he the founder of the Cuban Revolutionary Party, nor, of course, did he die on the battlefield. At stake here is not the 'dethroning' of Martí, nor his place in Cuban history, which is more than assured, but of trying to visualize a wider array of forces at play in Cuban culture and history that need to include less canonical voices.

Martí's example has precedent in nineteenth-century Latin America, with figures who were simultaneously writers, journalists, legislators, writers of constitutions, scholars, diplomats and politicians all rolled into one. Intellectuals like Andrés Bello (Chile), Eugenio María de Hostos (Puerto Rico), Domingo Sarmiento (Argentina) and Justo Sierra (México) were multifaceted (and tireless!) in their talents, and undertook with equal brilliance writings on literature, constitutional debates or governance. In part, it was the dire situation of the new republics, emerging from three centuries of colonialism, faced with the daunting tasks of building new nations, that motivated individuals to become writers, journalists, social scientists, politicians and legal scholars. Martí was similar to these figures, even if, due to Cuba's movement for independence some half a century after most of Latin America's, he came later.

He remains the prototype of the civic-minded author, the public intellectual and the poet-warrior, and many prominent intellectuals of the Republican period revisit Martí as biographical subject (Mañach), as emblem of moral and civic virtue (Varona), as anti-imperialist thinker (Marinello), as champion of a colour-blind Cuba (Ortiz) or as a writer and forger of national identity (Vitier). Historian Rafael Rojas has called Martí 'our imaginary monarch'.[7] He adds:

> For more than a hundred years the cult of Martí has gradually been losing its original republicanism and taking on a ritual aspect of a familial devotion more appropriate for a European Catholic monarchy. Martí becomes a family figure, intimate, like a father or a husband, and whose memory must be tenaciously defended against the enemies of the great Cuban family.[8]

Later we will return to this image of Cuba as a great family, but what Rojas touches on here is how large Martí looms in the Cuban imaginary and how his image functions, going from the monumental (his statue in Revolution Square, built by Batista not Fidel), to the educational (not only the prototypical white bust in the schools, but the recitation of his poetry, commemoration of his birthday and so on) to paintings and images of him in people's homes. Rojas mentions the intimacy surrounding Martí and that this is very Cuban. He evokes him as if he were a family member, but, one needs to add, a family member that one is in awe of because in many ways Martí represents an unattainable ideal as human being, artist and patriot. As a family man he was not exactly a role model, though, since he split up with his wife and rarely saw his children. There is a tension, then, between the intimate and the ideal, a distance that must be respected. It is that distance that some felt was deliberately transgressed in Fernando Peréz's film, *El ojo del canario* (The Eye of the Canary; 2010) based on the early years of Martí (the film ends with his first imprisonment at age sixteen). In one scene young José is with a friend and they explore their sexual urges by masturbating (not shown on screen but implied). Some critics considered the scene blasphemous, an outrage to the memory of Martí, and a desecration of a founding father. Others defended Pérez, saying it was refreshing to see Martí as a flesh-and-blood human (and teenager at that) and not as a kind of saintly figure, the iconic revolutionary who sacrificed everything for his country, including, presumably, all personal desires and urges. It is telling that Pérez, instead of shooting a full-blown biopic of his entire life, chose to focus on Martí before he became a celebrated figure, a little like Walter Salles Jr's treatment of Che Guevara in *The Motorcycle Diaries* (2004). Instead of an icon, we have a young passionate man who is moved by ideas (anti-colonialism, abolition of slavery, democracy), nature and friendship (and who has a healthy libido), who is eventually moved to act for Cuba's freedom from Spain.

The Soul of a Country: Cuba's Music

Martí described music as 'the soul of a country' and this is doubly true for Cuba. Cuban music was more fortunate than poetry (in not losing its best composers so young) and even by the early nineteenth century the island boasted three significant composers in Esteban Salas (1725–1803), Juan París (1759–1845) and Antonio Raffelin (1786–1881).

Others were to follow that set Cuba along its own musical path, with a wealth of genres. The *danzón* was the first of these, and its public launch in 1879 is credited to Matanzas composer Miguel Faílde (1852–1921), though clearly *danzónes* existed before that date. The first eight bars of Manuel Saumell's (1817–1870) *contradanza* 'La Tedezco', which was written in the 1840s, decades before Faílde was composing, already prefigure the *danzón*. The *danzón*'s origins are from the English country dance, which crossed the English Channel and became the French *contredanse* played on piano, flute and violin. This in turn became the Spanish *contradanza* and influenced the Cuban habanera. Brought by 'French blacks' as a result of Haitian independence (1791–1804), both Haitian and Afro-Cuban rhythms were incorporated into the *contradanza*. It was banned by the Spanish colonial authorities during the Ten Years War (1868–78) as a blatant symbol of Cuban nationalism, and they were right. Members of the elite or pro-autonomy forces (those who favoured neither independence nor a traditional colony) categorized it as 'music for savages' and a 'fire that consumes the flower of innocence'. These types of criticism tend to be levied at popular musical genres before they end up widely embraced in Cuban society. Part of the *danzón*'s scandal was that it was originally a figures dance where the partners did not touch, but over time that changed. The salons where the *danzón* was danced were some of the few places where black, mixed race and white Cubans mingled quite freely, and most of the musicians were non-white. Cuba, unlike most parts of the Caribbean, had a sizeable population of what was known as 'free people of colour', somewhere between 15 and 20 per cent (the Caribbean average, with exceptions, was less than 5 per cent, and usually between 1 and 3 per cent). These 'free people of colour' suffered under many limitations in terms of employment, education and social status, but they were not enslaved.

A 1982 film by Humberto Solás entitled *Cecilia* underscores the importance of the *danzón* as well as the prominence of 'free people of colour' in colonial Cuba. The film is based on the canonical Cuban novel of the nineteenth century, *Cecilia Valdés o la loma del Angel* by Cirilo Villaverde (1812–1894). There was a first edition from 1839, but the definitive second edition was published in 1882. Early in the film, the protagonist, Cecilia Valdés, who is mixed race and 'free', meets Leonardo Gamboa, a white aristocratic Spaniard at a dance. One of the musicians playing at the dance is a dark-skinned mulatto violinist by the name of José Dolores Pimienta, who is in love with Cecilia. Cecilia is being courted by an older white man, but it is Gamboa who entrances her, and they begin a torrid love affair, which displeases Gamboa's parents. Cecilia sees her relationship with Gamboa as a way of moving up the social ladder and, while some see her as the tragic mulatta figure who passively accepts her fate, the novel and more so the film show a mixed-race woman who through her wits and sexuality tries to better herself.

Cecilia's character contributed to the mulatta figure in Cuba's social, sexual and racial imaginary. Aside from fiction, her portrayal, even exaltation, has appeared in paintings, photography, music, poetry, film, dance and even in religious images (the Virgin of Charity or Oshún). Because of the high degree of miscegenation, she has become a symbol of national identity and racial harmony. But as Melissa Blanco reminds us,

> Yet as a living, breathing body, the mulata acts as a benign and aesthetically pleasing buffer against the legacies of racialist discourse in Cuba. In other words, how can there be tension between blackness and whiteness when they merge so well in the figure of the mulata? Historically she has been celebrated, denigrated, venerated and vilified.[9]

The mulatta, while often celebrated, was always a figure of appealing sexuality, and as such she was portrayed in the bufo theatre of the nineteenth and twentieth centuries (more on bufo later). Poet Nicolás Guillén wrote several poems showcasing the mulatta's hips, and countless songs speak again to the hips of a good dancer, with obvious sexual connotations. The mulatta is a woman to have fun with, but not necessarily to marry. And, of course, Cuba's patron saint is the Virgin of Charity, who is portrayed as mixed race and syncretized with Oshún in Santería, an Afro-Cuban religion based on Yoruba beliefs. Cuba even makes a rum Ron Mulata, that features a light-skinned mulatta on the label dressed in a yellow dress, the colours of both the Virgin and Oshún.

The *danzón* quickly became the musical-cultural emblem of the country from 1879 to 1920, after which it was surpassed by the *son*, an Afro-European hybrid genre and dance form. The traditional *danzón* has a march-like introduction (A), followed by a clarinet or flute section (B), then returns to the intro (A), then a slow songlike part dominated by the violins (C), returns again to the intro (A) and closes with a rapid section (D), yielding an overall structure of ABACAD, which was later simplified. *Danzónes* have often been called sound collages because show tunes, opera arias, *sones*, jazz melodies are inserted in either the B or C sections. For the dancers, the *danzón* moves are gentle, elegant, even restrained, with none of the acrobatic moves (especially in the hips and shoulders) that we associate with rumba or salsa. The *danzón* is no longer the national musical emblem of the island, but its legacy persists, not only in Cuba but also in Mexico, where it is actually more popular. What Cuban *danzón* reflects (or refracts) is how the island's culture, open to the most diverse of influences (Spanish ballads, German lieder, Italian opera, French *contredanse*, African polyrhythms, American jazz), is able to create diverse musical genres that are uniquely Cuban. Carpentier, in his classic work on Cuban music, sees the *danzón* as a true expression of national musical form, one that owes much to Manuel Saumell (1818–1870), whom he credits with being the father of the *danzón* and *contradanza* but also the habanera, the *clave*, the *guajira* and various forms of Cuban song.

One can also look at the *danzón* in the wider context of the island coming to terms with its African heritage, musically and socially. An Afro-European hybrid, the *son* gives more importance to the lyrics than does the *danzón* (which before 1929 did not have vocals), and was sometimes based on satirical *guarachas* from the nineteenth century and Congolese-derived rhythms. Although the *son* began in Oriente (Eastern) province in the nineteenth century, it was not until it became popular in Havana that it was considered the national musical genre. Originally, the *son* was played on guitar and/or *tres* (a guitar-like instrument, but more high-pitched, like a mandolin), marímbula (replaced by the bass), bongo, maracas and *claves* (two wooden sticks that kept a steady rhythm). Trumpets were added in the 1920s, followed later by other brass and piano. The *son* has an opening melodic part with fixed lyrics called the *largo*, a second section called the *montuno*, which often has an improvising *sonero* (singer) answered by a chorus singing a repeated phrase. Four rhythmic planes characterize the *son*: (1) an ostinato and melody (played by the guitar, *tres* or piano); (2) an improvisation section played by the bongos or congas; (3) a fixed pattern on *clave* and maracas; and (4) a syncopated figure (bass), which gives the harmonic foundation for the vocal part. The *son* and the rumba are among the primary sources of salsa music. Some of the great *son* composers were Ignacio Piñero (1888–1969), Miguel Matamoros (1894–1971) and Arsenio Rodríguez (1911–1971). More recently, composers such as Juan Formell (1942–2014), Adalberto Alvarez (b. 1948), Elio Revé (1930–1997) and Jose Luis Cortés (b. 1951), all distinguished bandleaders and performers, have penned *sones*.

One of the great *sones* of all times, 'Son de la loma' (Son from the Hills), was composed by Miguel Matamoros:

> *Son de la loma*
> *Mamá yo quiero saber,*
> *¿de dónde son los cantantes?*
> *que los encuentro tan galantes*
> *y los quiero conocer*
> *con sus trovas fascinantes*
> *que me las quiero aprender.*
> *De ¿dónde serán? ¿Serán de La Habana?*

¿Serán de Santiago, tierra soberana?
Son de la loma y cantan en llano. Ya verá. Tú verás.
Mamá, ellos son de la loma, pero mamá ellos cantan
en llano.
¿De dónde serán, mamá? Que ma las quiero aprender.
Ellos son de la loma y los quiero conocer, vamos a ver.
¡Sí señor!

Mama, I want to know where the singers are from
With all their charm I want to take them by the arm
With their fascinating songs I want to learn all day long
Where are they from? Are they from Havana?
Are they from Santiago, sovereign land?
They're from the hills and sing on the plain. You'll see
soon, you'll see.
Mama, they're from the hills but sing on the plain.
Mama, where are they from? I want to learn their songs.
They're from the hills, and I want to meet them, let's see
Yesiree![10]

What seems like a pretty straightforward song with an extremely catchy rhythm reveals important elements about Cuba and its culture. At first glance, the song is a playful look at the origins of the *son* itself, a musical genre that made its way from Oriente (the east, Santiago) to the west (Havana). This distinction between east and west in Cuba goes back to colonial times, when Santiago was actually the capital of the country, and also to the country's Ten Years War, when the pro-independence forces never fully succeeded in establishing a firm military and political presence in the east, which most historians feel ultimately cost the rebels their long-sought victory. Santiago feels much more like a Caribbean city than Havana in terms of climate, culture and people. The references to *loma* and *llano* are to the hills (or *el monte*) and the plains (cities); and saying that the singers sing in both places means they do so everywhere, indicating that the *son* has reached all parts of Cuba. The words *cantar en llano* are not only a geographical marker but also mean to sing in a plain, straightforward way; that aside from their charm the singers of *sones* are authentic. However, the singers are from the *loma* (eastern Cuba is known for the largest mountain ranges in the country), reaffirming their roots in the country's tradition of *guajiro* (peasant) music, even though the *son* is not, strictly speaking, *guajiro* music. The *loma* has associations with *el monte*, a profoundly charged term in the Cuban lexicon: in the nineteenth century it refers to the Cuban fighters for independence who went to the hills to fight against the Spanish for Cuban freedom, and for those influenced by Afro-Cuban religions it has sacred connotations of the religious practices of Ocha (aka Santería), Palo and Abakuá.

Cuba's music has been characterized as the successful marriage of the guitar and drum: the *son* best exemplifies that union, and further reaffirms the African influences on Cuban music. Rumba will further accentuate that African heritage: it is the most 'African' of Cuban musical genres, even though it has roots in the 'rumba flamenco' of Spain. It is played entirely on percussion instruments, the vocals have a classic call-and-response format, and the dance steps show a profound influence from the Congo and Calabar regions of West Africa. The *son* has an association with *el monte*, and this link is crucial to Cuba's culture and history, born out of slavery, resistance and a yearning for sovereignty. The *son* has become over time an emblem of Cuban-ness.

Cuban Identity: A Search for Origins and Symbols

One of Cuba's most experimental and gifted authors, Severo Sarduy (1937–1993) in his second novel, entitled *De donde son los cantantes* (1967; translated as *From Cuba With a Song*, 1972 and 1994), uses the Matamoros song as a way to examine Cuban cultural identity, specifically its Spanish, African and Chinese roots. Sarduy himself had Spanish, African and Chinese ancestry. Born in Camagüey of humble origins, Sarduy went to Paris on a government scholarship in 1960 and never returned. He published seven novels, three books of critical essays, several volumes of poetry, four plays (in one volume) and one book of creative autobiographical non-fiction. One could call this fictional identity romp Cuba's first postmodern novel (along with Caberera Infante's *Three Trapped Tigers*, from the same year). Sarduy's novel irreverently follows a pair of twins (Auxilio and Socorro, also known by various other names) who transform themselves into different characters, cross-dress and have many adventures. Drawing on the Yoruba mythology of the *ibeyis* or *jimaguas*, in Cuban Regla de Ocha (Santería) the twins are beloved by the major orishas from childhood, and known for their playful nature. The twins are known for having defeated 'the Devil' by playing drums until he was worn out; Auxilio and Socorro in the novel, in similar fashion, outwit the demons of identity and 'play their metaphoric drums, either by evading the traps of patriarchal and monocultural identity, or exhausting through parody traditional and canonical texts', be they literary, musical, folk or oral traditions.[11] The Devil is put in quotes because in Regla de Ocha there is no central Devil figure, so the reference to the *obeyis* defeating the Devil reveals a Christian influence (through Catholicism). Good and evil in Ocha are part of the avatars (roads) that characterize all the orishas, and these different roads can be beneficent or destructive.

Sarduy takes the question posed by the song ('Where are the singers from?') and debunks any idea of uncontaminated origins to explain Cuban culture or identity. In fact, the title of the novel uses the line from the song but not as a question; in effect, the author is showing his suspicion of the search for origins, or of crafting tidy narratives about either culture or identity. In a two-and-a-half-page note at the end of the book, he speaks of the three currents of Cuban culture (Spain, Africa, China) as being superimposed, a word that suggests a difference from the view of these elements as mixed or fused, as in standard accounts of the cultural heritages of Cuba. (Also of note is Sarduy's inclusion of the Chinese, often left out of the

narrative of Cuban identity.) The novel's queerness, with plurisexual
adventures involving several partners and genders, also questions the
patriarchal elements of Cuban culture, which remain strong to this
day. Sarduy's self-reflexive text is a heady mix of post-structuralism
(Barthes, Derrida, Tel Quel), baroque aesthetics, religious or mystical
references (Catholic, Sufi, Buddhist, Afro-Cuban), all written in a
lush, playful language that caused García Márquez to remark, 'he
wrote in the most beautiful Spanish of our time.'

Despite the popularity and diffusion of the *son*, nationally and
internationally (along with 'rumba'), most Cuban writers, artists
and thinkers in the first three decades of independence (1900–1930)
expressed deep dissatisfaction with public life and its accompanying politics. From the fervour and hope of an independent Cuba
the island lapsed into petty politics, turf wars, patronage and self-
enrichment. Nothing expresses this better than three poets writing
about the Cuban flag, whose colours are red, white and blue. The
first is from Martí, written in the early 1890s:

> Never has red been more beautiful
> than on our lovely flag;
> Nor a star brighter and whiter
> Nor has blue been more devout.[12]

The second from Bonifacio Byrne is from 1899, when Cuba was still
occupied by the U.S.:

> Where is my Cuban flag
> the most beautiful flag ever?
> I saw it from a boat this morning
> and never have I *seen* anything sadder!
> . . .
> there should not be two flags flying
> where only one is needed: mine![13]

Almost twenty years later Juan Manuel Poveda (1888–1926) wrote the following:

> Against a wall, smothered in a deplorable
> frame, almost filthy, they show it,
> colours faded . . .
> and thus the eminent sign that shines forth
> like a glorious moment of the past,
> resembles a cynical and odious vulture
> that exhibits the carrion of its ruin.[14]

Martí's images express hope, and are suffused with a kind of mystical vision of the flag as civic symbol that borders on religious devotion. Byrne, while still enchanted with the Cuban flag, expresses a concern that it will be overshadowed by the flag of its powerful neighbour, the u.s. Poveda's memorable sonnet is one of despair, of suffering and tragedy; at one moment he likens the flag to a rag. Twenty years after Poveda, Enrique Labrador Ruiz's character from his novel *Anteo* (1940) described the island as 'a country of pretentious nobodies, vain, exhausted and gone all soft – tricks, illusions, pastiche, and buffoonery'.[15]

Poveda was a remarkable poet, aesthetically more a follower of Casal than Martí, but his sensibility was of a post-*modernista* poet, with sumptuous verses. Are Poveda's verses and Labrador Ruiz's description an exaggeration? Was Cuba's plight that dire? Poveda was deeply distressed by Cuba's public life under the new Republic, and his depiction of the flag depicts the corruption, lack of sovereignty and immorality of a country full of 'pretentious nobodies'. Many Cuban intellectuals of the period sought to address these issues, attempting to analyse the culture and history in order to bring about change.

Varona and Mañach: From Public Service to *Choteo*

Despite the premature deaths of Martí and Casal, many Cuban intellectual and artistic figures who were their contemporaries straddled both centuries and were able to contribute to Cuba as a young nation in the early twentieth century. These included Enrique Piñeyro (1839–1911), Manuel Sanguily (1848–1925), Enrique José Varona (1849–1933), Rafael Montoro (1852–1933) and Juan Gualberto Gómez (1854–1925). Probably the most gifted was Varona, who began as a poet, then turned to philosophy and the social sciences. Later he was in charge of education under the U.S. occupation (1898–1902), eventually becoming vice president under García Menocal (1913–17). He also turned down an offer to be president. In his later years he returned to literary concerns, wrote aphorisms and became more involved again with the University of Havana, where he had taught for many years. Greatly admired by Martí, some felt that perhaps Varona would be his successor in the political and even the cultural sense; but Varona, despite his public service as politician, minister and vice president, was above all a thinker. He was a positivist and helped disseminate positivist thought in Cuba and Latin America but he was no orthodox follower of August Comte; as a result, he promoted a scientific and secular approach to education in Cuba. Steeped in the sociological, historical, literary, psychological and philosophical literature of his time, Varona was a wide-ranging intellectual who wrote incisively on many topics. He was a true liberal (à la Isaiah Berlin) with a healthy ambivalence – but not hostility – towards the state. He was a nationalist and anti-imperialist, so despite his embracing of liberal democratic principles he did not view the U.S. uncritically, particularly in regard to its interventionist policies in Latin America and the Caribbean.

His book of aphorisms, *Con el eslabón*, published first in Costa Rica in 1918, then in Cuba in 1927, contains some insightful, rueful, ironic and sardonic thoughts. The title itself is curious: literally it translates as 'with the link' (as in the links of a chain). Are the aphorisms links forming 'a chain of thought' or is Varona referring to the chains of bondage and slavery under Spain (still a recent memory for Cubans), or the dangers of U.S. hegemony in the Caribbean? In an obvious reference to the main concepts of the French Revolution, Varona underlines their non-existence in Cuba: 'Freedom? In the clouds. Equality? Underground. Fraternity? Nowhere to be found.'[16] Varona cleverly uses spatial metaphors to make his point that none of the three virtues are to be found on Cuban soil: they are out of reach, buried or gone. Two of his aphorisms anticipate Walter Benjamin by two decades: 'The annals of humanity: no matter where you open the page, they drip with blood'; and 'Barbarity is war with its face uncovered; civilization is war with a mask.'[17] Clearly, these aphorisms reflect Varona's revulsion at the horrors of the First World War. Who knows what aphorisms would have flowed from his pen if he had lived through the years of the Second World War? Varona was highly critical of the dictatorial turn of Machado's regime after 1928, and continued to serve as a beacon of public and intellectual integrity to many Cubans.

The 1920s saw increasing criticism from artists and intellectuals about Cuba's plight: issues of sovereignty, cultural degradation, political corruption and social anomie were seen as undermining the integrity of Cuban society. In 1923 the Protesta de los Trece (Thirteen Intellectuals Protest) expressed their discontent with the Zayas government in a declaration denouncing the purchase of a convent using public funds. Many of those who participated in the protest would become members of the Grupo Minorista, an influential group of writers and intellectuals who would exercise great influence in Cuban life for the next decades: Alejo Carpentier, Jorge Mañach, Juan Marinello, Enrique Serpa, Jorge Lamar Schweyer, Félix Lizaso, J. Z. Tallet, Max Henríquez Ureña, Emilio Roig de Leucheusring and feminist pioneer Mariblanca Sabas Alomá.

One of the key figures of this period was Jorge Mañach (1898–1961), a writer, journalist, politician and public figure whose life almost exactly coincided with the length of the Republican period. Mañach graduated from Harvard in 1920 and studied at the Sorbonne, later gaining further degrees from the University of Havana (1924, 1928). He was active in the Grupo Minorista and their 1923 protest against corruption in the Zayas administration. He penned two important essays, 'The Crisis in Cuban High Culture' (1925) and 'Inquiry into *Choteo*' (1928), as well as being one of the founders/editors of the vanguard journal *Revista de Avance* (1927–30). Opposed to the Machado dictatorship, Mañach founded a pioneer programme, University of the Air (waves) on Cuban radio (1932–3). Political repression sent him into exile in the mid-1930s, where he taught at Columbia University, then returned, taking part in the drafting of Cuba's 1940 constitution. He later served as a minister and as a leader of the Ortodoxo party. Mañach opposed the Batista dictatorship vigorously, went into self-imposed exile in 1957 and returned to Cuba after the rebels took power, initially enthusiastic about the revolutionary transformation. He quickly soured on what he saw as the growing Communist turn of the government, was forcibly made to retire from his position at the University of Havana, and after being offered a position at the University of Puerto Rico he left Cuba for good. He died in June 1961, having lived only a few months in San Juan.

Mañach was perhaps the emblematic intellectual of the Republican period: erudite and refined yet able to communicate to a wide audience, a public intellectual who moved between academia and politics with ease. As a writer, he wrote in almost all genres, but was best at journalism, the essay, biography and what today we would call creative non-fiction. Stylistically, he considered himself a classical writer who showed a sense of moderation and gracefulness in expression, free from passionate outbursts, reflecting the discipline of reason and exhibiting the sobriety of the scholar. Michael Walzer says that to be a good social critic you need to have courage (to criticize your own people), compassion (for victims of oppression or the less fortunate), a good eye (a sense of proportion that implies seeing and judging) and intellectual humility (the self-awareness and lack of arrogance required to admit you might be wrong).[18] On those terms one can say that Mañach was an excellent social critic (though not devoid of blind spots) – careful, respectful and even-handed as he took on major issues and engaged some of the better minds in Cuba at the time.

His 'Inquiry into *Choteo*' is a classic, one that looks into the social psychology of Cubans in trying to understand some of the conundrums of the Republic. Like other intellectuals of his time, Mañach was a nationalist and anti-imperialist (but not anti-capitalist nor anti-American) and in his writings was seeking to examine the social ills that had plagued the island post-1902: sugar monoculture, *latifundismo*, social dispersion, politicking, corruption, the need for cultural regeneration. *Choteo* is a very Cuban term that refers to an irreverent humour that mocks everything. It reflects an attitude where nothing is sacred, and thus expresses a powerful disenchantment with institutions, stripping them of their often-inflated claims to public legitimacy.[19] One could equally argue that *choteo* reveals one of the classical paradoxes of sovereignty: that between the name for absolute power (ruler, the state) and that of political freedom (autonomy and self-sufficiency of the people).

Mañach was not the first Cuban thinker to deal with *choteo*: Fernando Ortiz, as far back as 1906, had discussed it, as had José Antonio Ramos (1885–1946), Cuba's best playwright at the time, in his *Manual del perfecto fulanista* (Handbook for the Perfect Scoundrel; 1916), as well as José Manuel Poveda (1888–1926), a brilliant poet and essayist, and Mario Guiral Moreno (1882–1963). Ortiz, Poveda and Guiral Moreno viewed *choteo* as entirely negative; others, like Ramos, Virgilio Piñera (1912–1979) and the historian Jorge Ibarra (b. 1931), who has published extensively on the colonial and Republican Cuba, see it as a positive trait. Mañach, true to his classical and even-handed spirit, distinguishes between a benign *choteo* and a toxic one.

Mañach echoed the concerns of Martí about 'republics of paper', that is, countries that looked good on paper but were anything but robust, sovereign or well governed. Part of a generation that expressed a 'negative Cuban-ness and Republican frustration', Mañach lamented that the country had moved from *cubanía* (Cuban-ness) to *cubaneo* (an informal behaviour of exuberance, humour and docility). Mañach identified the former with the traits of altruism, patriotism, thought and transcendent pursuits, the latter with selfishness, evasiveness, personalism and narcissism, living for the moment, inability to think things through, and lack of respect for things that deserve some type of veneration. For Mañach, then, *cubaneo* would be associated with a toxic *choteo*.

In his inquiry, Mañach seeks first a definition, and then begins to contextualize the meanings of the word and its social repercussions. After saying it is an attitude that takes nothing seriously and turns everything into scorn, he adds that psychologically *choteo* exhibits 'a repugnance toward all authority'. Mañach does not mean healthy scepticism towards authority, but repugnance, adding that what makes *choteo* more pernicious is that it is 'an attitude set up into a habit'.[20] To his credit, Mañach distinguishes between different types of authority such as social, moral, political and religious, but clearly it is political and social authority that most interest him in the essay. He associates *choteo* with disorder, lack of respect and absence of hierarchy.

Disorder and disrespect can have a positive dimension in situations of arbitrary authority, misgovernment or outright oppression; the levelling effects of *choteo* have an inherently democratic impulse since it implies a critique of the powerful, a disruption of business as usual. *Choteo* is a cushion against the blows of adversity, an escape valve for political chicanery and a relief from all types of irritation and perfidy. When authority exceeds its limits, *choteo* has its place. *Choteo*, then, has a counter-hegemonic element that is undeniable, a way of speaking back to the powerful but avoiding open confrontation, or possibly reprisal. Mañach refers to *gracia o ingenio* (wit, charm, liveliness, creativity), which many Cubans possess; I would say this combination of wit, charm and improvisational creativity is really *choteo* with a conscience, with a political undertone that Mañach overlooks.

So what is toxic *choteo*? Making fun, or heaping scorn, for the sake of it; tearing things down (verbally, of course); it is not related to banter, to true conversation: '*Choteo* is not a genre related to dialectics but to verbal harassment.'[21] What seems like levelling the playing field in benign *choteo* becomes demolition in toxic *choteo*.

The corrosive humour mixed with a streak of nihilism is what worried Mañach because he felt that these attitudes translated to indifference, fatalism, pessimism and lack of collective spirit in the public sphere. *Choteo* is a manifestation of Cuban independence, a healthy trait, but it has a flipside: a need to be left alone and a manifestation of docility. One might be inclined to think that Cubans are emotional and melancholic and use *choteo* as a mask to hide their true emotions, that they fear appearing too tender, overly spiritual, too intellectual, sensible or elegant. Lest Mañach be considered to over-essentialize his characterization of Cubans, in a reissue of the essay in 1955 he claims that national character is not as immutable as most imagine, and can evolve or change due to historical circumstances. He says that in the ensuing two decades *choteo* had diminished, in part because of the revolutionary circumstances of the 1930s. He ends the essay on an optimistic note: '*Choteo* as mental libertinism is on the defensive. It is time for us to be critically joyful, audaciously disciplined, and irreverently conscientious.'[22] Was this the right comment to make during the middle of the Batista dictatorship, in the midst of the imprisonment and torture of political opponents, if not outright killings and the dumping of bodies on the streets as a way of intimidating dissidents?

One can detect a slight class bias by Mañach with regard to *choteo* in that the popular classes engage in it over other sectors of society. After all, disorder, unruliness and disrespect have often been considered uncouth (read lower class). And finally, despite the persistence of *choteo* in Cuban behaviour, Mañach and others have perhaps overestimated its influence, making it out to be too pervasive an element, perhaps crowding out other traits such as diligence, self-sacrifice, spirituality and solidarity that Cubans have also exhibited throughout their history.

Cuba Rediscovers its African Roots

As with other parts of the Caribbean, the U.S. and Europe, the 1920s in Cuba saw a renewed interest in things African and its diasporas. In the U.S. this was promoted by the Harlem Renaissance led by the likes of Langston Hughes, W.E.B. Du Bois and Alain Locke. In the Spanish-speaking Caribbean it sparked Afro-Antillanism, in the French-speaking world *Négritude* (Césaire, Senghor, Damas). Cuba was no exception. Called *afrocubanismo*, it began in the late 1920s and involved writers, musicians, visual artists, anthropologists and essayists. It was spearheaded by figures such as Nicolás Guillén (1902–1989), Alejo Carpentier (1904–1980), Fernando Ortiz (1881–1969), Lydia Cabrera (1901–1991), José Zacarías Tallet (1893–1989), Emilio Ballagas (1908–1958), Hernández Catá (1885–1940), Amadeo Roldán (1900–1939) and Wifredo Lam (1902–1982), among others. In Cuba the *afrocubanismo* movement was not made up of mostly black and mixed-race artists, as was the case in the English- and French-speaking worlds which, at times, led it to convey stereotypical images of blackness, some of them carry-overs from the bufo tradition of the nineteenth century.

Influenced by Spanish theatre, the *zarzuela* (light opera) and the *tonadilla* (a satirical musical comedy popular in eighteenth-century Spain), Cuba's bufo theatre relied on a series of stereotypes: the *negrito*, a comic black character usually played by a white actor in black face; the mulatta, a mixed-race woman who is a temptress; the *gallego*, a Spaniard of Galician origin, a bumbling, clumsy character unable to resist the sexual allure of the mulatta; the *negra*, a black woman, often older, usually associated with sorcery and witchcraft but not sexually attractive; and *el chino*, a Chinese man, hardworking and industrious, but always made fun of for the way he speaks Spanish. Despite these stereotypical portrayals, Cuban bufo theatre was an attempt to envision Cuban identity and nationality on stage. In an ever-changing nineteenth century, with Cuban nationalism asserting itself in one of Spain's last colonies with slavery still in existence, bufo theatre represented an entertaining and deeply flawed attempt to negotiate Cuba's growing sense of uniqueness and nationhood within the parameters of a colonial, racist and sexist discourse.

But most members of *afrocubanismo* transcended this exoticism and stereotyping. Poet Nicolás Guillén used the rhythms of the *son* to craft a series of eight poems in 1930 (*Motivos de Son*; Son Motifs) that caused a sensation. They are deceptively simple poems that evoke the lives of black and brown Cubans at that time, without a trace of exoticism or condescension, admirably capturing both their social and cultural lives, in quick brushstrokes, watercolours of street life. Guillén's best-known poem is 'The Ballad of the Two Grandfathers', a touching poem about his white and black grandfathers, whose spirits visit him. Guillén makes the poem both personal and historical, and a symbol for *mestizaje* (race mixing) that would become emblematic of how Cuba saw itself as a racial democracy. However, many saw *mestizaje* as a process of whitening, which was never the case for Guillén, even if he spoke optimistically about what he called a Cuban colour, neither black nor white. Guillen's poetry has inspired over five hundred musical compositions, and not just from Cuban composers (theirs were joined by works from Chile, Puerto Rico, Mexico, Peru and Venezuela, among others).

Carpentier's first novel *Ecue-Yamba-O* (Praised be God), written mostly in 1927 but not published until 1933, centres around an Abakuá initiation, and does so in a respectful manner. Carpentier also worked with Cuban classical composers in incorporating Afro-Cuban music into concert-style music. Aside from popular musicians who were composing *sones* and rumbas, even classical composers such as Amadeo Roldán and Alejandro García Caturla (1906–1940) brought Afro-Cuban themes into their work. Roldan used Afro-Cuban music in his *El milagro de Anaquillé* (with a text by Carpentier), and also set to music Guillén's *Motivos de Son*, both from 1931; García Caturla wrote *Manita en el suelo* (an opera, libretto by Carpentier), a ballet called *Olilé*, and *La rumba*, based on Tallet's poem. Painters also sought to capture the dynamism of Afro-Cuban culture, with Wifredo Lam being the best known, although his Afro-Cuban religious-inspired work would not become more prominent until the 1940s.

Crucial to the understanding of Afro-Cuban culture was the work of three Cuban scholars: Fernando Ortiz, Lydia Cabrera and Rómulo Lachatañeré (1909–1951). Ortiz, though trained as a lawyer, also wrote about sociology, history, anthropology, religion, politics and music. He first began as a scholar writing about the social issues related to Cuba's black population (*Los negros brujos*, 1906); at the time he was deeply influenced by the Italian criminologist Cesare Lombroso (1835–1909), who claimed that criminality was inherited and that it could be identified by a series of physical defects. Lombroso's ideas drew on early eugenics and Social Darwinism and defined the criminal as savage and atavistic. Ortiz made similar observations about Cuba's black and brown populations at the turn of the century, but over time, and after exposure to these populations and careful study, his views began to change. He claimed that Cuba would not be Cuba without its black population. He was not the first to coin the term Afro-Cuban, but he made it stick. Ortiz used the term as an adjective, not as a noun. This is an important distinction, one that most Cuban scholars observe to this day, using the term Afro-Cuban religions but not describing their non-white populations as Afro-Cubans. To a large degree this is consistent with Cuba's views on race, where culture and nationality trump race.

Later, Ortiz would write convincingly about different aspects of Afro-Cuban culture, particularly religion and music, culminating in his monumental five-volume work, *Los instrumentos de la música afrocubana* (1952–5, running over 2,100 pages). He was also among the first scholars to tease out the complexities of the term Afro by distinguishing each of the unique contributions as Yoruba, Abakuá, Congo, Wolof, Bantu and Arará, to name the most significant. Ortiz described Afro-Cuban music as a 'resonant rum for the ears', and argued that the Africans who came to Cuba became central to defining Cuban culture and identity. Ortiz, to describe the unique cultural mixtures of Cuba, coined the term transculturation in order to describe how traits of different cultures – Spanish, African, Middle Eastern, Chinese – were transformed to become something uniquely Cuban (to be discussed later).

Lydia Cabrera, unlike Ortiz, did write fiction – stories based on the lore of Yoruba culture, skilfully reworked by her narrative style and first published in the 1930s in French (1936) and finally in Cuba (*Cuentos negros de Cuba*, 1940; translated as *Afro-Cuban Tales*, 2004). Cabrera came from an educated and prominent family, her father being Raimundo Cabrera Bosch (1852–1923), owner and editor of the journal *Cuba y América*. Cabrera Bosch was also involved in the independence struggle against Spain, and was a jurist, writer and lawyer. However, Cabrera's great contribution to Cuban culture is her vast scholarship on the three main Afro-Cuban religions of Regla de Ocha, Reglas de Palo and the Abakuá society, publishing over eighteen books on these topics. Her most celebrated work was *El Monte* (1954), which includes a rich documentation of the practices of Ocha, Palo and Abakuá, along with a 275-page segment on all of the herbs used by practitioners of the religions for curative purposes. She then wrote books on the individual religions themselves, as well as three books on each of their ritual vocabularies. Cabrera wrote the first major book on the all-male Abakuá society (no small feat, being a woman), as well as writing the first (and only) book entirely dedicated to the ritual drawings of the Abakuá (*Anaforuana*, 1975; see the Abakuá section of this chapter).

Because she was almost a generation younger than Ortiz, as well as being his sister-in-law, Cabrera is often seen as someone who continued Ortiz's line of research, but in fact she often differed with him in both approach and sensibility. Her methods and approach to ethnography were much less paternalistic than Ortiz's and she was both a storyteller and ethnographer, in some ways a precursor to Cuba's testimonial novelists of the 1960s and '70s.

Her ethnographic voice was one that privileged the person she was speaking to. She was not interested in providing an 'authoritative voice' of the ethnographer, but in putting forth the voice of her informants, who were predominantly black or mixed race. In the words of scholar Edna Rodríguez-Mangual:

> Cabrera's work constitutes an escape valve for Cuba's national discourse precisely because it lays out an alternative view of the Cuban nation that in turn destabilizes traditional anthropological discourse itself. In this way, Cabrera's writings cannot be viewed as a prolongation of Ortiz's work or as a part of the larger body of studies produced within the mainstream of Cuban cultural studies, all of which define blacks and mulattoes as the Other ... In other words, Cabrera prefers to move from the periphery to the center.[23]

Rodríguez-Mangual might be overstating her case: without minimizing Cabrera's contributions, which are extraordinary (her studies of Reglas de Palo and the Abakuá go far beyond Ortiz), one must be careful in evaluating her work as totally removed from the contributions of Ortiz. After all, her magnum opus, *El Monte*, was dedicated to her illustrious brother-in-law.

One of the aspects that both Ortiz and Cabrera share is a rare combination of aesthetics and ethnography, witnessed in not only Cabrera's short stories but also in the unusual structure of Ortiz's *Cuban Counterpoint: Tobacco and Sugar*, which combines social science with a great literary flair. Cabrera reveals her literary abilities in *El Monte*. Does Cabrera's perspective reveal what does not come out overtly in her written work – a queer and gender perspective? Her lifetime partner, María Teresa Rojas, was integral to her work, including some wonderful photos. The first published photos of the Palo *nganga* were taken by Rojas and reproduced in *El Monte*. There is nothing overtly queer in her work, unless you understand the queer presence of so many Afro-Cuban religious practitioners (except the Abakuá). One can argue that Cabrera's work grew out of several passions: her love of art and aesthetics (painting), a gift for writing, an interest in public affairs, and her seven years in Paris, where she met many of the prominent black intellectuals of the *Négritude* movement like Césaire, Senghor, Damas and others. In this period she also befriended Wifredo Lam, the great Cuban painter whose work would gradually take on Afro-Cuban themes dear to Cabrera. She also did the Spanish translation of Césaire's *Notes of a Return to a Native Land* (1943), handsomely illustrated by Lam.

The core of Cabrera's work and thought is to be found in *El Monte*. The word *monte* in Cuba has special meanings. In English it could be translated as hill, forest, brush, wilderness, countryside, mount. In Cuba, *monte* certainly has these natural connotations, but also historical, cultural and spiritual ones. In the nineteenth century, to resist the Spanish in the pro-independence struggle was known as *irse al monte* or *irse a la manigua* (go to the brush), so here we see it as a place of refuge or resistance, with a strong anti-colonial meaning. But it is also a significant site for Afro-Cuban cosmologies and healing practices: the *monte* is a powerful spiritual place. It is where curative herbs are found, the *ceiba* tree (silk cottonwood) is a key part of *el monte*, and it is where the ancestral spirits dwell. One of Cabrera's informants says, 'Everything can be found in el monte . . . it gives us everything.'[24] She quotes others as saying, 'Life came from el monte', or 'We are children of the monte', as if the monte were the universal mother or the equivalent of the Earth. In making reference to the orishas, also called saints, one practitioner says: 'The Saints live more in the Monte than the sky (heaven).'[25] For Cabrera, it is the *monte* that quintessentially defines Cuba physically, spiritually and culturally.

The only major black scholar in this period to research these religions was Rómulo Lachatañeré, who, unlike either Ortiz or Cabrera, died very young. A grandson of the pro-independence general Flor Crombet, Lachatañeré was born in Santiago de Cuba in 1909. He published two important works on Regla de Ocha (*Oh mío, Yemaya* in 1938 and *Manual de Santería* in 1942). He was a pharmacist who worked in a lab in New York and was a member of the U.S. Communist Party, but despite his Marxism he maintained a keen interest in Afro-Cuban religions. His untimely death robbed Cuba of one of its most outstanding black scholars.

Afro-Cuban Religions: A Brief Overview

Afro-Cuban religions have often been described as cults or spiritual practices that do not attain the status of the major monotheistic religions such as Christianity, Judaism, Islam and Buddhism. Since they are viewed as polytheistic, or because they lack a hierarchical and/or central structure (like, say, the Vatican) or because for many generations believers did not have a printed scripture (Bible, Koran, Torah, Sutras) they were viewed as lacking the spiritual, philosophical and theological depth and coherence of a religion. All these assumptions are false. Most West African religions are not polytheistic (they have a central deity with a host of intermediary spiritual forces), the hierarchies are more diffuse (but do exist and command respect) and their scriptural sources have a long history with a vast oral tradition and in more recent times have been transcribed and written down. Even during its oral phase, the Ifá religious tradition (Nigeria) had a long heritage of commentary and interpretation.

The three major Afro-Cuban religions are Regla de Ocha (or Regla Lucumí, aka Santería), the Reglas de Palo and Abakuá. All of them are of West African or Central West African origin, and, as with most religions of the area, there is a belief in a Supreme Being or Creator, who after creating the world retires from human affairs, but intervenes through a series of spiritual intermediaries that go between the human and divine realms. (There are other Afro-inspired religious practices known as Arará and Vudú, but these will not be dealt with for reasons of space.)

Regla de Ocha or Santería

The most commonly practised of these is Regla de Ocha (Santería), derived from the Yoruba peoples of Benin and Nigeria, mostly.

Santeros (as practitioner-initiates are called) believe in Olodumare, or the equivalent of God in monotheistic religions. In fact, the Yoruba have a trinity which some say is analogous to the Catholic trinity of Father–Son–Holy Ghost. Olodumare, which means owner (*olo*) of the models (*odu* or *ordu*, which are the patterns and letters of the divination system) and the universe (*umare*), is the equivalent of the Holy Father. The second component of the trinity, Olofi (or Olofin), which means owner (*olo*) of the palace (*afin*), or the house, is associated with the Earth and linked to the Son (Jesus). Last is Olorun, owner (*olo*) of the eternal (*orun*), that which is everlasting (the Holy Ghost).

Olodumare embodies 'the divine vital energy in the cosmos', which in Ocha refers to the concept of *aché* (similar to ch'i or qi in Taoism), the spiritual energy to make things happen, the ability to create and transform ourselves and our surroundings. One of the major goals of *santeros* is to increase (receive more) *aché* and fashion a good life. *Santeros* believe in a give and take of opposites: light and dark, male and female, good and evil, yin and yang, so to speak. Olofi is concerned with how the divine expresses itself here on Earth, in nature, man and society.

Ocha is not a religion of salvation, where one is rewarded (or punished) for one's behaviour on Earth in the afterlife. On the contrary, the goal for *santeros* is to live a good life and die a good death. What does that mean? Scholar and *babalao* (a priest of Ifá) Juan Mesa Díaz defines a good life:

> From a conscious understanding of the interplay of energies, the believer must utilize the received Aché in order to achieve a good life – understood in terms of inner and outer harmony – and seek a good death – understood in the eschatological sense of reaching eternity. Since humans are at the center of divine creation, they are cosmo-biologically endowed with the conception of the aché, and with the concomitant ethical responsibility of guarding the harmonious interplay of forces

that define consonance within the self and its relation with all other manifestations of the cosmos.[26]

In seeking the good life, a believer seeks to achieve *Iwa Pele* (good character), which goes beyond having a sweet disposition. *Iwa Pele* is both a goal and a path towards self-realization. 'Iwa Pele means good health, fecund progeny, gratification in the performance of certain tasks, elimination of character distortions, realization of individual potential, exercise of self-control, and adherence to ethical behavior.'[27] If a person attains *Iwa Pele* s/he will have a good death and become Khu, or spirits of light, and become an ancestor or even possibly an orisha (a deity or spiritual intermediary), but this is quite rare; if not, they become Ba, spirits without light who can obstruct the spiritual lives of those on the Earth.

From the above we see that Ocha (and Ifá) are not religions of salvation. In that delicate search for *Iwa Pele*, a person seeks to obtain the power of *aché* from the orishas and have a good life. But as humans we have indissoluble bonds to the natural and spiritual realms, as well as to society. Since these links are so powerful and what one takes must also be restored, central to the notion of *aché* is that of sacrifice, since one cannot merely take without giving back; otherwise, the crucial balance of energies in the universe would be disrupted. According to the Yoruba, 'Nothing is more natural than the supernatural.' Yoruba thought accounts for every conceivable relationship, and 'any attempt to separate the parts from the whole would paralyse the energies flowing from all of the structures of the universe.'[28]

In Afro-Cuban religions the notion of sacrifice has been sensationalized, with a rather dramatic overemphasis on animal sacrifice. The narrow focus on the spilling of blood obscures a much deeper context and meaning:

The stereotype of Lucumí sacrifice is one of plain and simple bloodletting, yet nothing could be further from the truth. It is instead a complex ceremony, one that involves the skills of divination, humane slaughter, plucking, tanning, fastidious butchering, and careful cooking. Intricate songs, chants, and ceremonies, as old as the ancient African Yoruba culture, which is one of the oldest on the planet, accompany each step of the process.[29]

More importantly, animal sacrifice occurs only in major ceremonies, like a full initiation or urgent life-and-death matters. In most instances, the offerings related to a sacrifice are fruit, candles, non-animal food items, sweets, beverages (sometimes alcoholic), herbs and prayer. Because of the profound relationship that exists between different spiritual forces and their need to work in harmony, the notion of sacrifice is intricately involved in restoring the balance of cosmic forces and energies. As human beings we cannot simply take and take from our natural (and social) surroundings. We must give back and restore these balances in the natural world, which, as we have seen, includes the 'supernatural' as well.

Before animals can be sacrificed, one must seek the permission of the *eggún* (ancestors) as well as the orishas, in particular Elegguá and Oggún. If their permission is denied, one must find out what needs to be done for the sacrifice to be carried out (or it is postponed). In almost all cases of animal sacrifice, the *santeros* eat the flesh of the creatures in ritual meals, and the blood is for the orishas. Hence, what is not consumed is offered to the orishas, and this involves a real and symbolic exchange of forces/energies:

> [This] real and symbolic exchange ... seeks to create an equilibrium of cosmic forces, the creation (or reaffirmation) of a community, and the search for aché (the sacred life force). The *ebbó* (sacrifice) is ultimately a ritual of healing. The symbolic exchange is the giving of one life to sustain, nourish, and improve our own lives; the real exchange that precious loss in order to ward off obstacles, sickness, and death and create

both health and peace of mind. 'Life is but a process of giving in order to receive'.[30]

The notions of *aché*, *ebbó* and *Iwa Pele* are central to Ocha; they are the conceptual foundation of the religion and not difficult to comprehend. More complex are the ceremonies, rituals and initiations involving intricate and abundant preparation (food, altars, music, certain types of attire, divination, chants, prayer, dance). The ritual language is known as Lukumí (Lucumí), a nineteenth-century Yoruba, and it is not a conversational language.

One of the most significant aspects of the religion is divination, which in Ocha takes two forms: *obí* (the coconut) and the *diloggún* (performed with cowry shells). The coconut is interpreted with four pieces and read on whether the dark brown or white side is up: the permutations are yes, maybe or no, so it is a rudimentary form of divination, usually used to find out if an orisha (or spirit) is in favour of proceeding with a given ceremony.

The *diloggún* is far more complex. Of 21 shells, five are set apart as 'witnesses' and sixteen are read depending on whether the shell falls on the 'open' or 'closed' side. These readings are done in pairs, but each pattern has sixteen possibilities, making a total of 256 permutations. For example, a first casting with three shells up, followed by one with seven would be read as 3–7.

The patterns formed are called *odu* (or *ordu*) and carry messages related to good fortune (*iré*) or misfortune (*osogbo, osobbo*). Specific orishas speak through these patterns and the *odus* have proverbs associated with them. For example, three mouths open on the mat is known as Ogundá and the following orishas speak through this *odu*: Olofin, Oggún, Yemayá, Aganyú and Babalú-Ayé. Among the proverbs associated with the 3–7 pattern are 'tragedy, deception and despair are near', 'beware of those bearing gifts', 'as you have sown, so shall you reap'.[31]

These sayings are analysed in light of the circumstances in one's life, in dialogue with the person who does the reading (the *oriaté*).

More importantly, if the news is not good (as in 'tragedy, deception and despair are near'), the *oriaté* does not simply give the bad news and wish you luck but proceeds to ascertain, through the divination process, what is the nature of the misfortune (health, finances, family discord, death, accident, violence, job loss) and what can be done to prevent it (major sacrifice, offerings, spiritual cleansing, attending to an ancestor's or an orisha's wishes). In this regard it is clear that divination is not fortune-telling, but a consultation with the divine about one's life. Divination is a way of examining forces that are out of balance in one's life and determining how to restore social, familial or spiritual harmony. Ultimately, it is up to the individual to follow up the reading with actions. Of course, an individual can choose to do nothing, but at least the *oriaté* has helped them find out the what and why, as well as providing a road map to avoid tragedy.

Oriatés are also healers and can offer herbal and other natural sources of healing; however, there is no contradiction with science. If someone with cancer consults through the *diloggún*, an *oriaté* will suggest herbal remedies but will always tell the person to seek treatment by a doctor and undergo surgery or chemotherapy should that be necessary.

As healers and expert interpreters of the shells, many *oriatés* are sought out for help, even by those who do not practise Ocha, being a kind of psychologist and spiritual guide rolled into one. A person with a troubled marriage, someone in a difficult work situation or in ill health will go to an *oriaté* for guidance and help. This more practical side of the religion has led some to view Ocha in more pragmatic terms, as a results-based religion that does not have a deep philosophical or spiritual lineage; but, as we have seen, the Ocha-Ifá tradition has a long-established philosophy, cosmology and theology that rivals any of the major world religions.

Music is a central part of Ocha liturgy. Aside from the voices that chant to the orishas, the key instruments are the *batá* drums, a set of three double-sided hourglass-shaped drums played on each side, usually laid across the legs or lap of the drummer. The largest *batá* is the *Iyá*, or mother drum, followed by the medium-sized *Itótele*, and the *Okónkolo*, the smallest. This family of drums and its rhythms have carried the Yoruba faith all over the world, preserving a diasporic memory of great cultural value. In important ceremonies, aside from the intricate batá rhythms and the chanting, believers dance to the distinct beats of the different orishas; some call Ocha a 'danced religion', others, like the scholar-dancer Yvonne Daniel, refer to the relationship between body movement and spiritual truth as 'dancing wisdom'.

The *batá* drums played during initiations or special ceremonies must be consecrated, and the drummers initiates. Called *batás de fundamento* (foundational *batás*), these drums contain their own *aché* known as Añá, the spirit of the drum, as well as the spirit of the sound made by the drum. It takes years of study to master the three drums, usually under a rigorous apprenticeship with a recognized master. Given the complexity of the rhythms, drummers do not chant; that is left to the *akpwon*, a specialized singer, whose voice must penetrate the thick wave of sound produced by the *batá* trio. While the *batá* drummers must learn the traditional rhythms associated with each orisha (and this entails knowing the different sets of toques or rhythms for each orisha), they are also encouraged to develop their own style.

A person who becomes more involved with Ocha goes through several steps, the most important being the full initiation. In Ocha you are initiated into the religion by your tutelary orisha, determined by divinatory methods (a *babalao*, or priest of Ifá), and not out of personal preference. The full initiation process takes from seven to nine days, depending on circumstances, and is exhausting, exhilarating and costly. In most cases, the *iyawó* (the initiate) must wear white for a full year, avoid going out at night and keep the head covered. In Ocha, the head is spiritually important, since one receives *aché* via the head.

Reglas de Palo

Like Ocha/Santería, Reglas de Palo, as they are known in Cuba, have rites of initiation, divination methods, sacrifice, possession, an intimate relationship with the dead, and a spiritual world of intermediary forces that negotiate between natural, human and supernatural realms. They are derived from Bantu religions (the Congos, Angola) and have had a profound effect on Cuba's culture. Reglas de Palo, however, are viewed by Cubans with a bit more trepidation. *Paleros*, as initiates or practitioners are called, are often seen as engaging in acts of harm that *santeros* avoid. This obscures the fact that *paleros* mostly do good (even if they have the ability and training to inflict harm), and that their beliefs constitute a religion with a worldview, cosmology and a coherent philosophy.

Like *santeros*, *paleros* believe in one god, known as Sambi (or Nsambi, Sambi, Sambia). As Natalia Bolívar says:

> According to legends Sambia created man in the sky and then lowered him to the earth by a string hanging from a spider web. In the human spinal cord he embedded the mysteries of the road to be travelled; on the lines of the hand he engraved the text of existence; he blew into man's ear the soul and intelligence to glimpse it; and he gave man life with blood that made the body shake.[32]

Instead of being initiated into the world of a particular orisha, Palo centres on spirits of the dead and the manipulation of a sacred cauldron (*nganga* or *prenda*) containing many physical and spiritual forces that are made to work for the person who rules over the *nganga*. The *nganga* is a microcosm of the universe. Lydia Cabrera quotes a *palero* on the *prenda*:

> A prenda is like a little world unto its own and it is through it that you gain power. For this reason, the *nganguluero* . . . fills

his cauldron with all [kinds of] spirits; within it he has the cemetery, the bush, the river, the sea, lightning, the whirlwind, the sun, the moon, and the stars.[33]

The *nganga* also includes minerals and fluids found in bodies, including blood, bones, plants, protein, hair and so on. A *palero* says that Palo is 'nothing less than the encounter of man with the natural world'. Of course this encounter is mediated through the *nganga* and is also 'outside the bounds of social constraints, an errand into the wilderness'.[34]

Discussions of Palo lead to inevitable comparisons and contrasts with Ocha, with the latter seen in a more positive light. In fact, some *santeros* are adamant about their possible relationship, rejecting Palo altogether. They will admit that a *palero* can make Ocha, but say, if you have Ocha first, initiating into Palo would be a 'spiritual regression'. Stephan Palmié describes these two spiritual worlds and how they are viewed:

> practitioners of regla [de] ocha tend to represent the relation between 'their religion' and that of 'the paleros' in terms of a fairly straightforward dichotomy echoing conventional social constructions of nature and culture. In contrast to ocha, palo is said to be more crude ('rústico') but also very powerful ('muy fuerte'), violent but fast and effective ('violento', 'trabaja rápido', 'muy efectivo'), it is associated with the dead instead of divine beings ('cosa de muertos') and with the uncultivated landscape ('cosa del monte') instead of humanly inhabited, and therefore socialized, spaces . . . Individuals possessed by a *nfumbi* (spirit in the reglas de congo) present an image of violent motor behavior, uncouth speech, and generally 'uncivilized' demeanor. While a person possessed by an oricha notionally takes on a role circumscribed by images of awesome royal authority, the medium of a congo spirit is represented by an embodiment of brute force. To a certain extent, this

opposition between refinement and crudeness, civilization and wildness, has a gendered dimension . . . In contrast to regla de ocha, which counts a large number of homosexual adherents (sometimes euphemistically referred to as overly refined), palo cult groups are characterized by a pronounced homophobic atmosphere, and many women have told me that they dislike the machismo that pervades social relations within a 'casa de palo'.[35]

Even the spiritual relationships take on a different character. Between the orishas and their human interlocutors there is a feeling of mutuality, where the orisha is invited into the believer's home and becomes part of the family, not only spiritually but physically as well (altar, ritual objects, statues, necklaces and so on). With Palo there is an intimate relationship between the spirit residing in the *nganga* and its 'owner'; but it is often described differently than in Ocha. In Palo, the *nfumbi* responds to its human master. In a sense, this relationship is an overturning of the master–slave relationship from colonial times. Palmié describes this asymmetrical relationship as a pact or bargain established between the spirit and its human counterpart based on 'symbols of wage labor and payment, dominance and subalternity, enslavement and revolt'.[36]

Palmié traces the relationship between spirit and *nganga* owner to slavery and resistance to bondage. Drawing on the use of *nkisi* (*minkisi*, pl.) from the Congo that is both a healing charm but can also attack a source of affliction, he uses examples from Cuba's past where slaves used their *ngangas* to punish their masters for their misdeeds. In addition, he delves into how Africans saw the slave trade as a system of 'cannibalistic consumption'.[37] This feeling of being devoured was not literal but indicative of the dehumanization and wasting away of people through slavery, the loss of personhood it encompassed, the terror of being swallowed whole by its violent oppressiveness. Here, then, religion, healing and politics became entwined and because of the violence the use of *ngangas* was a 'healing by counter-attack'.[38]

None of this should obscure the fact that Palo is not only about inflicting harm; on the contrary, if the *nfumbi* is supposed to work for its owner, presumably this implies doing things to improve a person's life (health, work, relationships, family). The changed historical circumstances of the island would indicate that 'healing by counter-attack' is not needed as often as it was in the past.

Palo itself is intimately involved with Regla de Ocha, Spiritism, Catholicism and other religious manifestations. There are different types of Palo according to this intermingling with other religions: the 'purest' form is known as Mayombe, whereas Palo Briyumba (or Brillumba) is Palo mixed with Regla de Ocha and Spiritism. Initiations differ and the relationship with the orishas functions alongside the *nganga* (although ritual objects from the two are kept in different parts of the house). A third variant, Regla de Shamalongo (or Malongo), also influenced by Regla de Ocha, is considered 'very spiritual', where the initiate draws on protective spirits and other 'calming' practices. Finally, there is the Regla Kimbisa, combining Palo, Ocha, Spiritism, Catholicism and Masonic rituals. *Kimbiseros* (those who practise Regla Kimbisa) have a Catholic saint, Louis Bertrand (1526–1581), as their main spiritual guide and it is his *nganga* that is adored by its believers. Kimbisa is a truly Cuban creation founded by Andrés Petit (1829–1878), who was a Catholic, a believer in Ocha and also a practising Abakuá. Petit created liturgy specific to Regla de Kimbisa.

The Abakuá Society

A third major Afro-Cuban religion is known as Abakuá, an esoteric-religious mutual aid society for men that functions mostly in three port cities: Havana, Matanzas and Cárdenas. The Abakuá reorganized into lodges with a fairly strict hierarchy of officers, and they have often been described as a type of African masonry.

Like Ocha and Palo, Abakuá is African-based, has rituals of initiation (shorter for the Abakuá) and a ritual language (Brícamo), uses music in its ceremonies (drums are important, but different than the *batás* of Ocha and those of Palo), and believes in a central deity (Abasí) and intermediate spiritual forces similar to the orishas, although some believe that this is because many Abakuá also practise Ocha. Ancestral spirits are also important.

But there are notable differences as well: it is a male-only society, initiation is into the brotherhood itself, not to a specific orisha or to the spirit residing in an *nganga*, and the members pay dues instead of belonging to a house temple. They do not have a divination system, nor do they 'bring down' spirits of the dead or orishas, hence no states of possession. They have many sacrificial elements to their ceremonies (except in some major ones, like initiations or funerals). The graphic language of the religion, while similar to the *firmas* or secret drawings of Palo, also has significant differences in that it is used not only in ritual circumstances but also as symbols (names) of different lodges; it almost always indexes the foundational myth of the Abakuá.

The graphic system, called *anaforuana* (in Brícamo) or *firmas* (signatures, in Spanish), has been described in the following terms:

> Most of the ideographs are hypnotic variants of a leitmotif of mystic vision: four eyes, two worlds, God the father – the fish, the king [Tanze] – and the Efut princess [Sikán] who in death became his bride. The signs are written and re-written with mantraic power and pulsation. Mediatory forces, the sacred origins of the anaforuana corpus, indicate a realm beyond ordinary discourse. They are calligraphic features of erudition and black grandeur, spiritual presences traced in yellow or white chalk (yellow for life, white for death) on the ground of inner patios or on the floor of sacred rooms, bringing back the spirits of departed ancestors, describing the proprieties of initiation and funereal leave-taking.[39]

The ideographic system is ritual in the sense that it pertains to ceremonies, the recreation of certain myths, its appearance on ritual objects, and in the naming of certain lodges. In her monumental study, *Anaforuana* (1975), Lydia Cabrera identifies and explains over five hundred of these ideographs. Another singularity of the Abakuá is that they are found only in Cuba, unlike the Yoruba and Congolese influences that the island shares with other parts of the Caribbean, Brazil and northern South America.

The first publicly established lodge – known in Spanish as *juegos, potencias, tierras* or *partidos* – was in the port city of Regla in 1836. It grew out of the *cabildo* system (a mutual aid society of African origin usually organized on ethnic lines) by *nación* (ethnicity) and at first was open to blacks only, but that changed over time, with the first 'white lodge' (actually, it accepted black, white and mixed-race members) established by Andrés Petit, the founder of Regla Kimbisa. The Abakuá were very influential in port areas, particularly among stevedores, and in the working-class neighbourhoods of Havana and Matanzas. As lodges they functioned not only as mutual aid societies but also in landing jobs for their members, and in buying the freedom for their brethren (as did the *cabildos*). Different lodges often competed for jobs and this created tensions between lodges, sometimes leading to violent confrontations.

The hyper-masculine ethos of the Abakuá and its associations with violence and delinquency have caused misperceptions throughout their history. A popular saying has mothers trying to discipline unruly children by warning them, 'If you don't behave the *ñáñigo* [Abakuá] will come take you away,' the term functioning as the bogeyman. Some of this is attributable to old-fashioned racism and class bias, but some has to do with the strict code of conduct of the Abakuá. First, the Abakuá are supposed to be 'proven men' (in other words not to be homosexuals), and they cannot have been humiliated (especially struck) by a woman. They are expected to be ideal fathers, brothers and sons and to be faithful to their partners (even more important is not to get involved with the girlfriend or spouse of another Abakuá). Equally important is not to reveal the secrets of the society (or religion) and to uphold the respect and prestige of your lodge. Failure to comply with the rules can result in strong sanctions: demotion if you are an officer, fines, expulsion and, in extreme situations, death. During the 1860s, rivalry between different lodges led to violent incidents, mostly caused by turf wars over jobs with overlays about doctrinal or organizational differences as well. The Abakuás were closely watched – and sometimes persecuted – by the police during the twentieth century.

David Brown has pointed out what being an Abakuá meant in nineteenth-century Cuba: 'partly a phenomenon of [a] gendered Cuban social identity, *barrio* [neighbourhood] identity, mutual aid, proletarian organizing and self-defense'.[40] If one thinks about being an Abakuá in the 1860s, in what was still a Spanish colony with slavery still legal, joining an Abakuá lodge conferred a certain respectability or prestige. An average *potencia* had 25 or more officers (*plazas*); holding one of those positions meant respect, not to mention the secrecy they were sworn to, the mystique of overt manliness, public events which were splendid processions. The liberating psychic and spiritual space offered to members must have made the Abakuá lodges one of the few places in colonial times where black Cubans could feel their true worth politically, socially and culturally within their own neighbourhoods and society at large. Barely ten years after the founding of the first *potencia* in 1836, Havana alone had forty lodges. Between 1882 and 1940 Havana had over one hundred lodges, Matanzas twenty, Regla and Guanabacoa a dozen.[41]

Like *santeros* and *paleros*, the Abakuá build altars. Those found at lodges are elaborate, iconographically rich and laden with meaning. Brown discusses a particular altar by Jesús Nasakó when the lodge was renovated.[42] The top of the altar has the traditional *ibones* (staffs) that are used by the four principal officers, and the sacred drums, including the *seseribó*. These drums are not played or in some instances are struck once symbolically; they are not the drums played during ceremonies, known as the *biankomeko*. Also on the altar are a crucifix, a Catholic monstrance and the *delantal* (apron), silk embroidery on velvet that graphically represents the originating myth of the Abakuá, the founding date and the name of the lodge. As Nasakó explains the objects on the altar, it becomes clear that certain details related to the items have a certain meaning that derives from the Abakuá's personal and family history. As Brown states: 'Nasako's history and experience simply exceed the "bodies" of Catholic, African, and "religious" belief itself.'[43] There is a creativity in the construction of altars as well as other aspects of the religion that reveals enormous agency and creativity on the part of those who not only practise Abakuá, but Palo and Ocha as well. Another scholar refers to this creativity in altar building as 'ecumenical . . . additive, eclectic and non-exclusivistic'.[44]

These characteristics are an excellent description of Cuban culture and art in general. These religions, which on arrival in Cuba were treated with outright disdain and hostility, had such enormous power and resilience that they were not only able to survive, but to transform themselves and their colonial oppressors and create truly unique systems of meaning and religious expression.

One of the most identifiable icons of the Abakuá is the *íreme*, a dancing figure represented in unique garb with a conical mask and a set of eyes (but no mouth or ears). The *íremes* are spirit messengers and 'act as witnesses, supervise [ceremonies], they conduct purifications, they execute punishments'.[45] Their movements and sounds (they have bells around their waists) are an expression of joy that the Ekué drum is speaking and also ward off any evil influences. In Spanish they are called *diablitos* (little devils) but the term is not meant to be negative: the use of the diminutive connotes more a feeling of playfulness and mischief, no doubt related to the way in which they dance and their important presence in carnival.

During colonial times, one of the few days when Africans could publicly display their ways of dress, songs and musical instruments in the streets was 6 January, Three Kings Day (Epiphany). One of the most identifiable figures on the streets of Havana was the *íreme*, and there are numerous paintings and drawings from the nineteenth century that show this Abakuá spirit dancing or with an outstretched hand receiving their *aguinaldo*, a modest Christmas bonus. Many prominent Cuban artists of the twentieth century also depicted either the *íreme* or other aspects of the Abakuá faith. For example, Mario Carreño (1913–1999), in his 'Afro-Cuban Dance' (1943), depicts the *diablito* dancing with a bare-breasted *guajira* (peasant woman). Carreño's visual depiction of *mestizaje* (both racial and cultural) is given a modernist twist by the cubist nature of the painting, done in bright colours. Both Carreño and Wifredo Lam did paintings of the *fambá* room, a space where initiations and special ceremonies take place, where only initiates are allowed. Carreño's rendition depicts the drums, the *íreme* outfit on a chair, the staffs and the *anaforuana*, or sacred drawings, drawn on the wall. Lam's version is far more abstract and mysterious, but also evokes the signatures on the floor of the *fambá* room with a flurry of his own *firmas* – angular and highly geometric.

However, Belkis Ayón (1967–1999) engaged the Abakuá world most creatively. Her brooding prints (collographs) directly take on the foundational myths of the Abakuá. The narrative involves Sikán, an Efut princess who captured the soul of Tanze, an ancient Ejagham king who was the founder of a leopard society. Tanze's soul was transformed into a sacred fish and captured in Sikán's water gourd; she revealed the secrets to her husband Makongo, from the Efik tribe. For the transgression she was punished and sacrificed. A new sacred drum, the Ekue (Ekwe), was built with her skin, but it had no voice. Again the drum was made, using her blood, but it remained voiceless. Finally, the skin of a goat was used and the voice of the sacred fish roared. The Efor and Efik were united, and the graphic symbol of that union was the eyes of Sikán and Tanze.

Ayón inserted herself into the role of Sikán in her prints. Save for rare instances, the work is executed in whites, blacks, greys and browns, and the human figures have no faces except for very penetrating eyes, usually white pupils against a black eye socket. In other instances the eyes are all black (or white) slits. Ayón took one of the key icons of Abakuá visual culture and made it work to express her own concerns as a black woman artist in the 1980s and '90s. First, there is a temporal disjuncture in that she handles the

Abakuá foundational myth, an event from a remote past, and yet her rendering of it, while retaining all of its power and mystery, has a contemporary feel that gives agency to Sikán the princess, who has become Ayón's alter ego. In her startling 'La sentencia #1' (The Sentence #1) she represents Sikán in a dramatic pose: the skin is in grey tones and depicted like fish scales, and white serpentine silhouettes suggest the serpent around the tree that is shown on Abakuá renderings of their origins, while the head is all black, with white eye slits and black pupils. Her arms are tied by rope – this is a Sikán who is being punished and will be sacrificed, according to legend – and yet her left hand, white in stark contrast to the surrounding background, seems to suggest stopping the violence, as if to say do not make me the object of sacrifice, I do not need to be punished or to become a martyr.[46] Ayón's work, while nourished by Abakuá myth and ritual, clearly reworks some of the hyper-masculine aspects of the society into feminist statements of agency, while still retaining the awe and mystery of their practices.

Ocha and the Visual Arts

Another artist, Maria Magdalena Campos Pons (b. 1959), offers an example of artistic creativity and transculturation that draws on the imagery associated with Ocha, using performative and aesthetic characteristics of both religions with her own creative reclaiming of devalued sacred and domestic arts in the hands and homes of Cuban women of African descent. Campos Pons uses evolving multimedia installations, as well as large-scale Polaroid photography, constantly learning new techniques with which to creatively convey her understanding of African diaspora legacies, particularly through women's domestic lives.

For one of her early installations, building on the realization that her family home just outside of Matanzas, Cuba, was built on the ruins of a *barracón* (slave quarters), she learned how to make bricks to recreate the physical space as a deep well of history. Looking inside the well, the viewer could see and hear video images and sounds of children playing a Cuban version of 'Ring a Ring o' Roses'. Another multimedia installation using film and objects showed a larger-than-life video image of her mother sewing and ironing a white dress, the material now rich and sumptuous, the video surrounded by an installation that included blown-glass versions of the iron and its trivet.

One of the recurring images in Campos Pons's work is that of the orishas Yemayá and Ochún, both feminine representations of the waters – Yemayá of sea and maternity, Ochún of sweet river waters and marriage/partnerships. Campos Pons's installations and photographic work often directly incorporate ritual elements, blurring the boundary between quotidian, sacred and profane spaces. Her installation 'Las Siete Potencias/The Seven Powers' invokes the Middle Passage using wooden planks depicting the slave ships and the many lives lost to the unspeakable cruelty of enslavement. Yemayá is depicted in a drawing in her embracing oceanic and maternal roles, embracing the dead and caring for the survivors in a spiritual unity of tragic past and enduring survival. Campos Pons uses sculpture and photographs as both aesthetic and ritual objects, transforming the entire room-sized exhibition space into a sacred space resembling an altar, in which the viewer can bear witness to the horror, honour the lives lost to enslavement and the Middle Passage, yet feel comforted through the invocation of life's continuity through the sacred. In this and other work, Campos Pons photographs and represents her own body and those of other women to articulate and redefine the aesthetic space she configures, ever mindful of performative and ritual dimensions of spirituality.

Much of Campos Pons's work could be viewed within the Yoruba concept of *ori*, which represents the head of the body, but also mindfulness and consciousness: the internal experience revealing (and questioning) the self and identity, relationships (family, community), examination of the past (history, public and private) and envisioning the future (the creation of art). Campos Pons's use of *ori* is significant as she draws on the association between memory and water, especially when viewed within the context of Yemayá and water spirits as embodiments of *aché*. The orishas can be understood as archetypes with multifaceted manifestations, represented as embodying energies, relationships, forces in nature and principles that are a daily part of our lives. Adding to their magnificent complexity as resources for living, an individual orisha has different *avatares o caminos* (avatars or paths), which offer a rich spiritual and aesthetic vocabulary that Campos Pons uses in her work and millions of believers use to enrich and guide their everyday lives.

Afro-Cuban Religions and Music

Aside from the ritual music of Ocha, Palo and Abakuá, references, rhythms and refrains have made it into the popular (and dance) music of the island that derives from this music. One of the most famous is '¡Qué Viva Changó!' sung by Celina González and Reutilio Domínguez, a beautiful guaracha dedicated to the orisha of music and the drum, syncretized with the Catholic St Barbara. The song alternates between the names of the saint and the orisha within a very nationalist context. Written in 1948, the song quickly became a hit, one of the most recognizable tunes in the Cuban musical canon. What makes the song remarkable is that it is performed in the *punto guajiro* (music from the countryside) tradition, which is quite different from the Afro-musical traditions of the island; its crossover appeal brought it universal acclaim, and Celina González's booming voice gives the song a soaring, uplifting appeal.

Twenty years before Celina and Reutilio's hit, Ignacio Piñeiro (1888–1969), one of the island's great composers of *son* music, wrote 'No juegues con los santos' (Don't Mess Around with the Saints). The song is for believers and non-believers, but a warning to the latter in that one should respect these religious beliefs no matter what:

> Mayeya, don't mess around with the saints
> respect the necklaces

don't mess with saints
Don't mess with me
Because all of us in Cuba know each other,
Whoever doesn't wear yellow
wears blue or scarlet . . .
Oribea, the letter, oribab

Piñeiro is referencing all Cubans and their respect for the orishas (or saints, as they are popularly referred to). You do not want to have the orishas upset with you; better still, you want them in your corner helping you out, materially and spiritually. Specific mention is made of the necklaces that believers or initiates wear and the respective colours associated with the orishas: yellow (Oshún), blue (Yemayá), scarlet or red (Changó). The last line could be a reference in Lucumí to cocoa butter (*orí babá*), used in ritual cleansings; *orí* is a reference to the head, *oribá* to 'feeding the head', that is, acquiring *aché*. Cocoa butter is used in *rogaciones de cabeza* (spiritual cleansings of the head) and is linked to Obbatalá, an important orisha whose domain is the head, harmony, peace and purity. In just a few lines from a song we can see a rich layer of religious and popular references.

Perhaps one of the most popular songs in Cuba in recent decades is one by Los Van Van, entitled 'Soy Todo', aka '¡Ay Dios! ¡Ampáranos!' ('I am All' or 'Oh God! Protect Us!'). It is a popular dance number that revs up slowly and is based on a poem by Eloy Machado, aka el Ambia (One of the Tribe), about the roots of Cuban identity. He begins: 'I am the poet of the rumba', which alludes to one of Cuba's most identifiable musical genres and dance forms. The author references the *danzón*, Cuba's national musical genre during the nineteenth century (and part of the twentieth), his roots, his neighbourhood or slum, the necklaces (the *collar de mazo*), and then begins a long self-description that is linked to the orishas:

I am the step of Changó
the step of Obbatalá

the laughter of Yemayá
the bravery of Oggún
the spinning top of Elegba.[47]

Here we see direct references to the orishas, the self-confident step (almost swagger) of Changó, orisha of the drum and music, which is consistent with the beginning of the song; Obbatalá, the orisha of peace, harmony and the head (*orí*), who is followed by the mother of the orishas, Yemayá, also the owner of the ocean; Oggún, the warrior orisha; and finally, Elegba's (Elegguá's) top. Elegguá is often associated with children and is offered toys and candy during propitiations. Elegguá is the orisha of the crossroads, of fate.

The song shifts emphasis in the second half, saying 'I am Obbá' (I am the King), perhaps a reference to Changó, who was the king of Oyó before he became an orisha; then, 'I am Siré, siré', an allusion to a party in the Ocha tradition. The song maintains a celebratory mode as it references another Afro-Cuban religion, the Abakuá society. When the song invokes *Aberiñán* and *Aberisán*, it is referencing two officials (*íremes*) of an Abakuá lodge, with its bountiful hierarchy. Aberiñan and Aberisán are 'twins' who are involved with an important sacrifice that is part of Abakuá ritual. The ending lines reinforce not only affirmation but also a sense of relief and resolution – the reason in the puzzle (crossword puzzle) and he who brought light to Obedí, the orisha hunter of doubt. The poem ends: 'I am the hand of truth/ I am Arere/ I am conscience/ I am Orula.'[48] The first verse is a reference to the hand of Orula, a symbol of Orula that is given to a *babalao* when they have become consecrated. It also refers to those who receive Orula in a simpler ceremony, who do not become *babalaos*. Since Orula is the orisha of divination, and is considered to be the most impartial of all the orishas, he is seen as the purveyor of truth and wisdom. *Arere* is a whitewood used in thatching houses in Africa and perhaps a reference to Oggún Arere, an important warrior orisha. The ending perfectly brings together both the material and spiritual worlds of Cuba's African-ness.

Orula is one of the most highly regarded orishas (as Orúnmila or Orunla). As Mercedes Cros Sandoval says:

> He was present at the time human beings were created and their destiny sealed. Orúnmila knows the future. He also has the power to prescribe the remedies and sacrifices necessary to avoid any catastrophe forecast by him … He personifies destiny and hope, since destiny is neither blind nor unavoidable.[49]

It is in the sung/performed (and particularly live) version of the song that Orula becomes more prominent, because the last three lines become the refrain chanted by the chorus.

During the rest of the song, references to Orula become more overt, asking him to protect, help and have mercy not only on the singer, but also on all of the people of Cuba. Keep in mind that the song became popular in 1995, when Cuba's economy had hit rock bottom after the collapse of the USSR, a time of both material need and spiritual malaise. The refrain synthesizes all these concerns (material, mental, emotional and spiritual) while affirming Cuba's uniqueness culturally and as a nation.

Faith, music and conscience are all intertwined in the song, which ends with a question. This appears to be addressed to the audience as well as Orula: '¿Somos o no somos?' (Are we or are we not?). What is the question asking? Are we Cubans, believers in Orula, heirs of the orishas and the rumba, followers of our conscience, sworn to the drum, defenders of our cultural roots? Are all these synonymous? The song seems to infer as much, as well as suggesting that Cuba, through its faith, is part of a huge Latin American family: 'ampara a todos los latinoamericanos que estamos llenos de fe' (have mercy on all Latin Americans, we who are full of faith).[50]

The song does not evoke ritual music: it is a classic example of timba music, the dance music found in most salsa clubs. There isn't even a *batá* drum to give matters a more 'authentic' touch. When seen live ('Soy Todo' can be viewed on YouTube), one appreciates how the song combines the feeling of cultural affirmation, religious devotion (not blind faith) and deep spiritual yearning coupled with a let's-party-all-night groove. There are few places on the planet where this combination could come together so seamlessly.

Even Cuban hip hop artists are steeped in the Afro-Cuban religious traditions. On their first album, the group Orishas (formerly Amenaza) begin their intro with a chant in Yoruba, followed by 'Represent', a song that speaks freely about the orishas and the ancestral spirits within the context of their neighbourhood. Another track from the album is 'Canto para Elewá y Changó', a beautiful homage to two prominent orishas that conveys the importance of speaking the truth, thereby combining the hip hop dictum of 'keeping it real' with the Ifá teaching of 'Those who speak the truth will be helped by the orishas.'[51]

The list is long: Anónimo Consejo and their song 'Loma y Machete' use imagery of Palo Monte combined with references to Rastafarianism. Clan 537/MC Molano, Eleyó, Obsesión, among others, use Afro-Cuban religious references generously. This is something absent from U.S., European and Latin American hip hop. Tapping into Afro-Cuban religious imagery and practice is not only a way of reaffirming Afro-Cuban pride, but also a way of recovering a spirituality in our current globalized times that Cuban rappers see as an antidote to the crushing commodification of world culture on the one hand, and an impoverished (if not outdated) Marxism on the other (atheistic, treating religion as opiate). This rediscovery of their Afro-centric roots has been going on for over two decades and is one of the more significant changes in Cuban life in recent times.

The names, ritual concepts, music, ceremonies and even philosophical outlook of these religions have permeated all aspects of Cuban life, from the mundane to the sublime. For example, two friends might greet each other in the street and use the words 'Asere' or 'Ekobio' as a salutation (both are Abakuá terms that mean friend or brother). When a new bottle of rum is opened at a social gathering, the first few drops will be poured out onto the ground and said to be 'For the orishas!' One of the characters in the film *Strawberry and Chocolate* (1993) does this with whisky, a much rarer and more expensive commodity in Cuba. A man completely smitten by the charms of a woman might say, 'Me echó bilongo', quoting a famous song. The expression means something like 'She's put a spell on me' ('bilongo' in Kikongo means magic or spell). The healing aspects of the religions are deeply rooted in Cuban life, where people will seek help from a *santero* or *palero* in dealing with problems related to health, relationships or work. The concepts of *aché* and *ebbó* (sacrifice), while perhaps not articulated as such by Cubans, underlie their sense of personal and social harmony in trying to achieve a balance of forces and energies to make their lives more harmonious. All of these religions came from warrior cultures, and Cuba's history has been characterized by a kind of warrior aesthetic that becomes manifest not only in its struggle for independence (1868–78 and 1895–8), but also in the evolution (and belligerence) of its political realm, where giving one's life to the cause and the notion of revolutionary violence to affect change remains paramount.

TWO

Curses, Myths and Longing
(1930–1959)

The violet sea longs for the birth of the gods
since to be born here is an ineffable celebration.

José Lezama Lima, 1941

That accursed circumstance of water all around us.

Virgilio Piñera, 1942

I n his 1985 film *Un hombre de éxito* (A Successful Man), Humberto
Solás offers a panoramic story of a family and a period of Cuban
history spanning almost thirty years. The film begins towards
the end of the Machado presidency (1932) and centres around two
brothers from a well-to-do family, Javier and Darío Argüelles, both
of whom vigorously oppose the dictatorial regime that Machado
imposed. Javier is having a liaison with Rita, a former prostitute
and social climber who also happens to be the lover of Iriarte, a top
figure in the government. Javier has Rita drive a car for him while he
places a bomb at a theatre. Later, Rita is angry with Javier and says:
'Here everyone is afraid. You. Your brother. Even Machado is afraid.'
Both Javier and Rita seem to sense that this might be a turning
point for Javier. This is confirmed a few scenes later, when Javier's
mother reads him the Tarot cards: 'Something ends and something
begins. You are on the side of the forces of evil.' The rest of the film
documents Javier's slow, almost inevitable slide into compromises

with local and foreign forces that thwart Cuba as a republic, and his own personal dissolution that exacts a huge price on his family, including the death of his brother. As the film advances and Javier prospers economically and socially, you see photos of Cuban presidents change on the walls of his opulent study: Laredo Bru, Batista, Grau San Martín, Prío Socarrás and Batista again. After a while it becomes a blur, a rogue's gallery that serves as a background to the chicanery we see in the film.

Despite the succession of rogues, the considerable vitality of Cuban cultural life in the Republican period continued. Discontent with public life came from different perspectives, be it the liberal anti-imperialism of Mañach or Varona, the Marxist left (Marinello, Mella, Roa) or the more centre-right view that upheld a Hispanicist vision of the country's culture (see previous chapter). Because of different military interventions by the U.S. in the first three decades, Cuban nationalists were arguing for abolishing the Platt Amendment, a blatant symbol of the island's lack of sovereignty. To compound matters, President Machado's rule turned increasingly repressive and dictatorial after 1928. Machado (1871–1939) was elected with considerable political will in his favour. The son of a general who fought in the Ten Years War (1868–78), Machado fought in Cuba's second independence war of 1895–8. He later became a successful businessman and a minister of the interior under President Gómez (1909–13). Finally, he ran for president in 1924, promising to diversify Cuba's economy, protect Cuban businesses, abrogate the Platt Amendment, allow no re-election for the executive office, renovate the educational system and stamp out corruption. On this last issue it was thought that since he was already a wealthy man he would not need to feed at the public trough. His campaign slogan was 'Water, roads and schools'; he was elected and took office in May 1925. The beginning of his presidency was fairly successful as he embarked on a public works programme (building the central highway that traverses the country to this day, the Capitol building, expanding hospitals), as well as passing legislation that favoured Cuban businesses and/

or their export products. It is worth remembering that at the time much of the Cuban economy was in either U.S. or Spanish hands and so a politician like Machado was trying to satisfy a constituency that was demanding a greater role for local business and greater economic sovereignty. But soon sugar prices began to decline, labour unrest grew, and by 1929 the effects of the Great Depression were being felt on the island. In 1928, claiming he needed more than one term in office to implement his plan for the nation, Machado had the Constitution changed and ran for re-election. Despite growing opposition, Machado won easily. But the economy worsened with the stock market crash; the *zafra* (sugar harvesting period) was shortened, aggravating unemployment; wages spiralled downwards; and government employees were going for months without being paid. Workers, peasants and students went on strike, only to have their demands met with force. By 1930 civil liberties were suspended and a state of siege declared. In 1931 Machado closed fifteen newspapers and arrested their editors. Violent opposition to his regime grew, with assassination attempts and bombs becoming frequent, and various groups engaging in terrorism at times. It was open warfare between the regime and its opponents. This state of belligerence unleashed a crisis that concerned the U.S., and President Roosevelt appointed Sumner Welles as ambassador but also as a mediator with the ultimate purpose of having Machado resign. Fearing that the U.S. would intervene militarily, the armed forces pressured Machado, and on 12 August 1933 he flew to the Bahamas.

For many Cubans on the left, Machado's overthrow was a moment ripe for revolutionary change, and at first it seemed as though Cuba was going to have a nationalist and anti-imperialist government with Grau San Martín the president of a pentarchy made up of anti-Machado forces. However, Grau's presidency lasted merely a hundred days, as he was forced to resign by the army's chief of staff, Fulgencio Batista (1901–1973). Batista, a colonel who led the Sergeants' Revolt that eventually ousted Machado, became the strongman behind the scenes of several civilian governments from

1934 to 1940, and a dominant figure in Cuban politics for a quarter of a century, until he was overthrown by Fidel Castro's rebel forces in 1959. Despite the sometimes chaotic nature of Cuban political life after the overthrow of Machado, several positive changes came about: women obtained the vote, Cuba passed new laws regarding employment and business that protected Cuban nationals, civil liberties and freedom of the press improved, and in 1934 the Platt Amendment was abrogated. In 1940 Cuba adopted a new Constitution, which was a very progressive document for its time and which, in addition to reaffirming civil and political liberties (vote, association, press and so on), also included the obligation of the state to alleviate unemployment, compulsory social insurance, pensions, a minimum working age and the eight-hour day, and greater state sovereignty over citizenship. There was an enormous debate about legislation related to racial discrimination (specifically on enforcement), which never passed, but it did bring the issue to the fore. Cuba had changed after Machado's fall, even if for some it seemed that Cuba was back to politics as usual. Because of the mass movement to overthrow Machado, new governments could not ignore Cuban demands for greater sovereignty and political inclusion. Furthermore, the political system, no matter how authoritarian or anti-leftist, had to recognize unions and leftists and include (and often co-opt) them in the national political dialogue. And finally, the Machado aftermath ushered in a period of populism (both left and right) that legitimated calls for reform, both peaceful and violent.[1]

Looking at Cuba: Walker Evans, Molina and Solás

The photos of Walker Evans, taken in 1933, give us a glimpse of Machado's Cuba. Evans was sent by the publisher J. B. Lipincott to produce photos for a book by radical journalist Carleton Beals, *The Crime of Cuba* (1933). The book was meant to be a critique of the Machado regime and an indictment of U.S. imperialism in Cuba. The street scenes he captured, be it of a woman trying to avoid the gaze of a man on a corner, breadlines or coal workers with blackened skin, show an alert, wary and sometimes exhausted population. Very few photos have any overt political content (there is one of a wall with political slogans on it), and there are a few showing dire poverty – hardly surprising since Cuba had been hard hit by the Depression. One of these stands out: it is a shot of a black man dressed in a white three-piece suit in front of a news-stand. His expression is serious – almost (but not quite) angry. He is aware that he is being photographed but does not look directly at the camera. Who is he? A small businessman? A dandy? A cigar worker? A Machado agent? His suspicious look is framed by the news-stand, where we see *Bohemia* and *Carteles*, two of the most prominent magazines of the time (the former founded in 1908 and still publishing, the latter from 1919 to 1960). The press suffered greatly under Machado from 1931 onwards, but here we see at least some journalistic activity on display. The boy running the stand is reading *El País*, with a headline that blares 'Gran Triunfo de Chocolate', clearly a reference to Kid Chocolate (1910–1988), the great Cuban boxer. Chocolate was quite the dandy himself, had run-ins with the law and was extremely photogenic. In another photo taken of the news-stand, with the two young men who run it, we see more of what is on offer: *Cinelandia*, a film magazine, the newspapers *El País* and *Heraldo de Cuba* (pro-government), along with a union publication called *La Voz del Sindicato* at the top right. However, Cuba's two most prestigious papers, *El Diario de la Marina* and *El Mundo*, are not there. Looming above all the publications is a ubiquitous Coca-Cola sign. It is a slice of street life but revealing of Cuban interests in terms of what they read, their love of film (and Hollywood celebrities), u.s. commercial dominance (Coca-Cola), all mixed in with the weary alertness of the Machado period. It also reflects the growing middle class and consumer culture, much influenced by u.s. norms and advertising. In another photo by Evans, a man with his back to the viewer peers into a movie theatre with posters announcing Thursday's feature (*White Eagle*, with Buck Jones), Saturday's (*The Cabin in the Cotton*, with Richard Barthelmess and Bette Davis) and Sunday's (*A Farewell to Arms*, Helen Hayes and Gary Cooper), all from 1932.[2]

More dramatic are Emilio Molina's photos depicting the downfall of Machado, which unleashed widespread rioting and looting throughout the country, as well as reprisals against his supporters, many of whom were killed. In one we see the contents of the offices of the *Heraldo de Cuba* (a pro-Machado newspaper). Desks, furniture, lamps, print, paper and machinery are all out on the street, destroyed. Another photo shows an anti-Machado protest with a bust of the deposed dictator. Amazingly, it has not been smashed to pieces. A grisly shot by an anonymous photographer shows the dead body of a Machado assassin, Gustavo Sánchez, in the streets of Santiago. The 'contained' work of Walker Evans suddenly gives way to an explosive burst of fury.

A John Huston film from 1949 (*We Were Strangers*) is set in Cuba at the end of the Machado regime, and the film ends with his downfall, but it is nothing like Molina's photos. Despite the death of the hero, who is played by John Garfield, the action on the streets looks more like carnival than an insurrectionary movement. Even more baffling is the positive light in which the plot to kill the president of the senate in order to lure the president and his cabinet to the funeral, where a bomb would be detonated, is shown. The film is surprisingly sympathetic to this act of terrorism, given that the bomb would not only kill the president and his cabinet, but many of their family members as well. In today's climate of hyper-awareness of terrorism it is difficult to see how the film could even be made (unless it dealt with Nazis). Huston's film was based on historical events: Clemente Vázquez Bello was assassinated by the organization ABC on 28 September 1932. Only weeks later, Franklin D. Roosevelt was elected president, and after his inauguration he appointed Sumner Welles as ambassador and special envoy to Cuba. ABC's politics leaned to the right (some claim it was pro-fascist), other groups who opposed Machado leaned left (like the Communists), so the U.S. wanted to ensure an outcome that swung neither far right nor hard left.

What we see in the Evans and Molina photos, as well as the Solás film, are the vulnerabilities of Cuban society: poverty, social inequality, corruption and cultural malaise. Another film by Humberto Solás, *Lucía* (1968), deals with vulnerability from the perspective of three women all named Lucía from three different historical periods (1895, 1932 and the 1960s). With three different actresses, Solás highlights different elements of Cuban society and aesthetically shoots each major sequence differently. Musically, they differ as well. For example, the first Lucía is a member of the Creole landed aristocracy and, though she is pro-independence, she falls in love with a Spaniard. Solás shoots this segment in a very dreamlike style – expressionistic, and with high contrast. The over-the-top style is operatic and uses the music of Schumann. The second Lucía is of petit bourgeois background, not over the top. This part is shot in a more Hollywood style, realistically, with no abrupt camera movements. Musically, it uses Chopin and Dvorak, as well as some Cuban melodies. The second Lucía is caught up in the anti-Machado struggle. Her boyfriend Aldo eventually loses his life, and she winds up working in a factory. The third Lucía is a *campesina* (peasant) living in the countryside. She has a traditional husband who is insanely jealous of her and does not want her to learn to read and become involved with the social projects of the Revolution. It is shot in a realist, *cinéma-vérité* style, but combined with the music it has the feel of a musical comedy. The music throughout is the 'Guantanamera', one of the most popular and recognizable melodies in the Cuban song tradition. Solás structures the film not only in three historical periods but also under different regimes. In the first (1895) Cuba is still a colony; in the second (1932) it is a republic with limited sovereignty (what was subsequently called a neo-colony); in the third, socialist revolution. The three periods roughly break down class-wise as well: landed aristocracy, petit bourgeois and peasant worker. Racially, the first Lucía is white (of European descent), the second is also white but reflecting a mix, culturally speaking, and the third is clearly mixed race, with other characters darker-skinned. Stylistically, the first part is tragic, the second a drama, the third a comedy.

Solás never claimed that he had made a feminist film. In interviews he stated that he was interested in looking at three moments of Cuban history through the most vulnerable members of society, in this case women. The first Lucía is betrayed by her Spanish lover, leading her, in a fit of 'madness', to stab him. For the second the failure of a revolutionary outcome to the overthrow of Machado leads to death and disappointment; for the final one, there is what seems like a hopeful outcome in which Cuban women will take their place as equals in a new society. What is significant in *Lucía* is that despite obvious social limitations that affect the lives of women, no matter what the historical period, all three Lucías show considerable personal and social agency; they are not merely portrayed as victims.

After Machado: *Orígenes*

Because the Machado regime turned so repressive, many Cuban artists and intellectuals left Cuba, such as Alejo Carpentier, Fernando Ortiz, Lydia Cabrera; still others were jailed or killed, like Julio Antonio Mella. (Mella, one of the co-founders of the Cuban Communist Party, was killed in Mexico, where he was in exile; some attribute his death to Machado's agents, others to Stalin concerning divisions in the Communist movement surrounding the banishment of Trotsky.) After the downfall of Machado, cultural activity took a positive turn. Earlier we saw that Cuba, starting in the late 1920s, began to revisit and extol its African legacies. At the same time, it always maintained a close cultural relationship with Spain. Federico García Lorca, for example, had visited Cuba in 1930; his visit was quite the event and he was moved by Cuba, inspiring him to write poems about the island and its people. Perhaps more significant was the visit by Spanish poet Juan Ramón Jiménez (1881–1958), who had fled Spain because of the Civil War (1936–9). Jiménez's stay (November 1936 to January 1939) had a profound impact on a new generation of Cuban poets and writers that would come to be known as the *Orígenes* generation, named after the magazine that was founded in 1944. Jiménez, who won the Nobel Prize in Literature in 1956, took over the responsibility of the Institución Hispanocubana, and also co-edited the book *La poesía cubana en 1936* (Cuban Poetry in 1936). The prestige of an author like Jiménez helped put Cuban poetry on the international map, and legitimized a new group of poets who would be influential in Cuban letters for decades to come.

Cuba's cultural elites tirelessly worked during the first decades of the twentieth century to define and create new avenues of expression for Cuban artists, and the creation of magazines or journals was instrumental to these efforts. Previously we saw the efforts of a first generation of writers and artists, many of whom straddled both the nineteenth and twentieth centuries, as well as the Generation of '23 (the Minoristas) and those clustered around the *Revista de Avance* (1927–30). In the mid-1930s, energetic efforts at cultural renewal were undertaken by a group of poets who founded seven magazines over seven years before the creation of *Orígenes* (1944–56). Many of the small journals (*Verbum*, *Espuela de Plata* and *Nadie Parecía*) were founded by a gifted young poet, José Lezama Lima (1910–1976), who was a charismatic leader and mesmerizing conversationalist. Lezama's vision formed the aesthetic core of the journal and he infused it with his unique view of poetry as a way of knowing and as divine activity. Lezama used poetry in the Greek sense (*poiesis*) as synonymous with making, creating (all the creative arts), and argued that writing and poetry, through a certain intuitive logic, takes us to the divine. Unlike Heidegger, who defined humans as 'Beings-toward-Death', Lezama affirmed that we are 'Beings-toward-Resurrection', to paraphrase his words from his 'Preludio a las eras imaginarias'. His highly metaphorical language was imbued with spirituality; Lezama was a Catholic but he did not believe in heresy. In both his poetry and essays, Lezama practised a baroque aesthetic: his language was opulent, rich in metaphor, his allusions were dense and wide-ranging, his sentences were long cascades of images. He once said, 'I am ravished by being able to see words like fish in a waterfall.'[3]

Lezama's interest in the baroque had been inspired by Spain's Generation of '27 and their re-evaluation of some of the country's great Golden Age authors such as Góngora and Quevedo. Lezama saw the baroque of the Americas, especially authors like Sor Juana Inés de la Cruz, as an expression of an aesthetic that was not merely a copy of the European or Spanish baroque. In his celebrated *La expresión americana*, a book-length series of essays on Latin American cultural identity, he calls it a 'baroque of counter-conquest'. Due to Lezama's influence, both Cuban and Latin American writers in the 1960s were often called neo-baroque. In Cuba, the likes of Severo Sarduy, Reinaldo Arenas and, to a lesser degree, Guillermo Cabrera Infante often engage in baroque pyrotechnics in their playful and subversive use of language. Alejo Carpentier (1904–1980), the great novelist and contemporary of Lezama's, was considered a writer with a strong baroque flair.

Some have asked why there has been such a baroque tendency among Cuban writers. Certainly other Latin American countries (Mexico, Colombia, Puerto Rico) have had their own baroque authors, but why Cuba? Is it the influence of its lush natural beauty, an oral tradition that favours a rich use of language, the tropical sun and its colours, a literary tradition that is enthralled with the power of the word? These, perhaps, are partial (if superficial) explanations. More significant is the way both Spain and Latin America have revisited some of the authors of Golden Age literature, the historical importance of the baroque in Latin America (literature, art, architecture, music), and some of the affinities between *modernismo* and the baroque. Finally, one must acknowledge the incredible talent of those authors: Lezama Lima, Carpentier, Sarduy and Arenas are among the great voices of Cuban (and Latin American) literature in the twentieth century and have written some of the canonical works of Cuban narrative.

Other members of the *Orígenes* group were Father Angel Gaztelu (1914–2003), Cintio Vitier (1921–2009), Eliseo Diego (1920–1994), Gastón Baquero (1916–1997), Octavio Smith (1921–1986), Virgilio

Piñera (1912–1979), Justo Rodríguez Santos (1915–1999), José Rodríguez Feo (1920–1993) and Lorenzo García Vega (1926–2012). The only living member – and woman – of the inner circle of *Orígenes* is Fina García Marruz (b. 1923). In addition to these writers, two painters were important to the journal: Mariano Rodríguez (1912–1990) and René Portocarrero (1912–1985), as well as Spanish philosopher María Zambrano (1904–1991), musician-composer Julián Orbón (1925–1991) and art critic and diplomat Guy Pérez Cisneros (1915–1953). Though the magazine's emphasis was poetry, short stories, fragments of novels, essays (usually on literary, aesthetic or philosophical themes) and reviews were also included. The cover usually featured drawings by Cuban artists, many of them prominent (or to become so): Mariano Rodríguez, Amelia Peláez (1896–1968), Portocarrero, Wifredo Lam (1902–1982), Alfredo Lozano (1913–1997), Cundo Bermúdez (1914–2008), Mario Carreño (1913–1999) and Roberto Diago (1920–1955). The journal sought not only to showcase the best in Cuban writing, but also writing from abroad. Among the Spanish authors were Nobel laureate Vicente Aleixandre, Juan Ramón Jiménez, Luis Cernuda, Pedro Salinas and Jorge Guillén. Latin American authors included Octavio Paz, Juan Liscano and Alfonso Reyes. Among U.S. writers were Auden, Bishop, Eliot, Stevens, Santayana and James; and European authors included the likes of Aragon, Camus, Woolf, Weil, Chesterton, Heidegger, Mallarmé, Nin and Michaux.

The aesthetic was to a degree high modernism in the Anglo sense of the world, but at the same time rejecting some of the more avant-garde manifestations of the time. Fina García Marruz considers that the *origenistas* rejected Freudianism, Surrealism and existentialism, finding them too deterministic (presumably this includes Marxism as well). The first implied domination by impulse (the id, the unconscious), the second by unreason, the third by lack of meaning and the absurdity of our condition, the fourth by economy and society. The group was dismayed by the disunity, fragmentation and degradation of values of the modern world, symbolized by the materialism, corruption and shallowness of Cuban life in the Republic. The bickering between parties, the levels of graft, the lack of national purpose, the economic dependence on the U.S., the recurrence of political violence, the island's limited sovereignty, were issues that concerned the *origenistas*, but unlike the Generation of '23 they chose not to be 'public intellectuals' in the way of Guerra, Ortiz, Mañach, Marinello, Martínez Villena and others. None of them held government positions, with the exception of Pérez Cisneros, nor did they hold academic positions, even if at times they might give a lecture or a seminar in a university setting. *Orígenes* kept a political and economic distance from the centres of power, the latter thanks to the largesse of José Rodríguez Feo, whose inheritance allowed the journal to be financed privately.

Not that the group was indifferent to politics. They welcomed many Spanish writers and artists who had fled the Civil War, and they shared their Republican sympathies, as was the case with Jiménez and Zambrano, both of whom lived for periods of time on the island, in exile from Franco's Spain. During the Cold War years they did not take sides, although presumably their religious faith would have made them wary of the atheism of Communist societies. Yet they published authors of all political stripes, from deeply conservative (Eliot, Heidegger) to radical or Communist (Aragon, Weil, Carpentier). Their aesthetic preference, however, was not realism or a socially committed literature, nor radically avant-garde work, nor art for art's sake; they practised a well-crafted, elegant literature that was deeply spiritual and resolutely humanistic.

The magazine was highly praised by Octavio Paz, who called it the best of its kind in the Spanish-speaking world. In a sense it followed two great examples of the Hispanic-speaking world: Spain's *Revista de Occidente*, founded by José Ortega y Gasset (1923–36; reappearing in 1962 and still published), and Argentina's *Sur*, founded by Victoria Ocampo (1931–66; then sporadically from 1967 to 1992). In fact *Orígenes* maintained a cordial relationship with *Sur* and its authors, in part because Virgilio Piñera lived in Buenos Aires from

1946 to 1958 and solicited works from Argentine authors. But in addition to artistic excellence and creativity, *Orígenes* also represented an ethical stance among certain Cuban intellectuals that was deeply linked to their efforts at cultural renewal.

Not everyone shared the *Orígenes* approach. In 1949, Mañach himself criticized the type of writing in its pages, claiming it was difficult to understand, obscure and removed from engagement in Cuba's public life. To a degree, Mañach was reviving the dichotomy of Martí versus Casal. Others criticized the journal for its 'hermeticism, cultural elitism, and fanaticism in the cultivation of poetry'.[4] The criticisms levelled at it came from the left, the centre and the right: from the left for its lack of social concerns and commitment, from the centre for its unwillingness to be more involved in public life (and its obscurity), from the right for its being a lofty conversation among poets. Some of these criticisms (minus any personal animosity, of course) have a grain of truth to them. While not true of all the writing in its pages, the texts by Lezama were – and are to this day – challenging: his baroque style, serpentine sentences, cascading metaphors and richly allusive digressions produce both astonishment and consternation. Not surprisingly, most of his work has not been translated into English, except the novel *Paradiso* (unevenly) and some of his poetry, with varying degrees of success. The difficulty with Lezama is that the language he uses for poetry, essay and the novel is the same: dense, layered, filled with a wide range of cultural analogies or allusions, not to mention the sheer audacity of his insights.

Lezama's response to Mañach and others was swift and pointed, criticizing those who have wasted their intellectual talents in government or academe, defending the group's right to their autonomy, competence and integrity. He rejected socially minded literature as sociology, conversational poetry as facile and the avant-garde as lacking philosophical depth. One could point to the opening line of Lezama's famous essay, *La expresión americana,* which reads, 'Only that which is difficult is stimulating.' By that definition, all his work was stimulating.[5]

Virgilio Piñera: Cuba as Dystopian and Surreal

The *Orígenes* writers were not a monolithic group: Rodríguez Feo, Piñera and García Vega were non-believers. And aesthetically, writers like Piñera (always referred to by his first name, Virgilio) and García Vega did not go in for baroque pyrotechnics. Virgilio has often been depicted as the anti-Lezama, for trivial reasons and not: if Lezama was big (and round), Piñera was rail-thin; Lezama was opulent with words and metaphorical, Piñera's language was blunt and cut to the bone; Lezama displayed his erudition, Piñera hid his behind a dark colloquial humour; Lezama's faith was often celebratory, Piñera's atheism leaned towards the bleak; Lezama's humour was ornate and literary, Virgilio's wickedly sarcastic as it hid its literary antecedents. Nothing illustrates this better than the following quotes, the first by Lezama, the second by Virgilio: 'The violet sea longs for the birth of the gods/ since to be born here is an ineffable celebration'; 'That accursed circumstance of water all around us'.[6] Both make reference to the ocean and, of course, to Cuba itself, but the vision offered by each is diametrically opposite. Both allude to a long history of exalting the natural beauty of Cuba: Lezama lovingly cites that tradition, but Piñera finds it a curse. Virgilio's long poem ('La isla en peso'/Island in the balance; 1943) is a grim but often hilarious romp through Cuban history. He destroys all attempts to mythologize the island's past and deals unflinchingly with the legacy of colonialism and slavery. Unlike most *origenista* poets, he makes several references to the island's black population, as well as to Afro-Cuban religions; the references to Catholicism in the poem are critical. Even the light of the tropics, extolled by many writers, is subjected to withering comments: 'the clarity is an enormous sucker that devours the shadow'; 'An entire people can die of light as easily as it can from the plague.'[7]

Piñera's poem was not critically acclaimed by the *origenistas*, particularly Cintio Vitier, who did not include it in the two anthologies he edited, *Ten Cuban Poets, 1937–1947* (1948) and *Fifty Years of Cuban Poetry, 1902–1952* (1953). In his celebrated book *Lo cubano en la poesía*

(1958, revd edn 1970), Vitier is highly critical of the poem, saying it does not exhibit *cubanía* (Cuban-ness), and also suggests that the poem is derivative, owing much to Aimé Césaire's *Notebook of a Return to the Native Land* (1939). But Piñera's poem is not a return (at that point he had not left Cuba), his language was not dense and metaphorical like Césaire's, and instead of Surrealism he offers a corrosive, humorous, almost blasphemous existentialism. Piñera's poem demolishes the entire poetic exaltation of Cuba's natural beauty and any kind of possible redemptive future: for Virgilio Cuba was a wild, uncontrollable and historical disaster. Vitier was a brilliant literary critic, but even great critics can sometimes make mistakes, and his evaluation of Piñera counts as one of the great misreadings in Cuban literary criticism.

Piñera's literary reputation, however, rested on his theatre, his short fiction and one extraordinary novel, *La Carne de René* (1952; *René's Flesh*, 1989). As a playwright, Virgilio's place in twentieth-century Cuban theatre is unquestionable, from *Electra Garrigó* (1941; staged in 1948) to *Aire Frío* (Cold Air, 1958; staged 1962), culminating in his 1968 Casa de las Américas award for *Dos viejos pánicos* (Two Panicked Geezers). His *Falsa Alarma* (False Alarm, 1948; staged in 1957) could be considered the first play of the theatre of the absurd along with *The Bald Soprano* and *Waiting for Godot*, all written in the same year, but the European plays were staged earlier (1950, 1953). Some claim *Jesús*, written in the same year and staged in 1950, is also an absurdist work, as well as being a wicked satire on Catholicism. The importance of Piñera's work belies the often-repeated notion that Latin American art and literature is always borrowing its aesthetic models from Europe, somehow always lagging behind.

Virgilio was also an excellent short story writer and some of these works are considered classics: 'The Fall', 'Meat', 'The Face', 'The Dummy', 'The Candy', 'The One Who Came to Save Me'. His universe is bleak, and he emphasizes the fate of the human body in extreme situations (death, mutilation, sacrifice, domination), foregrounding issues of sexuality and power. Nowhere is that more evident than in his first novel *La Carne de René*, a chilling tale that offers an unflinching and grotesquely comical look at pleasure, power and pain. Published in Buenos Aires, only two people reviewed it, José Rodríguez Feo (in Cuba) and Polish author Witold Gombrowicz, who lived in Argentina at the time and knew Piñera. A mix of Kafka and Sade told with Virgilio's trademark deadpan humour, the novel narrates the travails of René and his body and how it is fought over by different people and forces. At one point, René is sent for instruction to The School of Pain, where the motto is 'To suffer in silence'. Virgilio's examination of the sadomasochistic nature of power is about as far removed from *Orígenes* as you can possibly imagine, yet the novel insightfully explores the dark side of our most cherished institutions: family, school, church, the military and the state.

Virgilio, along with Rodríguez Feo, were the guiding forces in the creation of *Ciclón*, the magazine that was both successor and challenger to *Orígenes*. Starting in January 1955, it published fifteen issues, appearing bi-monthly in 1955 and 1956, twice in 1957 (after which they stopped publishing, claiming the country was at war) and one final time in early 1959. The first issue began with an editorial that was a direct and hostile reference to its predecessor ('Reader, behold *Ciclón*, the new journal. With it we erase *Orígenes* with one stroke. *Orígenes*, which, as everyone knows is now nothing but dead weight after ten years of service to Cuban culture . . .').[8] To make matters worse, the same issue had an excerpt from Sade's *120 Days of Sodom*, with an introductory note by Virgilio himself. It was the first time that Sade had been published in a Cuban journal, and some called for *Ciclón* to be closed down. In issue 5 (September 1955) Virgilio wrote one of his most significant essays, 'Ballagas en persona', openly discussing the nature of Emilio Ballagas's (1908–1954) homosexuality, another first in Cuban literary criticism. In the same issue, Gombrowicz's essay 'Contra los poetas' (Against Poets) also appeared. For those in the know, the text seemed to be a not very veiled attack on *origenista* authors; at one point Gombrowicz compares pure poetry to sugar, in that pure sugar is not eaten, only put in coffee. Otherwise it is too much, excessive:

It is the excess which exhausts one in poetry: an excess of poetry, an excess of poetic words, an excess of metaphors, an excess of nobility, an excess of purity and condensation that make verses seem like a chemical product.[9]

In the next issue (November 1955) Virgilio published one of his most prescient plays, *Los siervos* (The Serfs), a hilarious fable on the nature of power and ideology. Set in the future, when the entire planet has gone Communist, the chief ideologist of the party, Nikita, declares he wants to become a serf. From there, all hell breaks loose and the play turns into a succession of philosophical and physical pratfalls that highlight the brittle nature of Communist ideology. Written at a moment when the USSR was living through post-Stalinist upheaval (and barely months before Khrushchev's famous Twentieth Congress speech), its themes foreshadow the events that would mark the end of 'actually existing socialism' in 1989. The play had a dramatic reading in Spain (1958) and was not staged in Cuba until 1999, with references to Communism changed to 'carolism', and the characters having Cuban (not Russian) names. When Piñera's anthology, *Teatro*, was published in 1960, it included seven plays, but not 'The Serfs', no doubt a wise decision given the leftward tilt of the Cuban Revolution and its growing relationship with the USSR.

Ciclón, like *Orígenes*, published a mix of Cuban, Latin American, European and U.S. writers and it was a platform for a host of upcoming writers who became known in the 1960s and beyond: Antón Arrufat (b. 1935), César López (b. 1933), Guillermo Cabrera Infante (1929–2005), Severo Sarduy (1937–1993), Fayad Jamís (1930–1988), Calvert Casey (1924–1969), Nivaria Tejera (1929–2016), Luis Marré (1929–2013), Manuel Díaz Martínez (b. 1936) and Rolando Escardó (1925–1960). Many of them would join Piñera in forming part of *Lunes de la Revolución*, an important weekly cultural supplement that began publishing after the Revolution.

Cuba's Living History as Poet: Dulce María Loynaz

A solitary figure whose presence went virtually unknown for decades was Dulce María Loynaz, whose life spanned almost the entire twentieth century (1902–1997). Although she was well acquainted with the *Orígenes* poets, Loynaz was a loner and carried on her literary endeavours away from the mainstream of Cuba's literary culture. She was not a recluse: the Loynaz home was a true cultural hub, and well-known foreign writers like Juan Ramón Jiménez, Federico García Lorca and Gabriela Mistral stayed at the Loynaz home when visiting Cuba. Her two brothers were poets, and her sister Flor was both a painter and a poet.

Loynaz was from Cuba's independence aristocracy. Her greatuncle was Ignacio Agramonte, a general in the Ten Years War, and her father fought in the Spanish-American-Cuban War (1895–8), becoming a general. Loynaz's upbringing was unconventional; she did not receive formal schooling until she went to law school and passed the bar exam (1927). She published her first poem at the age of ten.

Despite an intriguing novel, *Jardín* (Garden; 1951), a travel book (1958) and a collection of literary essays, Loynaz's work is almost all poetry. She published six books of poetry in her lifetime, most of it by 1958. Her verses have a disarming simplicity that reveal a world of solitude, unhappiness in love or the anguish of physical decay. Many of her poems use nature imagery to reflect on time, creation and memory. Deeply influenced by the mystical tradition (St John of the Cross, St Teresa of Ávila), Loynaz was not a mystic writer, grounding her imagery in the concrete, the daily objects that surround us. She was fully aware that poetry is neither an escape nor an untroubled beauty: 'Poetry, divine and savage beast ... When will I be able to mark your flanks with my branding iron!'[10]

Loynaz was a great admirer of the poetry of Casal and wrote about him on several occasions. Her commitment to art and aesthetics was total, but that does not mean her work was totally unconnected to Cuban history or reality. Her poetry was intensely lyrical and personal, and not political or 'socially committed' in any conventional way. For example, her last major poem before the Revolution, 'Ultimos días de una casa' (Last Days of a House; 1958), is a sombre meditation on a house that is symbolically crumbling. Many have interpreted the poem as a premonition of the Cuban Revolution and the forces it would unleash. Loynaz's long narrative poem was the last published for a very long time. The crumbling house of the poem could be interpreted not only as a symbol of the Cuban nation, but also as the place to dream of an alternative to what Cuba was living through in the 1950s.

The Cuban Revolution meant the end of the world she had grown up in, as well as a radical change in cultural policy. As of 1959, she withdrew from an active literary life and stopped writing poetry, not publishing any of her verses until 1991. She would give an occasional lecture, write some journalistic pieces and the Royal Academy of the Spanish Language (Cuba Section) would meet at her house. After the Cuban Revolution she became a kind of non-person and was basically forgotten for decades. Finally, in 1987, she was awarded the National Literary Prize, a Casa de las Américas collection of criticism and testimony on her work and life (1991) appeared and, finally, she received the Cervantes Prize (1992), which renewed interest in her work, leading to new editions of her poetry, essays and her novel.

From a gender perspective one could argue that as a woman writer Loynaz was being marginalized by a literary establishment that was predominantly male, but that does not seem to be the case pre-1959, when her work was certainly recognized and received critical attention. However, it is interesting to note that many of her works before 1959 were edited in Spain. Her first important collection of poetry, *Versos* (1920–38), was first published in Cuba in 1938, but two subsequent editions (1947, 1950) were published in Spain. Still, publishing three editions of a collection of poetry in twelve years is impressive.

One must look at the changes in Cuban society post-1959 to understand the indifference to her work: her aesthetic, her worldview, her lifestyle were not compatible with the revolutionary ethos of the times. As a result, she withdrew into the world that she had grown up in, maintaining a fierce independence. When asked why she did not just leave Cuba, she responded: 'The daughter of an Independence War general does not abandon her country.'[11] Spoken like a true warrior.

The Visual Arts: From Avant-garde to Hallucinatory to Exuberant

The second half of the Republican period represented a true flowering of the visual arts in Cuba, with over a dozen world-class painters. Victor Manuel García (1897–1969) was credited with being one of the precursors of vanguardism, even if his work was highly figurative (portraits, peasants, city scenes). Eduardo Abela (1889–1965) combined a lively impressionism with some elements of a naïve style. His *Triumph of the Rumba* (1928) captured the beauty and movement of one of the island's major dance forms. Marcelo Pogolotti (1902–1988), who depicted humans in a Leger-type style, portrayed social realities with a strong anti-capitalist message. The monochromatic work of Fidelio Ponce (1895–1949) is haunting; the human figures look like ghosts, the landscapes are images of desolation.

The antithesis of Ponce was Jorge Arche (1905–1956), whose paintings are brightly coloured, with robust human figures (though not quite Botero-round), set in lush landscapes. His portrait of Martí (1943) is one of the first to depict him in white (he is almost invariably shown in black); his right hand is over his heart, where one can see a split or tear in the shirt. In the background are the mountains and royal palm tree that echo his love for nature, so prevalent in his poetry. In the foreground, his left hand reaches over as if to come right out of the picture. Is the hand reaching over a window, a bannister? Where is Martí actually standing? Arche's piece is an oddly serene mix of icon, realism and the surreal.

Arístides Fernández (1904–1934) was equally gifted as painter and short story writer; his palette tilted towards brownish hues (in group portraits or landscapes). He was deeply admired by the *Orígenes* generation.

Cuba's most renowned artist of the twentieth century was Wifredo Lam. His work was influenced by cubism, Surrealism and expressionism, filtered through an Afro-Cuban religious sensibility. Lam himself was the quintessence of Cuban *mestizaje*, having African, Chinese and European ancestry. His best-known work is *The Jungle* (1943), a profusion of faces, bodies and vegetation done mostly in blues, greens and oranges. It is not a real jungle (and there are none in Cuba) of the type that we associate with tropical rainforests, but a metaphorical and symbolic representation of *el monte*, that catch-all term for a place for slave runaways and independence fighters, as well as a sacred environment where a dialogue between man and nature is mediated by the orishas. Many of Lam's paintings have references to the orishas, such as Eleggúa (the crossroads, destiny), Changó (a warrior, guardian of lightning and music), Oggún (metals, creator-destroyer), Oyá (the winds, cemeteries) and Yemayá (the ocean, motherhood). Though he spent most of his life in Paris, Lam travelled frequently to Cuba both before and after 1959. His circle of friends included the French Surrealist poets, Picasso and the Martinican poet Aimé Césaire (1913–2008) whose books he often illustrated. It was a perfect match: Césaire's violently beautiful surreal imagery was ideally suited to Lam's elongated spiky figures that whirled about in constant transformation.

Carlos Enríquez (1900–1957) was a painter of rare talent who used colour to construct dreamlike portraits and landscapes that were often layered but in a way that suggested you could look through certain colours or forms. His use of colour was exuberant to say the least, if not hallucinatory. Although he produced some excellent work on Afro-Cuban themes, he is best known for his female nudes and landscapes, usually with horses. Enríquez had a fascination with horses and they appear in much of his work. Two of his best-known works, *El Rapto de las Mulatas* (The Abduction of the Mulatto Women; 1938) and *Dos Ríos* (Two Rivers; 1939), feature horses. The first is clearly a reference to the Poussin, Rubens and David renderings of the 'The Rape of the Sabine Women'. It is a period when Enríquez sought to paint the ballads of rural life, capturing its beauty, roughness and violence. Its bold use of colour adds to the drama depicted with two bandits grabbing two mulattas, with a horse in the foreground staring at the viewer. In the background can be seen the bucolic Cuban countryside with royal palm trees. The mix of violence, sadism, pleasure and natural beauty is disturbing. 'Dos Ríos' refers to the place where José Martí died, and Enríquez captures the moment Martí is shot while riding his horse into combat. One can see Martí is wounded but at the same time he has a serene look. The drama and agony of the painting is reflected in the horse, with its head turned back towards Martí, surging out of a vortex of colour. Enríquez's *Happy Peasants* (1938) is a blistering critique of rural poverty, showing emaciated rural dwellers (and an equally emaciated dog) amongst hallucinatory squalor.

If Enríquez was fascinated with horses, Mariano Rodríguez (1912–1990) was enthralled by roosters, and painted hundreds of them in his career in realistic, cubist, impressionist and abstract styles. The expressionist work of Mariano, who was part of the *Orígenes* group inner circle, is often playful, and his humour is steeped in the knowledge of Cuban culture. His rooster paintings, for example, acknowledge that roosters are a symbol of male virility (cockfighting was popular before 1959), but at the same time he makes nuanced statements about them, either by showing them tenderly with women, or debunking some of their masculinist strutting.

Also close to the *Orígenes* circle was René Portocarrero (1912–1985), whose work often mirrors the baroque language of Lezama Lima. Portocarrero's imagery is dense, boldly coloured and layered almost to the point of dizziness. Equally gifted in portraits, landscapes and cityscapes, Portocarrero often worked on certain themes (interiors of houses in the Cerro neighbourhood, cathedrals, flowers, masks, landscapes), churning out dozens if not hundreds of examples (his total artistic output is estimated at some ten thousand works).

He illustrated many literary works, including Lezama's seminal novel *Paradiso* (1966), and he received an award for the totality of his work from the São Paulo Biennial in 1963.

Yet another artist close to *Orígenes* was Amelia Peláez (1896–1968), the most acclaimed female painter of the time, known for her cubist/stained-glass effect in portraying still lifes and interiors. She also did the gigantic mural on the front façade of the Hilton Hotel (now Habana Libre); its rich use of blue hues evokes the marine life of the island. Peláez's work uses bold colours and the geometry/architecture of interior space to create a unique world that is immensely appealing to viewers.

Popular Culture: Television and Radio

Cuba's close relationship with the u.s. meant that it was the first Latin American country to have broadcast radio (1922) and TV (1950). Cuban radio developed quickly, and was instrumental in the diffusion of Cuban music. It not only played *danzas, contradanzas, danzónes, canciones* (songs), *boleros* (torch songs), which were already popular, but over the decades featured new genres: the *son* and *danzonete* (1920s), rumba and the *charanga* sound (including what some called *danzón-mambo*) in the 1930s; Latin jazz, *filin* and mambo (1940s), and mambo and cha-cha-chá in the 1950s. Cuban radio was known for its soap operas as well. The first serial broadcast of a radio soap was *La serpiente roja* (The Red Serpent; 1937), featuring a Chinese detective Chan Li Po. It ran for ten years, and was written by one of Cuba's most prolific and successful writers of soaps, Félix B. Caignet (1892–1976). He also wrote *El monstruo en la sombra* (The Monster in the Shadow), a soap that dealt with heroin addiction, a first for Cuban radio. But it is Caignet's 1948 *El derecho de nacer* (The Right to Be Born), which ran for 314 episodes, that put him on the map of Latin America. The radio soap was not only hugely successful in Cuba, it was also remade throughout Latin America (Mexico, Venezuela, Puerto Rico, Brazil, Colombia,

Nicaragua, Peru) and Spain, and in the TV era shot for TV audiences as well, with TV remakes into the 2000s. By 1956, radio reached some six million people (out of 6.5 million) and two-thirds of Havana's vehicles had radios.[12]

Cuban TV was a leader for the region and by the time of the Revolution the island had a higher per capita rate of TVs than Italy. Cuban TV was known for its advanced technology, the artistic and acting excellence of its performers, and its sophistication in linking entertainment, popular culture and commerce. The programming was varied: sports, news, variety shows, comedy, cooking shows, high art (ballet, contemporary dance), soaps, serials, sitcoms, charity telethons and, of course, films. In the latter case, U.S. Hollywood productions dominated, but Mexico's films were tremendously popular on the island, with the likes of Pedro Infante, María Félix and El Indio Fernández becoming household names for Cuban audiences. Because Mexico's film industry was much larger, Cuban singers, actors and musicians often performed there and, in some cases, helped jump-start their careers. It was in Mexico that Dámaso Pérez Prado (1916–1989) was able to popularize the mambo, before it became a craze in the U.S. in the 1950s.

Of course, the most popular Cuban performer on television in the 1950s was on U.S., not Cuban, TV: Desiderio Arnaz (1917–1986), known as Desi, the husband of Lucille Ball on the *I Love Lucy* show, which ran for six seasons (1951–7, and in a different format for another three). It is easy to dismiss Arnaz's character on the sitcom as a Latin (and, specifically, Cuban) stereotype: he talks loudly, he has a 'hot' Latin temper, he speaks English with a strong accent, he sports the good looks and suave demeanour of the Latin lover, he plays a conga drum and is the leader of a Latin music band. But, as Gustavo Pérez-Firmat points out, Ricky Ricardo is more than that:

> He is neither straight enough to be the straight man nor flat enough to be a stereotype. Richer and deeper than the common sense view of him, Ricky Ricardo lives out the dilemmas and

delights of bi-culturation. He is not only a central presence within 'I Love Lucy'; he is also the exemplary Cuban-American subject.[13]

Even though the show makes fun of Ricky's tendency to mangle the English language, his wife never tires of saying she loves him *because* of the accent, his otherness (and foreignness) and the fact that he is not like American men. There is a hilarious episode from the second season where Lucy hires a Mr Livermore to tutor Ricky in order to improve his English and improve his accent. The attempt fails miserably, with the tutor adopting a Cuban accent and singing 'Babalú', Ricky's trademark song. Seeing that the tutor is an aspiring singer, Ricky sets him up for auditions and possible record company contracts. Lucy admits defeat: 'It was a battle of the accents, and Mr Livermore lost.'[14]

Pérez-Firmat further claims that Desi Arnaz embodied the notion of *viveza*. The *vivo* is someone who prospers because they are on the ball, instinctively knowing how to navigate life's trials: 'What the *vivo* lacks in formal education or native talent, he makes up in plain smarts. His intelligence is a species of ingenuity, his wit a species of cleverness.'[15] Not trained as a musician, Arnaz joined Xavier Cugat's band, but eventually started his own, which became successful; he was not a trained actor but then quickly made it into the movies and became Lucille Ball's co-star; he was not a businessman, but through wit and grit formed Desilu Productions and even bought RKO studios. The Cuban *vivo* lives on, both on and off the island.

Cubaneo, Transculturation and Ajiacos

If in the 1950s Desi Arnaz's TV personality was defining Cuban-American biculturalism, a decade before, and in a more serious vein, Fernando Ortiz was defining Cuba's culture as an example of transculturation, an *ajiaco* (a type of stew) that has become a metaphor for Cuba's racial and cultural mix. The term came from his best-known work, *Contrapunteo cubano del tabaco y azúcar* (1940; *Cuban Counterpoint: Tobacco and Sugar*, 1947 and 1995). Using tobacco and sugar as organizing metaphors of Cuban reality, Ortiz traces out their evolving identities: tobacco is associated with prestige, myth, craftsmanship, individual talent and ingenuity, while sugar is linked with power, industry, history, slavery and mass production. Their relationship is complex and transmutational, and to understand Cuba required studying, in Ortiz's words, 'the history of its intermeshed transculturations'. What does Ortiz mean by it? Nancy Morejón offers a succinct definition of the concept:

Transculturation signifies constant interaction, transmutation between two or more cultural components, whose unconscious end is the creation of a third cultural whole – that is, culture – new and independent, although its bases, its roots, rest on preceding elements. The reciprocal influence here is determining. No element is superimposed on the other; on the contrary, each one becomes a third entity. None remains immutable. All change and grow in a 'give and take' which engenders a new texture.[16]

A good example of transculturation would be Regla de Ocha, which combines Yoruba beliefs, Catholic practices and elements of Spiritism into something uniquely Cuban.

Morejón's definition stresses culture, as does the work of Ortiz, but *Cuban Counterpoint* seems to be a work of economic history, albeit a highly unusual one. The most 'successful' Caribbean examples of transculturation are based on race, religion and music; in terms of economy and politics Cuba had definitely followed Eurocentric models (market-based economies and parliamentary systems of government). Ortiz makes a further distinction, saying that in many cases deculturation (or exculturation) characterizes the beginning of an encounter between cultures, especially when one dominates the other (as in colonization and slavery), followed by acculturation, finalizing in transculturation. These distinctions are important in that they recognize that transculturation is a social process marked by history and power relationships.

Ortiz famously defined Cuban culture as an *ajiaco*, a stew of Amerindian origin that eventually incorporated foods and condiments from Africa, Europe, Asia and the Middle East. It has meats, vegetables, tubers and condiments that are constantly being added to the mix, and while the stew has its own flavour, it also retains the taste of its individual elements. To call Cuba a melting pot is to confuse it with U.S. notions of assimilation and acculturation. For example, in the case of Santería, the religion is predominantly Yoruba even though it is overlaid with Catholic and Spiritist elements. Despite these Catholic elements, one cannot consider it Catholicism with Yoruba touches; on the contrary, it is profoundly African with European influences and, ultimately, Cuban, without forgetting its ancestral roots. One could say that the *ajiaco* has an additive and associative logic, the melting pot a subtractive and reductive one. It bears remembering that Ortiz coined his two terms around 1940, and in the context of the Second World War (especially given Nazi racial theories) and Jim Crow laws in the U.S., Cuba in comparison seemed like a racial paradise.

Although later questioned by scholars and activists working on race, the *ajiaco* metaphor still has some resonance: in a 2011 documentary by Henry Louis Gates Jr on race in contemporary Cuba, historian and director of the National Library Eduardo Torres-Cuevas invites Gates to his house, where he has prepared an *ajiaco* for him. As they eat, Torres-Cuevas explains to him Ortiz's metaphor of the *ajiaco*. Other voices in the film, however, argue that despite the *ajiaco* Cuba is still faced with issues of racism, and that the *ajiaco* metaphor has perhaps run its course.

Another Cuban author who dealt with cultural *ajiacos* from this period was Alejo Carpentier (1904–1980). His history of the island's music (*La música en Cuba*, 1946; *Music in Cuba*, 2001) beautifully describes the many cultural streams that fed the music of the country

(Spain, West Africa, France, Italy, the U.S.). His *Kingdom of the World* (1949; English translation 1957), his first major novel, is set in Haiti during its revolution and deals mostly with the aftermath during the rule of Henri Christophe and beyond. It is a highly poetic novel that deals with the cycles of repression and liberation in history, and includes a positive look at Vodou as a significant cultural element of resistance in Haiti's struggle to abolish slavery and achieve independence. In the original 1949 edition, Carpentier spoke about Haiti and coined the term *lo real maravilloso* to describe aspects of Vodou and Christophe's projects of building the Citadelle and Sans Souci (his palace). Many have translated the term to English as magical realism, but more accurate would be 'the marvellous real'. Carpentier did not like the term magical realism, which he associated with a literary gimmick akin to Surrealism. For Carpentier, 'the marvellous real' entailed something deeper than a literary technique; it was a cultural practice or belief system that was able to transform the reality of people (whether it is Vodou in fighting oppression or Christophe's visions for resisting possible French invasion). After writing three further important works in the 1950s, Carpentier published his magnum opus, *El siglo de las luces* (1962; *Explosion in a Cathedral*, 1962), an exhilarating novel about the influence of the French Revolution in the Caribbean. It begins, ominously, with the boat transporting the first guillotine to be brought to the New World. The novel is a true epic, with revolution, betrayals, love stories and discussions about art. All of the work in this period was written in Venezuela, where he lived between 1946 and 1959 and had a radio programme. He wrote extensively on music for many newspapers (mostly for *El Nacional*, Caracas) and journals. His published writings on music cover over 1,800 pages in three volumes, and encompass classical music (Wagner, Varese, Strauss, Schoenberg) to Cuban popular music, light opera (*zarzuela*) and *Porgy and Bess*, to the musics of India and Brazil. Carpentier had a solid musical education; however, as a journalist he was able to keep the technical aspects understandable to his readers. His reviews were learned, witty and enjoyably informative.

Binaries of the Republican Period: Sacrifice over *Choteo*?

In her insightful book on Cuba, Velia Cecilia Bobes outlines traits of Cuban politics during the Republican period. What is interesting about her typology is that it recognizes a continuum of attitudes and actions. Her list is intriguing, albeit frustrating, in that the traits can seem contradictory. Some of the more salient distinctions she makes are a belief in democracy but a belittling attitude towards its institutions, a sacrificial attitude towards patriotism with unabashed *choteo*, or anti-imperialist sentiments, co-mingling with a fascination with the American Way of Life.[17] While Bobes's traits are intriguing, is it really the case that they are all uniquely Cuban? Many of the attitudes she outlines are applicable to other Latin American nations, and even to the U.S. or Europe.

For the moment, let's focus on the notion of sacrifice for a cause, which goes back to the nineteenth-century independence movements, and is embodied in the figures of Antonio Maceo (1845–1896), Máximo Gómez (1836–1905) and, of course, José Martí, poet-warrior. Their examples would continue to resonate in Republican Cuba, as we have seen in the constant evocation and re-evaluation of Martí during the twentieth century. The belief in the virtue of revolutionary violence could be seen in acts that were not aimed at overthrowing a government (or system). For example, if a group of people had a political grievance, they often joined together twenty or thirty armed men, took over a building or part of a small town and made their demands known. After some negotiation with the authorities a political settlement would be reached. Despite participants being armed, most of these incidents did not to lead to bloodshed. However, at other moments things could turn bloody, as when members of the PIC (Independent Party of the Colored), founded in 1908, staged an armed protest in May 1912. They were seeking to overturn a law prohibiting the founding of parties based on class, religion or race, which was clearly aimed at the PIC. The reaction was swift and alarming: the government and the elites claimed the PIC was fomenting a race war. The results were disastrous: the government unleashed its troops and violently suppressed the PIC, killing between three thousand and six thousand black and mixed-raced Cubans over the next two and a half months.

Interpreting Cuban History: Absolution, Redemption, Exhaustion?

During the Machado dictatorship, many underground groups turned to violence, especially after 1931, often engaging in acts of terrorism or political assassination. In the 1940s the rise of one of Cuba's most charismatic politicians, Eduardo Chibás (1907–1951), energized civil society; his motto was 'Vergüenza contra dinero' (Shame Against Money). A vociferous critic of the corruption, gangsterism and cronyism of Cuban politics, he ran for president on the Ortodoxo Party ticket and lost, but he seemed destined to win the 1952 elections. Chibás had a popular Sunday radio show that attracted over half a million listeners, almost one out of every ten Cubans. On his show, he accused the education minister of fraud and misuse of funds; he was challenged to provide the proof, but only provided photos of the miserable state of rural schools. People began to question his integrity, and in the spirit of Cuban *choteo*, mocked his claims. Ever the media-savvy politician, on 5 August 1951 he planned to fire a pistol and wound himself at the end of his radio show, in a kind of wake-up shot to the citizenry to rally around his cause and against corruption. Chibás fired the shot, but no one heard it because he had exceeded his time on air and by then a commercial was running. However, it made the news and for ten agonizing days he was in hospital before dying from his self-inflicted wound. Despite an outpouring of grief and an unruly funeral, the Ortodoxos never really recovered from his death. Their candidate for the 1952 election was impeccably honest, but no match for Chibás's charisma, and before the elections could be held, Batista and the military stepped in on 10 March 1952. (In 1952, the Ortodoxos ran a young lawyer for the Cuban legislature, Fidel Castro. He lost.)

The Batista coup went fairly smoothly and at the beginning not much changed in Cuban society and politics. Despite the Cold War and Batista's anti-Communist credentials, he did not even outlaw the Communist Party until a year later. Eventually, though, the regime began to censor the press, repress trade union activity, crack down on student activism and brutally persecute political opponents. Barely sixteen months after taking power, a group of over 160 young rebels, led by Fidel Castro, launched an attack on the Moncada Barracks in Santiago de Cuba on 26 July 1953. The insurrection would become a defining moment in Cuban history and politics. The plan was for the group, which included two women, to attack the barracks, capture it and its weaponry and use these for a general insurrection that would inspire the people to resist and topple the government. Militarily, the plan was a total failure, with the rebel forces being routed and most of them captured. In battle or captivity, many were tortured and executed (61 in total). Among those captured were Fidel, his brother Raúl, Juan Almeida, Ramiro Valdés, Haydée Santamaría, Gustavo Arcos and other leaders who would become prominent in the struggle against Batista. Part of the failure of Moncada was poor execution, lack of weapons and a belief that the righteousness of the cause would lead to certain victory. The Communists severely criticized the Moncada attack as 'putschist' and 'adventurist'. Others simply called it 'crazy' or 'suicidal', and these criticisms have some merit, but the critics were not able to discern some of the unforeseen elements that played into the great dissatisfaction that Cubans felt at the time. Fidel and his forces were determined to make Moncada a political victory and they succeeded.

Barely two months after the attack, the government put several of the rebels on trial. The most significant was Fidel Castro himself who, as a lawyer, prepared his own defence. He gave a four-hour speech (later entitled 'History Will Absolve Me') in which he denounced the illegitimacy of the Batista government and laid out his plan for a future Cuba. The speech became the political platform of what would become the 26th of July Movement (abbreviated as M-26-7), named in honour of the date of the attack on the Moncada barracks. Fidel's rhetorical strategy was brilliant. He established three discursive devices: the lone man versus the powers of the state; the accused versus the accuser; and truth versus lies. In the first case he reminded the judges that he was simply a patriotic Cuban pursuing the ideals of Martí – who was quoted nine times during the speech – facing the military, political and juridical machinery of the Cuban state. Quickly, he made his appeal to being the underdog. In the second case, Fidel became the accuser, turning the tables on his prosecutors. He accused the regime of violating the 1940 Constitution, called Batista a monarch and 'miserable tyrant', and branded the government illegitimate; he further argued that precedents for rebelling against a government like Batista's went all the way back to Christian antiquity, the philosophers of India, Greece and Rome, Aquinas, Luther, Calvin and beyond. But ultimately, it was before the tribunal of history that Fidel made his plea, one that again alluded to Martí, since 1953 was the centenary of his birth. Fidel and his rebels unequivocally stated that the Moncada attack was inspired by Martí and was a vindication of his historical legacy.

This is why Fidel ended his speech with 'Condemn me. It does not matter. History will absolve me.'[18] What tribunal of history was he referring to here? Is it some secular god judging humankind through history, a Hegelian world spirit that sees all, or some law of history that sifts through the evidence and renders its sentence? In his speech Fidel not only referred to world historical examples to buttress his arguments – especially in justifying the right of rebellion – but he drew on Cuba's own history, recalling the nationalist heroes of the nineteenth century: Maceo, Gómez, Martí and Céspedes, those who defended the homeland and tried to free it from foreign domination. Nicola Miller sums up this appeal to history, saying that its centrality to Fidel's speech and 'to the revolutionary struggle meant that history rather than constitutionalism or ideology, was the key legitimating force behind the Cuban revolution'.[19] Fidel, ever aware of politics and history as performative event, saw that performance as a decolonizing and anti-imperialist event.

Miller additionally observes that Castro's vision of history was influenced by Cuban revisionist historians, who had been arguing for seeing greater agency of Cuba during the Spanish-Cuban-American War, arguing that Cuba was not freed solely because of the U.S. intervention in that war. These historians also upheld an anti-imperialist perspective in seeing that Cuba's sovereignty was compromised by U.S. hegemony; hence, their interest in the Platt Amendment and the trope of the 'frustrated republic'.

Influenced by the Annales School, they also began to look at other strata of society (workers, peasants) to compose histories of 'those without a history'. And, finally, some of them maintained that Cuba's revolutionary trajectory was one long history (punctuated by moments of less activity) that began with the Ten Years War (1868–78), was reaffirmed by the war of 1895–8, was resurrected briefly in 1933, and reclaimed and successfully brought to fruition by the 26th of July Movement (1953–9) and the subsequent socialist revolution (1959 to the present). Later, of course, as the Revolution adopted Marxist-Leninist thought, some of these ideas were reworked from a Marxist perspective. Fidel clearly subscribes to this interpretation. A visual reminder of this appeal to Cuban history, while interpreting it with new actors in new ways, is exemplified in the backdrop to the main stage where the Second Cuban Communist Party Congress of 1980 was held. Nine figures were on display: on the left Marx, Engels and Lenin; in the middle Martí, Maceo and Gómez; on the right Mella, Camilo and Che Guevara.

How should we view this appeal to history and this view of history, and how do they relate (or not) to perspectives of Cuban history by either Cuban or non-Cuban historians and in the country's wider culture? What Fidel argued for, and in this he was no different from most historians, is a particular narrative of Cuban history. Most histories are told as narratives and I would like to examine some of the rhetorical strategies involved in the plotting of these narratives, as well as their modes of argument and ideological meanings.

In his renowned book *Metahistory*, Hayden White discusses the way in which history is represented and outlines four elements: (1) mode of emplotment; (2) mode of argument; (3) rhetorical strategy; (4) mode of ideological implication. Mode of emplotment refers to an aesthetic approach, of which there are four: (1) Romantic (redemption of hero or humankind); (2) Tragic (a fall but a revelation and lesson for the rest); (3) Comic (reconciliation); (4) Satirical ('inadequacy of consciousness to live in the world happily or to comprehend it fully').[20] The mode of argument is both a cognitive and a narrative strategy, of how history is narrated but also exploration of its themes and organizing metaphors. There are four of these as well: the first is associated with the Romantic mode and is Formist and defined as dispersive, offering vivid and colourful details but not sweeping generalizations. Formist argument establishes the uniqueness of individuals or collectivities with regard to history, focusing more on the events than what grounds them. The second, mechanistic, is tied to the Tragic mode; it is integrative and often reductive (offering one guiding explanation for history). It seeks out the 'laws of history' and almost views these laws as extra-historical agencies. The Marxist notion of class struggle or the centrality of economics would be examples of a mechanistic argument. The third approach would be organicist, associated with the Comic mode. It takes the many parts of a narrative as part of a synthetic and integrative process, and is not reductive like the mechanistic argument. Instead of the laws of history, it talks about principles and ideas. Hegel's notion of the Idea (or the spirit of history) would be a good example. Finally, the contextualist argument, linked to the Satirical mode, avoids reduction and abstraction and looks at history in wide contexts. Instead of laws or guiding ideas it seeks to establish certain threads or influences that run through a historical period, but its claims are modest. Ideologically, the Romantic-Formist mode is described as Anarchist, the Tragic-Mechanistic mode as Radical, the Comic-Organicist as Conservative, and the Satirical-Contextualist as Liberal; but these are seen as attitudes more than adherence to parties. Historians and thinkers, as well as political figures, can sometimes use different modes of emplotment, argument and ideology, which may allow us to see someone like Fidel Castro in a more complex fashion, since he will combine different modes of emplotment and argument with differing rhetorical strategies as well.

The Romantic mode involves the redemption of humankind, clearly something that would resonate with both Martí and Fidel. Both were Romantics in that they believed in the triumph of good over evil, and in the perfectibility of humankind; but they equally showed the influence of the Christian theology of martyrdom and sacrifice to achieve the redemption of the people. (Recall that Fidel studied with the Jesuits, an upbringing that gave a moral tinge to his politics.) In the Romantic plot the hero transcends the world. As White says, 'It is a drama of triumph of good over evil, of virtue over vice, of light over darkness, and of the ultimate transcendence of man over the world in which he is imprisoned by the Fall.'[21] Both believed in the perfectibility of humans and, obviously, after 1959 Cuba promoted the concept of the 'New Man', a Bolshevik notion recycled and popularized by Che Guevara himself. Fidel clearly saw himself fulfilling what Martí had left unfinished.

However, Fidel's political goals also belong to the Comic mode of emplotment that seeks reconciliation and, above all, national unity; its mode of argument is organicist (integrative). Organicists see the whole as greater than the sum of the parts; they believe in goals, in teleological explanations, repeatedly appealing to notions of 'the people', nation and culture. After 1959 Fidel and others would add the term Revolution, always with a capital letter. In this sense, Fidel is a Hegelian at the macrocosmic level, who endorsed a comic view, as well as saying that history was to be the world's court of justice and final judgement.

How do we reconcile this conservative ideology of comedic emplotment with a Marxist revolutionary like Fidel Castro? This requires arguing for a dual aspect to Fidel's thought: at the microcosmic level he saw history as Tragically emplotted, with a mechanistic mode of argument, where the laws that govern history inform their narrative and imply a radical ideology. Tragedy requires people to struggle and it requires sacrifice, and Fidel's constant references to struggle and martyrdom were a consistent refrain not only in the 1950s when Batista and the military was the main enemy, but after 1959, when counter-revolutionaries, internally, and U.S. imperialism, externally, became the main enemy. Fidel embodied the utopian vision of a better society free of classism, racism, sexism and so on (a comic plot with a happy ending), but realized that to get there requires a titanic effort (tragic plot, strife), an epic struggle that delivers redemption to the people (Romantic plot). We can see how Fidel's thought borrowed from three different modes of emplotment, types of argument and ideological implications. But none of this should be a surprise since it has often been pointed out that, after the period of initial revolutionary upheaval and dramatic social change, most socialist revolutions of the twentieth century settled down and often became set in their ways: conservative, if you will (Comic mode).

The one mode Fidel did not embrace for interpreting history was the Satirical one, associated with a contextualist mode of argument – irony – and ideologically liberal. Satire would be the opposite of Romance: it states that humankind is a captive of the world, not master of it. Human consciousness and will cannot overcome the dark forces of life and the eventuality of death. This need not imply pessimism or passivity towards social problems, just a certain humility in accepting the human, social and material limitations to change. The Satirical mode raises doubt, has a certain relativizing tone. It is 'dialectical' in that it is aware of 'the capacity of language to obscure more than it clarifies in any act of verbal figuration'.[22] For Fidel's ability to transmit thought and exhort followers to achieve revolutionary goals cannot be Satirical because it would undermine revolutionary morale or muddle the message.

In the case of Fidel, we are not dealing with a formal historian in a book-lined study, moving around dusty archives, but a political leader and a man of action. His study and understanding of history were tools for political struggle with a concrete objective: the eventual overthrow of the Batista regime. History was not merely a guide to the past, but a way of putting that past into the service of revolutionary insurrection, propaganda of the deed. Although not a Marxist at the time of the Moncada attack (1953), Fidel's thought and actions coincided with Marx's on some points. First, he would agree in seeing Marx's view of history as a way of changing society, as in Marx's famous thesis on Feuerbach: 'The philosophers have only *interpreted* the world in different ways; the point, however, is to change it.'[23] Second, like Marx, Fidel would be able to perceive capitalist society from a Satirical mode, in that this mode of emplotment enables one to see the paradoxical nature of our social realities. How else can one perceive a society 'which breeds poverty in the midst of plenty, war [or violence] in a situation in which peace is possible, scarcity (both material and psychic) in the midst of affluence'?[24] One could add to the list unemployment, lack of health care, violation of human rights, racial and sexual discrimination. Finally, Marx, this time following Hegel's dual emplotment (Tragedy, Comedy), also resonated with Fidel's thinking. Marx's emplotment of history had him associate the bourgeoisie with Tragedy, the proletariat with Comedy. The fall of the bourgeoisie and their being eclipsed by the proletariat, who culminate a historical process that eliminates social conflict, becomes a Comedic fulfilment. If you replace bourgeoisie with Batista's forces (which did include some elements of the bourgeoisie, the military, some trade unions, some small businesspeople, some sectors of the church, and the U.S. – at least until 1958) and the proletariat with the people (peasants, workers, students, professionals), you have the argument made by Fidel and others in their search for revolutionary change. Given these affinities in emplotment, argument, rhetoric and ideology, Fidel's later embrace of Marxism might not seem so surprising. This also allows us to see his thinking post-1959 not as a betrayal of the Moncada period but one that has both continuities and ruptures with his earlier thinking.

The Satirical mode and the use of irony is evident with some of the thinkers we have seen: Sarduy and his questioning of Cuban national identity and debunking of binaries, Piñera in his fables about power and the body as well as the nature of ideology, Mañach and his investigation into *choteo*. However, only Mañach would qualify as a liberal in the most conventional sense of the term. Sarduy is almost impossible to categorize ideologically: openly queer, radical, neo-baroque, postmodernist and quasi-Buddhist. Piñera, not openly queer (but not in the closet), was an atheist, a materialist in the philosophical sense, a Kafka with a wickedly developed sense of *choteo*, maybe a lapsed existentialist. With his Sadean overtones, Piñera mixed tragic and satirical modes brilliantly. Did this make him an anarchist-radical-liberal? What does this mean? Apart from the fact that Piñera is hard to pin down, he was also a thinker who was able to straddle these aesthetic and cognitive modes. Fernando Ortiz and his tobacco-sugar metaphor evolved an organicist argument to explain transculturation in a Comic mode (with a motif of racial conciliation) that some might view as conservative nowadays, but was certainly couched in liberal terms in his time. Appreciating the complexities of these thinkers and their respective historical visions allows us to look at the island's history in a richer way. It avoids (or at least complicates) some of the well-known tropes or binaries of nationalism versus cosmopolitanism; progressive versus conservative or revolutionary versus counter-revolutionary; anti-imperialist versus pro-imperialist; elitist versus populist; authoritarian versus democratic; and warrior-intellectual versus aesthete.

Fidel's absolution or redemption through history carries both responsibility and a burden: to always be better; to work harder; to make sacrifices for the future. It is no easy task and requires enormous discipline, revolutionary fervour and unshakeable conviction. Reaffirming these values, all Cuban schoolchildren chant in unison at the beginning of each school day: 'Pioneers for Communism, we will be like Che!'

Leonardo Padura's novel *La neblina del ayer* (2005; *Havana Fever*, 2010), set in contemporary Havana, is part of his cycle on detective Mario Conde (more in the next chapter). In a conversation between the protagonist and his group of friends – Rabbit, an amateur historian; Candito, formerly into illicit business and now a Seventh Day Adventist; and Skinny Carlos, a wheelchair-using Angola vet – Cuba's plight and its role in history are discussed. Parts of the conversation follow here, all stated by Rabbit:

> All the time, day in and day out, we've been living out our responsibility for this moment in history. They were bent on forcing us to be better.

> After being so exceptional, so historical and so transcendent, people get tired and want to be normal. I have a name for that 'historical exhaustion'.

> This is a country predestined to exaggeration, Christopher Columbus started the rot when he said that this was the most beautiful land ever seen by man and all that jazz . . . This exaggeration is also our greatest burden: it threw us into the midst of history.[25]

Conde, while listening to these comments by Rabbit, describes the whole process as 'historical exhaustion syndrome'.[26] Padura's use of the Satirical mode argues for accepting the frailties and limitations of humans. In the conversation the idea of a normal existence seems like an antidote to the idea of exceptionalism, transcendence, grandeur, History with a capital 'H'. Padura also alludes to the idea of Cuban exceptionalism, which has had a long history, as the quote suggests – from the time of Columbus. This has led many Cubans to argue for that exceptionality (Martí, Mañach, Lezama, Fidel, Guerra, Ortiz) and Cuba's destiny of achieving greatness. Very few of the artists and/ or writers discussed in this book go against that trend: Piñera, García Vega, Arenas, Ponte and Bruguera, among others.

Padura critiques the revolutionary perspective on progress, which is linear, something it inherited from Enlightenment thought. Rabbit again explains the contradictory path, one that must go straight as an arrow into the future:

> Life was passing us by on all sides . . . and to protect us they gave us blinkers. Like mules. We should only look ahead and strive towards the shining future awaiting for us at the end of history and, obviously, we weren't allowed to get tired on that road . . . I sometimes think they dazzled us with all that glare and we walked past the future and didn't even see it . . . Now we're halfway round the track and are going blind, as well as bald and cirrhotic, and there's not even all that much we want to see anymore.[27]

From these quotes, it would be tempting to say that Conde and his friends are thoroughly disillusioned with 'el proyecto' (the revolutionary project, as it is referred to in Cuba). No doubt, there is a sense of missed opportunities in life, of the high price of revolutionary commitments (Carlos as a vet with disabilities), of certain choices made by the Revolution (censorship, elimination of small businesses, limitations on personal life), not to mention the age-old argument about the ends justifying the means. But at the same time, Padura is expressing these criticisms against the backdrop of a Cuba with universal education and health care, almost full employment (at least until the early 1990s), a level of social violence that is negligible (especially when compared to most Latin American countries) and a cultural life that is vibrant. Most Cuban readers would understand that context; many foreign readers would only see these quotes as Cubans 'suffering under Communism'.

As we have seen in these first two chapters, Cuba had a vibrant, musical, literary and visual arts culture before the 1959 Revolution that swept Fidel Castro and his guerrilla army into power. In the literary field there were established authors writing fiction such as Alejo Carpentier, Virgilio Piñera, Lino Novás Calvo, Carlos Montenegro, Lino Novás Calvo, Enrique Labrador Ruiz, Dulce María Loynaz and Onelio Jorge Cardoso; in poetry the likes of José Lezama Lima, Eliseo Diego, Cintio Vitier, Mariano Brull, Eugenio Florit, Piñera, Ballagas, Loynaz, Guillén, Baquero, Acosta and José Zacarías Tallet. In the field of criticism or non-fiction an excellent cohort that included Fernando Ortiz, Lydia Cabrera, Juan Marinello, Mañach, Lazo, Ramiro Guerra, Félix Ichaso, Medardo Vitier, Carpentier, Portuondo, Lezama, Juan Marinello and José Rodríguez Feo. In the visual arts a host of painters and sculptors came to the fore from the late 1920s on: Víctor Manuel, Abela, Pogolotti, Peláez, Enríquez, Ponce de León, Lam, Mariano, Portocarrero, Arche, Bermúdez and Carreño among many others. Cuba's musical culture was exceptional during this period, led by extraordinary composer-musicians such as Ernesto Lecuona, Ignacio Piñeiro, Roldán, García Caturla, Miguel Matamoros, Arsenio Rodríguez, the López brothers (Orestes and Israel, better known as 'Cachao'), Antonio María Romeu, or singers of the stature of Rita Montaner, Celia Cruz and Benny Moré. Cuban music was known throughout the world, from the habanera and *son* to the rumba and cha-cha-chá, as well as the mambo. The level of development of radio and television in Cuba was high, especially in comparison to the rest of Latin America. The one area with less creative vitality – with exceptions – was film.

Despite the cultural significance of the Republican period, all was not perfect. Almost no authors could live from their writing and many had to self-publish. The Batista dictatorship (1952–9) was a harsh environment for anyone who openly opposed the regime, and that included many artists, writers and thinkers. For personal or political reasons many authors spent time abroad (Carpentier, Piñera, Lydia Cabrera, Florit, Guillén, Ramos), something that was equally true of Cuba's painters (Lam, Carreño, Peláez). The fall of Batista and the triumph of the revolutionary forces led by Fidel Castro would alter Cuba's culture and history indelibly.

THREE

A Revolution in Culture
(1959–1980)

In some respects, a revolution is a miracle.

Lenin, 1921

A revolution is certainly the most authoritarian thing there
is; it is the act whereby one part of the population imposes
its will upon another part by means of rifles, bayonets, and
cannon – authoritarian means, if such there be at all . . .

Friedrich Engels, 'On Authority', 1872

Nothing captures the joy, spontaneity, even magic of the early
moments of the Cuban Revolution more than the photos of
Raúl Corrales, Alberto Korda, Mario García Joya, Osvaldo
Salas and José Agraz. García Joya's 'We Are Cuban' (1959) depicts
a rickety old truck with a *guajiro* (peasant) holding a Cuban flag;
in front of him is a placard that reads: 'Today We Are Cuban More
Than Ever. Proud to be So. Now or Never. Long Live a Free Cuba.
Onward Cubans.' It distils a moment of tremendous celebration
at the overthrow of Batista and the hope of building a new future.
Corrales's 'Cavalry' (1960) shows revolutionary *guajiros* on horse-
back waving Cuban flags. Clearly, it is in the countryside and, if
not for the militia uniforms, it could be a scene of *mambises* (pro-
independence guerrilla fighters, mostly black and mulatto) fighting
the Spanish for Cuban independence from seventy years earlier.

Korda's 'Lamppost Quixote' (1959) is perched above the crowd at a huge rally in Revolution Square; he embodies beautifully the soaring ideals of the time, combining both individual and collective longing. And, of course, there are iconic photos of Fidel Castro: the Corrales shot (1960) from behind as he gives the 'First Havana Declaration' speech with a sea of followers in Revolution Square filling almost all the frame; the Agraz photo (1959) of a speech when doves landed on the podium and Fidel's shoulder; and Korda's 1959 'David and Goliath' that shows Fidel looking up at Lincoln at the Lincoln Memorial, in his guerrilla fatigues, but with his cap off to show respect. Fidel looks tiny and pensive, perhaps thinking he will have to struggle long and hard to keep such a powerful neighbour at bay. The photo captures the David and Goliath imagery that would define U.S.-Cuba relations, and that still persists in Latin America to this day. The Corrales shot shows one among many remarkable moments when the Cuban leader and the people seem fused in what some have called the 'direct democracy' of the early years. The moment captured by Agraz conjures up supernatural associations: for Catholics the symbol of the Holy Spirit (or even peace), for *santeros*, the orisha Obbatalá, who rules over things to do with the head and the mind. All these photos seem to reinforce Lenin's remark: 'In some respects, a revolution is a miracle.'[1]

Cuba's Revolution had been unusual in that it had broken a few rules. Although it was a nationalist, anti-imperialist, radical revolution, it had not been led by a Communist party, as was the case with Russia, China, Vietnam and Korea. (The countries in Eastern Europe are a separate case and we cannot truthfully count their turns to socialism as revolutions, with the possible exception of Yugoslavia.) Cuba's was not a proletarian revolution, either, or focused in the city, but in the countryside (in this it shares some similarities with China and Vietnam). However, its revolution was not a long war of national liberation, such as in China or Vietnam, taking decades, nor an anti-colonial struggle like Vietnam's. And, finally, despite being a Third World nation, Cuba was nowhere near as impoverished as the three Asian nations: it had a significant middle class, a relatively good educational and health system, even if unequally distributed, a fairly robust press, and a better than average infrastructure in Latin American terms.

Swiftly, Cuban society changed as the new government implemented new measures: agrarian reform (which included expropriating large landowners, among them U.S. companies), urban reform (drastic lowering of rents, telephone and electricity rates), educational reform (including a literacy programme in 1961), socialized medicine, public works projects, raising of worker salaries and an attempt at industrialization. Major utilities (water, telephone, gas) and banks were nationalized. Many of these measures led to confrontation with the U.S. until the Cuban government ended up nationalizing all U.S. businesses, which led to the severing of diplomatic relations (1961) and the imposition of the U.S. trade embargo on Cuba (1962). By 1960 the U.S. was making plans to overthrow the Cuban government by training Cuban exiles and, with CIA backing, invading the island and sparking an insurrection. This occurred in April 1961: known as the Bay of Pigs invasion, it was one of the worst foreign policy disasters in U.S. history, which ended with the anti-Castro forces being routed. This increased tensions between the two nations, and eventually led to the Cuban Missile Crisis (October–November 1962). By then any possibility of improving relations had been dashed and Cuba drew closer and closer to the Soviet bloc, even if from 1963 to 1968 relations were often strained between the USSR and Cuba. (After the invasion of Czechoslovakia, which Fidel grudgingly supported, relations improved significantly.)

With the sweeping political and economic changes came cultural ones as well. In a short period of time Cuba set up a National Publishing House (run by Carpentier), a National Ballet (under Alicia Alonso), Casa de las Américas (CASA) – a pan-Latin cultural centre with a strong emphasis on literature – a National Cultural Council, the ICAIC (a film institute) and the UNEAC (National Union of Cuban Writers and Artists). As private media outlets closed or were nationalized, the Cuban Institute of Radio and Television (the ICRT) was formed. All were financed by the state. Cuba, like many socialist revolutions of the twentieth century, placed great emphasis on culture as a human and social right and strove to make access to culture either free or at a rate affordable to the vast majority of the population. To a large degree Cuba has made good on this promise.

Cuba's culture after 1959 would develop some unique characteristics: an innovative film industry, a vibrant flowering of poster art, the *Nueva Trova* song movement, the creation of a new genre (testimonial literature), and the reworking of a traditional genre of detective fiction that would reflect revolutionary values. In discussing these unique facets of Cuban culture we will also examine how more traditional expressions of Cuban culture were transformed by revolution.

After 1959 and as part of the newspaper *Revolución*, founded by Carlos Franqui while the M-26-7 was still fighting its guerrilla war against Batista, a cultural supplement was added, published on Mondays, known as *Lunes de la Revolución* (*Lunes*). It began as a twelve-page insert, had an initial run of 100,000 copies, and was directed by Guillermo Cabrera Infante, with Pablo Armando Fernández second in charge. *Lunes* began publishing in March 1959 and lasted until November 1961, producing 131 issues in its two-and-a-half-year history. Its last issue, dedicated to Pablo Picasso, had a run of 250,000 copies. Despite Cabrera and Fernandez's leadership, *Lunes* had a fluid editorial team and issues were often parcelled out to members of the team. Though it leaned left and was both nationalist and anti-imperialist, *Lunes* did not have a specific political orientation: it included work by Marxists, existentialists, Surrealists, high modernists and the avant-garde. Most of the editorial team were from a younger generation of writers and some of them were highly critical of the *Orígenes* group, who were attacked for being politically inactive, ivory-tower types and for living in a poetic bubble removed from the concerns of Cuban society. These criticisms would be repeated later on with dire consequences for these writers.[2]

Carlos Franqui (1921–2010) remarked that *Lunes* was disliked by both the left and the right. More conservative publications like *El Diario de la Marina*, Cuba's oldest newspaper, criticized its avant-gardism and anti-imperialism; the Communist left (under the name of the Popular Socialist Party, or PSP) in its paper *Hoy* chided it for its cosmopolitanism, its flirtation with existentialism and its lack of ideological discipline. In a way, *Lunes* was the successor to *Ciclón*, not *Orígenes* or *Nuestro Tiempo* (the cultural publication of the PSP from 1954 to 1959) but it was much more openly political than *Ciclón* and, of course, unlike any of the previous publications, had the financial backing of the Cuban state and the 26th of July Movement. *Lunes* also had a weekly half-hour TV show, which aired on Mondays.

Lunes and some of its members would become embroiled in a controversy concerning politics and art and what it means to be a revolutionary intellectual. These issues were not new to revolutionary societies and the example of the USSR allows us to see some of the similarities (and differences) between the cultural experiences of the two countries. Scholars such as Tzvetan Todorov and Boris Groys have pointed out some of the analogies between avant-garde artistic movements and their political counterparts.

Groys, in explaining how the building of a future society was similar to the artistic process, argues that both society and the individual can be sculpted, like clay:

The world promised by the leaders of the October Revolution was not merely supposed to be a more just one or one that would provide greater economic security, but it was also and in perhaps greater measure meant to be beautiful. The unordered chaotic life of past ages was to be replaced by a life that was harmonious and organized according to a unitary artistic plan. When the entire economic, social, and everyday life of a nation was totally subordinated to a single planning authority commissioned to regulate, harmonize, and create a single whole out of even the most minute details, this authority – the

Communist party leadership – was transformed into a kind
of artist whose material was the entire world and whose goal
was to 'overcome the resistance' of the material and make it
pliant, malleable, capable of assuming any desired form.[3]

This 'desired form', of course, was socialism, and eventually
Communism. Both the promise and temptation of this utopian
impulse can be gleaned from Groys's comments. If the Communist
Party leadership has become an artist, what does that make the leader
of the Party – the 'supreme artist'? It reminds one of Stalin's famous
phrase that writers are 'the engineers of human souls'. (In Spanish
the word *constructor* is used, which seems more benign: building
or constructing sounds less ominous than engineering.) Stalin, of
course, meant this as a compliment to writers, in recognition of how
important they were to building a new society, but if authors accepted
this definition, did it not mean that Stalin himself was the Grand
Architect?

In 1959, with an enthusiasm that would later be tempered,
Lezama Lima wrote that 'the Revolution was the last of the imaginary eras', where 'all negative incantations have been decapitated'.[4]
Angel Augier, a literary critic, said, 'The Cuban Revolution, a truly
historical event is – by the same token – an amazing poetic deed.'[5]
Poet Eliseo Diego declared: 'Lezama's thesis has been fulfilled; that
is, Fidel did the impossible, he was able to bring about the impossible.
The Revolution is a work of poetry; it is the greatest surprise imagin-
able.'[6] These metaphors of Revolution as a work of art, as poetry,
are consistent with the efforts of the Soviet artistic avant-garde of
the 1920s.

The artistic remaking of society poses a question for writers and
artists: what is their new role in society? Are they to remain aloof
from social concerns, creating art in splendid isolation, or do they
commit themselves through art to revolutionary change? Aside from
wanting to bring art to the people, both in terms of aesthetic and
financial access, how does one break down the barriers between elite

and popular concepts of art? Do you actively seek the possibility that the general population gains opportunities to create art?

These are some of the questions that were being discussed in the pages of *Lunes*, and also in wider cultural circles in Cuba after 1959, and which in 1961 led to three meetings scheduled between intellectuals, artists and representatives of the new government. At the third meeting, held on 30 June 1961, Fidel Castro spoke, and his speech is known as 'Palabras a los intelectuales' (Words to Intellectuals). Held at the José Martí National Library, Fidel spoke for some 75 minutes about issues of artistic freedom, the relationship between art and revolution, and what constitutes revolutionary art. The speech was a multifaceted oration, legendary for one sentence, often quoted, which obscures the rest of the speech.

Before discussing Fidel's words, a bit of context might help. The three meetings had been prompted by the banning of the film *P.M.* by Sabá Cabrera Infante (brother of the famed novelist Guillermo Cabrera Infante and director of *Lunes*) and Orlando Jiménez Leal, who would later direct *El Super*. *P.M.* was a fourteen-minute experiment in free cinema that explored nightlife in Havana, with people dancing, drinking and conversing, mostly in bars. It was praised by many at *Lunes*, and given a glowing review by Néstor Almendros in *Bohemia* magazine, but those close to the ICAIC and old-line members of the PSP (Alfredo Guevara et al.) were highly critical of it, calling it undignified and claiming that it lacked revolutionary ethos. The film had been made outside the parameters of the ICAIC. After one initial showing it was yanked from theatres. Letters and phone calls ensued, protesting this action, setting in motion the three June meetings.

Some scholars have argued that *P.M.* suffered from bad timing and that if the film had been released at another moment in history nothing would have happened. Its release coincided with the U.S.-backed invasion of Cuban exiles at the Bay of Pigs (14–18 April 1961). Despite the defeat of the Cuban exile force, the country was clearly on edge, albeit combined with an intense nationalist fervour, which Fidel used to declare the socialist nature of the Revolution.

The meetings were held at the National Library. Built in 1957, this was an important symbol of Cuban culture, housing an important collection of Cuban works and providing an extensive archive for scholars. The library is located on one of the 'corners' of Revolution Square, not far from the gigantic monument to José Martí, and from which Fidel has delivered some of his most memorable speeches. The Martí monument features an 18-m (60-ft) sculpture of Martí and a 139-m (456-ft) obelisk, finished in 1958, intended to commemorate the one hundredth anniversary of his birth (1953). These are imposing structures that dwarf the plaza. Having the meetings at the National Library both created an intimate setting between the revolutionary leader and Cuba's intellectual-artistic elite and underlined wider concerns, since literally yards away was the regime's most coveted and celebratory public square. Private conversation and public sphere came together in this fragile moment that would leave an indelible mark on Cuban culture.

Fidel prefaced his main remarks by saying that as a representative of the government –and leader of the Revolution – he was no expert on matters cultural and artistic, and that the three dialogues had not been set up to 'lecture' artists and intellectuals, but to learn from them as well. Rhetorically, Fidel brilliantly undercut his position of authority, even if at other points in the speech he asserted that authority, although almost always couched in a collective 'we' that implied not only the government but all revolutionaries in a wider sense.

Central to this meeting was a conversation about what it meant to be a revolutionary intellectual or artist. Are they a contradiction in terms? Does being a revolutionary mean forfeiting artistic status and integrity and vice versa? Fidel was conscious of the imprudence of trying to narrowly define what made an intellectual a revolutionary, and he was equally aware that some audience members were intellectuals who had come to maturity before 1959 and, even though they had opposed Batista and were sympathetic to the goals of the revolutionary government, might not consider themselves full-blown revolutionaries (or Marxists). Fidel claimed to have no problem with that, insisting that he did not expect every artist and intellectual to be on the front lines of the barricades in the revolutionary struggle.

Jean-Paul Sartre had visited Cuba the previous year (1960) with Simone de Beauvoir, and had met with Fidel and Che Guevara. For some in Cuba, Sartre represented a model of the revolutionary intellectual: socially engaged, politically committed, someone who saw the intellectual as a representative of the masses, as an activist who stands up to injustice and the wrongs of society. Sartre had been a partisan in the Second World War, a staunch defender of workers' rights, was against nuclear proliferation and was adamant in his anti-colonial denunciations of France's war in Algeria, as well as his future role in the Russell Tribunal on Vietnam (1966). His position on Algeria resonated strongly with Cuba, since many in the revolutionary struggle saw Cuba's revolution not only as anti-imperialist but also as decolonizing. Cuba was not a 'classic colony' in the way that Algeria was, but it was still viewed as a neo-colony of the U.S. by many on the left, and its revolution was grouped with the great anti-colonial struggles of the 1950s and '60s. Sartre wrote favourably about the island's social transformation (*Sartre on Cuba*, 1961), but a decade later was very critical of the regime and its handling of the brief incarceration of poet Heberto Padilla in 1971, signing a letter drafted and signed by Latin American, U.S. and European intellectuals demanding Padilla's release (more on this further on).

In his book *Cuba and Western Intellectuals Since 1959*, Kepa Artaraz discusses some of the models that Cuba was examining in how to define a revolutionary intellectual: among the options are those of Sartre, Gramsci, Lenin and Marcuse (Fanon). While many elements of his analysis are useful, Artaraz overlooks a home-grown model: José Martí. Before discussing Martí, it will be useful to discuss Gramsci, Lenin and Marcuse.

Gramsci's model was an influential one, especially what he termed 'the organic intellectual', linked to issues of class and rooted in working-class organizations. Gramsci saw traditional intellectuals as subservient to the ruling classes and, thus, willingly or not, serving elite interests. He sought a new 'organic intellectual' to serve the workers; even better if they were of proletarian origin. Gramsci's major theoretical contribution was his definition and use of the word hegemony, which refers to the ability of groups, classes or parties to dominate through consent and persuasion, so that political rule is exercised through non-coercive means.[7]

The Leninist model is that of the professional revolutionary who brings revolutionary theory from outside the working class by way of a vanguard party (in the USSR the Bolshevik Party). Like Gramsci's model, it is inspired by Marx, and certainly PSP cadres like of Juan Marinello, Carlos Rafael Rodríguez, Mirta Aguirre, Blas Roca and Edith García Buchaca embodied this Leninist model in Cuba. A more New Left model of the revolutionary intellectual was exemplified by Herbert Marcuse, who was anti-Leninist but a Marxist in his approach to the arts and sympathetic to new subjects of liberation beyond the traditional Marxist emphasis on the working class. Marcuse argued for the revolutionary potential of youth and students, of blacks, Latinos and other racial minorities, women and gays. He also saw Third World revolutionary struggles as an inspiration for similar action in the First World. In his discussion of Marcuse, Artaraz mentions Frantz Fanon, the Martinican activist, theorist and revolutionary who fought with the Algerians in their quest for independence. His ideas on racial oppression, colonial subjection and the pitfalls of national liberation (do not rely on the 'nationalist bourgeoisie') resonated with Cuban revolutionaries. However, Fanon was not widely known in Cuba until after his death in December 1961, so neither Fidel nor those in attendance would have been able to see him as a revolutionary intellectual model at that time.

Cuba's home-grown model of a revolutionary intellectual was José Martí, who was a poet, journalist, playwright, orator, activist and premier spokesperson for Cuban independence in the late nineteenth century. Martí's life was exemplary in many ways, being the inspiration for the Moncada attack of 1953, as well as the moral compass of the anti-Batista struggle. Those who took up arms against Batista were known as the Centennial Generation, since they initiated their uprising a hundred years after Martí's birth.

Martí the warrior-poet, however, is a unique example. As a writer and artist he was one of a kind; as a politician-activist his actions were equally unique, historically speaking, since Cuba became independent shortly after his death. More troubling is Martí the warrior. As a warrior he was not very successful, dying in his first action (less of a battle than a skirmish). True, he gave his life for Cuba's freedom and independence, but if he had been a bit more prudent he might have become the island's first president.

Fidel's guerrilla warriors, unlike Martí, were successful, and here they were in the National Library discussing cultural politics with Cuba's creative elite. Many Cuban intellectuals during the second Batista years had lived outside Cuba (Latin America, France, the U.S.), returning after the revolutionary triumph. Many others remained on the island, and despite widespread antipathy towards the repressive aspects of the Batista regime were not very active in the armed struggle. What some have called 'guerrilla envy'[8] was a prevalent attitude among these groups of artists, not having been active warriors or even part of the clandestine urban underground working secretly to overthrow Batista.

Of course, a more recent example of the intellectual who was a guerrilla warrior would be Che Guevara himself, someone who Sartre called 'the most complete man of his time'. Löwy describes his Renaissance man qualities: 'doctor and economist, revolutionary and banker, military theoretician and ambassador, deep political thinker, and popular agitator, able to wield the pen and the submachine gun with equal skill'.[9] Guevara addressed the issue of intellectuals in his influential essay 'Man and Socialism in Cuba' (1965), and despite his criticism of socialist realism he states the following:

> To sum up, the fault of many of our artists and intellectuals lies in their original sin; they are not true revolutionaries. We

can try and graft the elm tree so that it will bear pears, but at the same time we must plant pear trees. New generations will come that will be free of original sin.[10]

Sartre addresses this 'original sin' in his writings, and later in his life thought that intellectuals had to suppress themselves to be with the people, and to do so implied making a concerted effort to go against their natural interests. And yet at the same time Sartre was concerned that intellectuals conserve independence of thought and not be subservient to those in power, and that serving the interests of the people need not imply abandoning one's ability to think autonomously. Not surprisingly, Sartre never formally joined a political party in the 1950s when he was close to the French Communist Party, or later in his Maoist phase, nor did he ever become a minister like André Malraux. In a meeting he held with Cuban intellectuals and writers (which appears in the Spanish edition of his book) Sartre said to his audience, 'Intellectuals are not happy in any society.'[11] Sartre never resolved that dilemma satisfactorily, and neither has the Cuban Revolution, though not for want of trying.

It bears noting that in the intellectual models discussed, none of the cases other than that of Sartre are of artists: Gramsci, Lenin, Marcuse, Guevara and Fanon did not write fiction, poetry or plays. Guevara wrote a few mediocre poems, Gramsci and Lenin headed parties, Fanon was a psychiatrist who became a militant of the Algerian Front for National Liberation (FLN), Guevara was a guerrilla leader and government minister, Marcuse a philosopher and academic. In addressing what makes literature revolutionary, Marcuse's words are cautionary, maybe even a warning:

This thesis [content must be overtly social] implies that literature is not revolutionary because it is written for the working class or for 'the revolution'. Literature can be called revolutionary in a meaningful sense only with reference to itself, as content having become form. The political dimension of art lies only in its own aesthetic dimension. Its relation to praxis is inexorably indirect, mediated, and frustrating. The more immediately political the work of art, the more it reduces its power of estrangement, and the radical, transcendent goals of change. In this sense, there may be more subversive potential in the poetry of Baudelaire and Rimbaud than in the didactic plays of Brecht.[12]

Marcuse's words from 1977 echo the debates about realism and the politics of culture that raged around the likes of T. W. Adorno, Walter Benjamin, Gyorgy Lukács, Ernst Bloch and Bertolt Brecht from the mid-1920s onwards, and that had also played themselves out in the USSR, often with disastrous effects for the arts with the adoption of socialist realism that argued for a relationship between the arts and politics that was direct, unmediated and uncomplicated. Marcuse sides with Benjamin and Adorno, who would argue that authors like Beckett or Kafka are revolutionary not because of their content but because their work examines the dimensions of power in society in such uniquely subversive ways, even if they do not appeal overtly to working-class rebellion or call for the establishment of a future socialist society.

Fidel's speech does not directly address these different intellectual models but his comments do leave some clues as to his thoughts on the matter. He does say that what defines a revolutionary is that they are with the people, that they defend the interests of the great majority, suggesting that Cuban intellectuals keep this in mind as they create their work (Sartre model). However, Fidel prescribes that literary and artistic creations must be didactic, formulaic or pamphleteering in nature. In terms of the forms of the artwork, the young Cuban revolutionaries rejected the tired and ineffective formulas of socialist realism. In early 1960, Fidel and some Russian dignitaries visited an abstract mural by a Cuban artist. The Russians voiced their discontent, and Fidel responded, 'Our problem is with imperialists not abstract artists.' He repeated this comment to French reporter Claude Julien in 1963.[13]

In terms of the formal aspects of a work of art, the matter seemed decided: freedom of formal expression was not a problem. Cuba's artists and writers were not expected to adhere to certain standards of realism, heroism, exaltation of the 'New Man' being created by socialism, portrayal of the old dominant classes as uniformly evil, creation of good guy versus bad guy stereotypes, and so forth. But what about the content of the artwork? (Here Marcuse's words offer a way of looking at this issue that avoids outdated binaries about content and form, base and superstructure, realism and modernism (the avant-garde), personal subjectivity and collective struggle, emotion and rationality, identification with protagonists and estrangement.) Fidel refers to certain rights within Cuban society, and artists and intellectuals as part of a revolutionary society partake of these rights, but he underlines that, above all, the most important rights are the rights of the Revolution:

> In other words: within the revolution, everything, against the revolution, nothing. Against the revolution nothing because the revolution has its rights and the first right of the revolution is the right to exist, and no one can oppose the revolution's right to exist. Inasmuch as the revolution embodies the interests of the people, inasmuch as the revolution symbolizes the interests of the whole nation, no one can justly claim a right to oppose it … Within the revolution, everything, against the revolution, there are no rights [*ningún derecho*].[14]

This last phrase is the one most often quoted, and usually out of context. It is significant that Fidel does not use the words 'from without' to finish the statement that begins 'within the revolution'. He uses the word *contra* in Spanish, which means against. *Contra*, of course, evokes the word *contrarrevolucionario* (or counter-revolutionary), someone who actively opposes and wants to destroy the Revolution. The difference between contra and 'without' leaves the interpretation open: one could be an artist who is indifferent to politics and the

Revolution and presumably still be an artist and continue to create work. However, to be fully against the Revolution is another matter.

Still, Fidel's dictum raises many questions. Is the revolutionary aspect of art mostly an issue of content? If so, who decides what is revolutionary or, more crucially, what is counter-revolutionary? The National Union of Writers and Artists (UNEAC)? The National Cultural Council (now the Ministry of Culture)? Those in charge of ideological matters in the Communist Party? Some other organ of government? Is this not admitting that writers and artists have to face the possibility of censorship and self-censorship as a way of preserving their artistic careers?

In his speech Fidel attempts to assuage the fears of those present, their pessimism about the stifling of art. Ever the optimist, he states that the Revolution does not smother artistic creativity. Late in the speech he even mocks the 'Stalinist Revolution' that the government has been accused of creating by anti-revolutionary critics. He talks about the difficult situation artists had in pre-1959 Cuba and then exalts all the cultural achievements of the revolutionary government: the creation of the film institute (ICAIC), the National Symphony, the National Ballet (under Alicia Alonso), the programmes at the National Library, the creation of new publishing houses, and the National Cultural Council (CNC). He defends the latter institution as promoting the interests of not only Cuban artists, but of Cuban culture in general. He agrees with the CNC's decision to remove the film *P.M.* from circulation, admitting that he had not seen it. His honesty in this admission does not detract from his dereliction of duty: could he not make time to see a film under fifteen minutes? On the other hand, not seeing *P.M.* might make it seem that he does not want to get involved in being the ultimate judge on the film's merits.

In the latter part of the speech he refers to the inequalities of Cuba and the importance of promoting culture in the countryside, culturally under-served before 1959, as well as his own privileged upbringing. He underlines the importance of culture for all the people, and urges those present to go beyond an elitist concept of culture. Towards the end, he reminds his audience that they are privileged to be living during the Revolution, the most transcendent event in twentieth-century Latin America. He finishes with two comments, one about a woman over a hundred years old who had been a slave and how crucial it would be for her story to be known. Then, always looking to an ever-brighter future, Fidel tries to reassure his audience that they have nothing to fear in the present, neither from 'imaginary authoritarian judges' nor 'cultural executioners'; only from the future generations, who will have the last word.[15]

The challenge posed by Fidel relating to the hundred-year-old ex-slave was taken to heart buy one of the artists present. Five years later (1966) Miguel Barnet would publish *Biografía de un cimarrón* (Autobiography of a Runaway Slave; 1968), a 'testimonial novel' which inaugurated a genre that would become popular in Cuba and Latin America, later acquiring more legitimacy when CASA included the genre in its awards starting in 1970.

Barnet claims to have been inspired by Truman Capote's *In Cold Blood* when he interviewed the 106-year-old ex-slave Esteban Montejo, who recounts his life as slave and runaway, providing much useful information on the realities and mores of a population that had been little studied. Not surprisingly, the first Cuban edition was published by the Institute of Ethnology and Folklore. Later it was published by Siglo XXI in Mexico and became widely known, read and acclaimed. Barnet followed up with *Canción de Rachel* (1969; *Rachel's Song*, 1991) about a vedette who performed at the Alhambra Theater. The novel covers the first three decades of Cuban life in the twentieth century, ending with Machado's overthrow (1933). Unlike *Cimarrón*, *Rachel* has six other narrators besides Rachel, and often these voices contradict her or supply a different version of her tale. Its kaleidoscopic vision is often fascinating, offering glimpses of the joys and frustrations of Cuba in the first half of the Republican period. *Rachel* was followed by two more testimonial novels, *Gallego* (1981) and *La vida real* (A True Story; 1986), the former about a Spaniard from Galicia who emigrates to Cuba (as did hundreds of thousands of Galicians), the latter about a Cuban emigrant in New York City. The four novels round out a portrait of what makes up Cuba's identity (Africa, Europe, its Creole mix and the diaspora).

The *novela testimonio* was a hybrid form: though it told stories with a literary flair, it was not fiction, since the protagonists lived through or witnessed what they are narrating. Therefore, the narrative has a degree of authenticity – not to mention historical relevance – that is undeniable. Casa de las Américas defines the genre as such:

> Testimonios must document some aspect of Latin American or Caribbean reality from a direct source. A direct source is understood as knowledge of the facts by the author or his or her compilation of narratives or evidence obtained from the individuals involved or qualified witnesses. In both cases reliable documentation, written or graphic, is indispensable. The form is at the author's discretion, but literary quality is also indispensable.[16]

John Beverley adds the following, arguing that 'sincerity is valued more than literariness', which might seem to disagree with the CASA definition slightly. He further concludes, 'Testimonio, in other words, is an instance of the New Left and feminist slogan "The personal is political".'[17] The individual story is important, but it must fit into a larger scheme of things: a community, an ethnic group, a revolutionary movement or a nation.

One of the inspirations for *testimonio* was Che Guevara's own *Reminiscences from the Cuban Revolutionary War* (1959), an interesting and well-written account of his involvement in the insurrection against Batista. Perhaps it is not surprising that after CASA established the prize, many of the winners had taken part in guerrilla struggles. Given the politics of Central America in the 1970s and '80s, some of the best-known testimonies of the genre won the award: *Los días de la selva* (Days of the Jungle; 1980) by Mario Payeras (Guatemala);

Corresponsales de guerra (War Dispatches; 1981) by Fernando Pérez Valdés (Cuba, but writing on the Sandinista struggle); *La montaña es algo más que una inmensa estepa verde* (Fire from the Mountain; 1982) by Omar Cabezas (Nicaragua); *Me llamo Rigoberta Menchú* (My Name is Rigoberta Menchú; 1983) by Menchú and Elizabeth Burgos (Guatemala); *Mi general Torrijos* (My General Torrijos; 1987) by José de Jesús Martínez (Nicaragua, but on President Torrijos); and *La paciente impaciencia* (The Patient Impatience; 1989) by Tomás Borge (Nicaragua). The dominance of Central American narratives reflects Cuban interest in the revolutionary movements of the time. The Sandinistas had defeated Somoza and taken power in 1979, and guerrilla movements in El Salvador (FMLN) and Guatemala (URNG) came to the fore in the early 1980s until 1992. The taking of power by the New Jewel Movement in Grenada under Maurice Bishop (1979) also lifted spirits in Havana. For Cuba, the Sandinista victory in Nicaragua had vindicated the Cuban ideology of social transformation through armed struggle, which had been tried in the 1960s and '70s throughout Latin America. All had met with crushing defeat. Cuba, of course, was hoping that the Sandinista example would soon spread to El Salvador and Guatemala, creating a nucleus of revolutionary states in Central America.

The *testimonio* genre as defined by CASA stresses its 'indispensable literary quality'. While not denying the literary quality of the 1980s narratives (Payeras, Cabezas, Borge), what seemed to be of utmost importance was the historical significance of these writings. Be it a narrative of time spent with the Guatemalan guerrillas (Payeras), the Sandinista Revolution (Cabezas, Borge) or the travails of the Maya in Guatemala under a policy of genocide (Menchú), the intimate stories of these historical struggles are what makes these books so compelling. In the forty or so years that the prize has been awarded, Cubans have won eight times and most have written on historical themes: Bay of Pigs, Moncada Barracks attack, the struggles against anti-Castro guerrillas in the Escambray, the Sandinista revolution, corruption and organized crime under Batista, Che in Africa, a memoir of Raúl

Roa by his son. Only two were on more cultural themes: one on the circus (co-winner in 1972), another on singer Rita Montaner (1997).

What is interesting is that the supposed creator of the genre, Miguel Barnet himself, never won the CASA award. One could argue that his first two *testimonios* were published before the award was created (1967, 1969), but the second could easily have made it into the contest's first year (1970). His other two from 1981 and 1986 certainly could have been winners. Barnet's literary talent is without question and the fact that he never won the award leaves one wondering whether the literary aspect remained secondary to political ones.

In a sense, the *testimonio* will be a kind of revolutionary literary genre that, like Cuban crime fiction and espionage novels, will be a test of how to (or not to) combine a revolutionary ideology with artistic and aesthetic excellence. These issues will continue to define the dilemmas that writers and artists had after the meeting with Fidel and the closing of *Lunes de la Revolución*.

Revolutionary Cultural Policy in the Wake of Fidel's Speech

Of course, many writers and artists were faced with a novel situation, since the state became more invested in culture and for those who identified with the Revolution many opportunities flourished. The state, through its cultural institutions, now published and distributed the work of Cuban authors, often in large print runs. Early on even poetry books had runs of anywhere from five thousand to thirty thousand copies, a phenomenal number considering the size of the country. Books were amazingly inexpensive, due to government subsidy, and accessible to all the population. The state was an employer as well, offering many writers opportunities as editors, staff writers, journalists, professors and translators. Different institutions, magazines and journals sponsored literary awards (CASA, UNEAC, Caimán Barbudo, La Gaceta, Unión), as well as facilitating access to writers seeking awards in Spain and Latin America. Travel opportunities were significant, which was no small thing at a time when few Cubans could travel abroad. Giving talks and readings abroad facilitated the opportunity for foreign translations of one's work, and greater recognition globally. Cuban writers were also cultural ambassadors (sometimes literally), offering a different face or voice of the Cuban Revolution for foreign audiences.

While many writers saw these changes as positive, there were some negative aspects of state involvement and control of the arts. One ran the risk of being censored, or confronted with the tricky challenge of self-censorship. How did different institutions and magazines interpret the dictum of 'Within the Revolution everything, against the Revolution, nothing'? This dilemma has undergone different periods of interpretations, from rigid to less strict, to somewhat flexible, to a blurring line under constant negotiation.

The writers behind *Lunes* would have significant issues in Cuba over the decade following Fidel's speech. Guillermo Cabrera Infante (1929–2005) would leave Cuba in 1965, Franqui in 1968, poet Heberto Padilla (1932–2000) would be imprisoned in 1971 and would eventually emigrate in 1980. Virgilio Piñera, after briefly being jailed for one night in the early 1960s, would not be published during the last decade of his life (1969–79), even after winning the prestigious CASA prize for his play *Dos viejos pánicos* (Two Panicked Geezers; 1968). Still others would have difficulties with the cultural establishment in the late 1960s all the way through to the early 1980s. These included Lezama Lima, Antón Arrufat, César López, Manuel Díaz Martínez, Miguel Barnet, Norberto Fuentes and Pablo Armando Fernández.

In the 1960s, Cabrera became one of the best-known authors both inside and outside of Cuba, if only because his novel *Tres Tristes Tigres* (1967; *Three Trapped Tigers*, 1971) was one of the signature novels of the Latin American boom. A raucous recreation of Havana of the late 1950s, the novel has been described as a tropical *Ulysses*, brimming with all kinds of word play and puns. One of the more memorable (and funny) segments of the book is when he has seven great Cuban writers describe the death of Leon Trotsky, conjuring up the rich baroque metaphors of Lezama Lima, the caustic prose of Virgilio Piñera and the grandiloquent lyricism of Guillén (the other parodied writers are Alejo Carpentier, Lydia Cabrera, Lino Novás Calvo and José Martí). Unlike most Cuban authors, Cabrera's literary and cultural models were not from France or Spain, but the Anglo world (the u.s. and uk). An admirer of Laurence Sterne, Lewis Carroll and Faulkner, Cabrera was a born storyteller and had an incredible ear for Cuban spoken Spanish, which lovingly and hilariously permeates all his work. Cabrera was also an unabashed cinephile, having been a film critic for *Carteles* magazine. Here again, he was a great admirer of u.s. cinema, his favourite directors being Welles, Hitchcock, Minnelli, Hawks and Huston. He wrote on European cinema, but was not a big fan of its more experimental directors like Godard, Fassbinder or Straub-Huillet (he did like Bresson). As well as publishing several books of film criticism and essays, in most of his novels there are references to film: his characters talk about films they've seen, and he often uses cinematic techniques in his narrations. He also wrote the screenplay for the film *Vanishing Point* (1971).

Though Cabrera left the island in 1965, he did not make any public declarations about Cuban politics until 1968, when he openly came out against the Revolution, as well as harshly criticizing Fidel Castro. He was perhaps the most vocal of Cuban exile writers and certainly the most humorous. His criticisms of Cuban socialism and those associated with it, and that includes a list of the likes of Reinaldo Arenas, Carlos Alberto Montaner and Carlos Franqui, to mention some of the most prominent, are barbed, if not venomous. His political essays and commentaries often had ingenious insights and flashes of wit, but were ultimately marred by an inability to see anything positive about Cuba post-1959.

His *Vista de amanecer en el trópico* (View of Dawn in the Tropics; 1974) offers his view of Cuban history, one that would be considered both tragic and ironic in its emplotment. Structured as a series of vignettes from colonial times to the present (originally to appear in *Three Trapped Tigers*, but removed), it is a chilling and bloody narrative that swings between lyrical interludes, blind illusion, nihilism and the lies of the powerful.

Cabrera's colleague at *Lunes*, Heberto Padilla, poet and translator (from both English and Russian) fared far worse. After initial praise for his first book of poems, *El justo tiempo humano* (A Just Human Time; 1962), Padilla spent time in Czechoslovakia and the USSR as a promoter of Cuban culture, experiences that made him wary about the fate of poets under state socialism. He befriended poet Yevgeny Yevtushenko who personally talked to him about the lives of prominent writers like Blok, Yesenin, Mayakovsky, Mandelstam, Akhmatova, Pasternak and others before and during the Stalinist period and the thaw (post-1953). The controversy surrounding Pasternak's publication of *Doctor Zhivago* and his winning of the Nobel Prize (1958) were fairly recent reminders that the Soviet cultural thaw was by no means smooth. Yevtushenko was present at the meetings between Cuban intellectuals and artists and Fidel in the National Library. In 1967, Padilla published an article praising Cabrera's *Three Trapped Tigers* over Lisandro Otero's *Pasión de Urbino* (Urbino's Passion; 1966). Otero had won the prestigious CASA prize for his first novel, *La situación* (1963), and held an important post in the writers' union (UNEAC). By then, Cabrera had left Cuba and was considered politically suspect, even though he had not made any public declarations.

The following year Padilla's book *Fuera del juego* (Out of the Game; 1968) won the Julián del Casal UNEAC award for poetry. Padilla had written most of these poems in Moscow, Budapest and Prague. The jury, composed of three Cubans, a Peruvian and a British author, was unanimous in its decision. The book overall is supportive of the Cuban Revolution, but there are several poems that are highly critical of what he saw as negative trends of socialism, particularly one titled 'Instructions for Joining a New Society'.

In a mere nine lines, using a kind of Brechtian sarcasm, Padilla, from the title onwards, is already letting the reader know that the advice being given is for those in the know. Instruction one speaks to the inherent optimism of revolutionary societies and their ultimate faith in the future of utopian realization. Instruction two concerns dress and behaviour; the model of the new citizen who is 'clean' in all senses of the word. It carries a triple aspect: how one is to be seen by others, how one is supposed to treat others, how one behaves toward authority (the leadership, the Party). The parenthetical instruction deals with the physical, but in the age-old sense of sound body, sound mind, and refers back to the 'clean' of the previous line and the mental attitude of the first. And finally, the walking straight ahead seems to indicate that faith in progress proceeds along a linear path, except that the author modifies the instruction (a step forward and two or three going backwards). The line is not so straight; maybe it's a zig-zag. Of course, Padilla echoes Lenin's famous tract 'One Step Forward, Two Steps Back' (1904), where he recommends that the Bolsheviks be patient and not hastily rush into doing something foolish. Here, good old-fashioned Cuban *choteo* has collided with Marxist political analysis. And, of course, the applause at the end refers to the need for unanimity in helping build the new society. Padilla offers a satirical look at the 'New Man': on the one hand, there is optimism, cleanliness, a movement forwards, unity; on the other, obedience, backtracking and a lack of critical thought. The ending, perhaps, recalls the conversation that Sartre had with Cuban writers sponsored by *Lunes*. Sartre mentions that writers often say no: no to injustice, corruption, inequality, discrimination and war. But Cuban writers, after 1959, are supposedly living in a society where these ills, if not wiped out, are being tackled by the government, which claims to be on the 'right side of history'. To this, Sartre argues, writers must say yes. What does that yes imply? Does it mean that writers must give up their critical faculties and always say yes? Is it the Revolution, right or wrong?

In a later poem, 'At Times it is Necessary' (from his *Provocaciones*, 1972), Padilla tackles the issue of revolutionary leadership and the sacrifices needed to build a better future. Here again, he plays with the reader's possible interpretation. The first stanza seems to be a criticism of rulers who sacrifice their own people for either personal gain or for a cause, or maybe a mixture of both. After the first four lines the reader assumes that Padilla is speaking about Fidel Castro. But then he claims that the first four lines actually belong to Salvador Espriú (1913–1985), the great Catalonian poet, which means that those lines were originally meant about Franco who dictatorially ruled Spain for almost forty years, a true example of the Hispanic *caudillo* (strong man). Padilla sort of admits to a 'misquotation', or at least a quotation out of context, except that he says he knows it by heart, has set the words to music and his friends sing it. He ends with a reference to another poet and writer, Malcolm Lowry (1909–1957), author of *Under the Volcano* (1947).[18]

Is Padilla trying to have it both ways here, criticizing Fidel while quoting Espriú, evoking Brecht's saying that one needs cunning to tell the truth? And why the reference to Lowry and his ukulele, which ends the poem? Padilla is quoting again: this time Lowry's epitaph, which the author himself wrote:

> Malcolm Lowry,
> Late of the Bowery
> His prose was flowery
> And Often Glowery
> He lived, nightly, and drank daily,
> And died playing the ukulele.

This playful epitaph brings us back to the first stanza (Espriú's words), – that is, death. Is Padilla suggesting that criticizing *caudillos* can be risky? Is he contrasting the music of poetry to the Siren song of power? Certainly death was an important theme for Lowry: *Under the Volcano* takes place during the Mexican Day of the Dead.

In quoting Espriú, Padilla begins with what he sees as legitimate circumstances for sacrifice: the defence of one's homeland. What is interesting is that despite the collective purpose, the decision to die for one's country is an individual one, since one can also choose not to die for one's country. The reverse is not true: to die for a *caudillo* is the *caudillo*'s decision, not one made by the individual citizen. One critic has described Lowry as 'a man of astonishing extremes', dwelling 'either in heaven or hell, and the two realms existed side by side for him'.[19] Could Padilla – in this poem and the previous one – be referring to the polarizing ways in which Cuba is portrayed as either inferno or paradise?

The poems quoted here also earned Padilla harsh criticism from more old-guard elements of the cultural bureaucracy. Despite winning the poetry award, *Fuera del juego* was published with a disclaimer by the UNEAC that the book did not reflect the revolutionary ethos of the organization. Although the book was published, it was not promoted and was eventually withdrawn from circulation. Padilla did not receive the monetary award or a trip to Moscow. That, however, was the least of his problems.

Over the next three years Padilla's life became more difficult: he was rarely published, he could not travel, and finally, in March 1971, he was imprisoned. There was an immediate outcry, first by the Mexican PEN Club, then a week later with an open letter in *Le Monde* to Fidel Castro asking for Padilla's release. It was signed by Latin American and European intellectuals, among them Calvino, Duras, Moravia, Semprún, Enzensberger, Octavio Paz, Carlos Fuentes and Mario Vargas Llosa. It was also signed by Sartre and Simone de Beauvoir: their honeymoon with Cuba was over. Eighteen days later Padilla was released, and he gave a public recantation of his sins before a crowd of writers at the UNEAC. There he confessed to his pessimism about the Revolution, sharing these thoughts and rumours with foreign journalists; he also named names, other writers, most of them present at this 'confession'. This prompted a second letter published in Spain with even more signatories (Sontag, Pasolini, Resnais, Metzsáros, Gorz) added to those from the first, in which they denounced Padilla's recantation as a 'charade' and reminiscent of the 'more sordid moments of the Stalinist era, with show trials and witch hunts'. The letter ends by reminding the reader that Cuba's socialist revolution was inspired by deep humanist values, and asks that it return to those values.

The Cuban response was swift, coming even before the second letter, during the First National Congress on Education and Culture, which was being held when Padilla gave his confession. Fidel gave the closing speech of the congress and he thundered against foreign intellectuals, calling them 'minor agents of colonialism', 'pseudo-leftists' that are 'trying to win their laurels while living in Paris, London or Rome'. Further, he considered many of these critical voices from abroad agents of imperialism, of the CIA, and spies. During the same Congress, resolutions were passed calling for a refusal to allow homosexuals to be teachers and to have contact with students.[20]

Although released from prison, Padilla was closely watched, and relegated to translation work. His wife at the time, poet Belkis Cuza Malé (b. 1942), who had been imprisoned with him, was able to leave Cuba in 1979. There she lobbied for Padilla's right to leave the country, which he was able to do in 1980, weeks before the Mariel Boatlift Crisis. In 1982, they both founded *Linden Lane Magazine*, a journal for Cuban exiled writers and artists that continues to be published.

The fallout from the Padilla Affair, as it is now known, was significant. Many Latin American and European artists and intellectuals either broke with Cuba or became much more distant. This was costly to Cuba, since many of its writers and artists who travelled abroad were true and more sympathetic ambassadors for the Revolution than the usual functionaries. And despite the enormous changes in cultural policy since the 1970s, the legacy of what happened to Padilla has left an indelible mark, either as a negative example of what to avoid, or as a warning to writers of how to proceed in issues of expressive freedom.

Culturally, Cuba was now in a period where a more hard-line, conservative, if you will, policy towards art and artists was the norm. Critic Ambrosio Fornet coined the term *quinquenio gris*, using the

Spanish term of the Five Year Plan with the adjective grey to indicate this hardline policy. Most scholars agree that the five years were closer to a decade, and that cultural policy began to loosen up around 1981, although there were signs of liberalization starting in 1976.

For many, it was tempting to view the Padilla Affair and its aftermath as good old-fashioned tropical Stalinism, but one must tread carefully with these analogies. Cuba has never experienced the terror that was unleashed in the USSR in the 1936–9 period of massive purges and show trials. The Cuban revolutionary government never adopted a policy of 'socialist realism' as an official artistic policy as did the USSR in 1934, although it tried a variant of it through crime and espionage fiction. Revolutionary Cuba did not pursue an excessive persecution or incarceration of its artists and writers, and had a more flexible policy in discerning cultural from political dissent, though not successfully in all cases (witness Padilla, Arenas, Benítez Rojo). Cuba treats political dissent rather harshly, but at the same time it has always had an official policy of allowing those in disagreement with the government to leave the country. From the government's perspective, conveniently having disgruntled citizens out of the way provides an enormous safety valve. Many prominent Cuban writers have chosen this path: Enrique Labrador Ruiz, Lino Novás Calvo, Guillermo Cabrera Infante, Severo Sarduy, Reinaldo Arenas, Antonio Benítez Rojo, Lydia Cabrera, Gastón Baquero, Lorenzo García Vega, Calvert Casey, Jorge Mañach and, of course, Padilla and Cuza Malé. Previously, when these writers left, their work would no longer be published in Cuba, but since the late 1980s Cuba has in some cases recognized their contributions to Cuban letters and begun to publish them (Cabrera, Sarduy, Casey, even Padilla).

Nueva Trova or the New Song Movement

As Cuban society changed under revolutionary leadership, similar changes occurred in some of the art forms. *Nueva Trova* (or new song) came to the fore in the 1960s and its name implies that it is both building on existing Cuban traditions, and adding or creating something new. Cuba had a formidable song tradition that dates from the nineteenth century, with the likes of Sindo Garay, Manuel Corona, Alberto Villalón, Patricio Ballagas, Rosendo Ruiz, María Teresa Vera and many others. This 'old song' (*trova* in Spanish) was mostly a singer-composer who expressed the values of the people: patriotic songs, songs of love, nature, exaltation of women, and also satire and humour. Much of it fed into the *bolero* (torch-song tradition) that is well rooted not only in Cuba but in all of Latin America. In the 1940s, the *trova* tradition incorporated some elements of jazz and became known as *filin* (from the English word feeling), showing influences from Nat King Cole, Billy Eckstine and Cab Calloway. In both the music and the lyrics there was greater freedom, and composers like César Portillo de la Luz and José Antonio Méndez made the *filin* movement a popular one, even through the age of the mambo and cha-cha-chá of the 1950s.

All these traditions fed the *Nueva Trova* movement, which musically speaking was also influenced by rock, r'n'b and jazz. What made New Song more distinct were the lyrics: no longer was the emphasis on love songs, although these did not disappear, and some were reworked to give a revolutionary feel. Songs focused on the new realities of Cuba: building a revolutionary society, new changes in gender relationships, songs about Che Guevara and the New Man, the understanding of history (contemporary or from the past), the creation of new institutions or civic engagement, and songs about revolutionary struggles in other parts of the world, particularly Latin America and, of course, Vietnam. In the 1970s, songs were written denouncing military dictatorships, especially those of the Southern Cone (Chile, Argentina, Uruguay, Bolivia, Brazil, Paraguay). As the movement grew it sponsored festivals, often inviting artists throughout Latin America and Puerto Rico; in some cases, artists who had to flee were given safe haven in Cuba. The New Song movement grew throughout Latin America, and was particularly strong in Chile, Argentina, Brazil, Mexico, Venezuela and Puerto Rico.

Silvio Rodríguez (b. 1946) is one of the best-known *cantoautores* (singer-songwriters) of Cuba, having recorded more than 25 albums and toured internationally. Rodríguez has a singular – though not spectacular – voice, and is a very gifted poet as a songwriter, even if sometimes his images are a bit enigmatic. Many of his songs have become classics, and have been sung by other singers. These include 'Unicornio' (Unicorn), 'Días y flores' (Days and Flowers), 'Rabo de nube' (Watersprout) and 'Canción del elegido' (Song of the Chosen One). This last song, from 1969, is an intriguing homage to Che Guevara. What is interesting about it is that it never mentions Che by name, but through the use of certain metaphors it alludes to him as being a 'galactic figure', wandering from planet to planet in search of peace but only finding war. At one point the song says: 'The most terrible things are learnt at once/ the most beautiful things cost us our lives'.[21] The song is a stirring portrait; yes, revolutionary, too, but without forgetting that it is art and poetry. Rodríguez, like some of the other *Nueva Trova* singers, has been a cultural ambassador for Cuba, touring widely throughout the world. When he and Pablo Milanés performed in Buenos Aires after the junta, they played to full soccer stadiums. Most recently (2015–16), Silvio, as he is known in and outside Cuba, did a series of more than seventy free concerts in different and mostly poor neighbourhoods of Havana. The performances were well received, although criticized by some as hypocritical because of the fact Rodriguez spends so much time touring and earning quantities of money most Cubans could only dream of.

Pablo Milanés (b. 1943) is one of the other leading voices of *Nueva Trova*. While his own lyrics do not have the poetic flair of Silvio's, he often uses the poetry of others (Martí, Guillén) for his composition, and he has an enviable soaring voice that can sing love songs, political hymns, salsa and even rock with equal skill. Physically, he forms a counterpoint to Silvio: he is mixed-race, for years sported an Afro, is clean-shaven, and is ample-bodied; Silvio is pale, with stringy hair and a goatee or beard, and rail-thin (though he has added a gut in his later years). He has also written signature songs that have been performed by many singers, like 'Yolanda' (a love song), 'Amo esta isla' (I Love This Island; patriotic without being schmaltzy), 'Pobre del cantor' (Pity the Singer; about the importance of singers laying it on the line) and 'Años' (Years; about ageing and one's dreams). His 'No vivo en una sociedad perfecta' (I Don't Live in a Perfect Society) is a disarmingly simple song whose title is pretty self-explanatory. What makes it so effective is that without discarding the idea of making a better society, Pablito (as he is known in and out of Cuba) insists that because flesh-and-blood men and women are trying to create this new vision, it will always be imperfect because we humans are that way. But that is no reason to give up trying. In more recent years Pablito has been very outspoken on cultural and racial matters in Cuba, and in the 1960s had been sent to the UMAP (Military Units to Aid Production) camps. He and Silvio have had public disagreements and what had been a long-standing friendship seems to have soured in more recent times.

Noel Nicola (1946–2005) was another important figure of the Cuban *Nueva Trova* movement who recorded several albums and toured widely. He was the son of Isaac Nicola, a well-known guitarist and teacher, and Eva Reyes, a violinist with the National Symphonic Orchestra and also a singer. His best-known compositions were 'María del Carmen', a tribute to the new Cuban revolutionary woman, unconcerned with traditional concepts of femininity (virginity, being a housekeeper and mother) and 'Comienza el día', a perky and optimistic song, which captures the revolutionary enthusiasm of the 1970s. True to the *Nueva Trova* principles, Nicola recorded songs based on the poetry of Peruvian poet César Vallejo, even performing some of the poems of *Trilce*, a notoriously difficult avant-garde work.

Cuban *Nueva Trova* was both part of a Latin American phenomenon and uniquely Cuban. Outside Cuba the music was known as *canción protesta* (protest song) since in most cases the singers were protesting against their governments about social inequality, lack of democracy, military rule and often flagrant violations of human rights. But in Cuba the term *canción protesta* could be problematic, since the government was committed to employment, social equality and serving the people. What would the singers be protesting against if the government was working for the people? So Cuban singers had to tread a fine line between their support for the Revolution and finding a way to be critical without seeming to be against the new society, or counter-revolutionaries. Some singers who became better known later, such as Pedro Luis Ferrer, Carlos Varela and Frank Delgado, were going to have a more complex view of the Cuban Revolution.

What is important in *Nueva Trova* is that a whole generation in Cuba grew up with their music – not just that of Silvio, Pablito and Noel Nicola, but also Sara González, Augusto Blanco, Vicente Feliú, Virulo and many others. They also listened to New Song artists from Latin America: Mercedes Sosa (Argentina), Daniel Viglietti (Uruguay), Chico Buarque and Milton Nascimento (Brazil), Joan Manuel Serrat and Luis Eduardo Aute (Spain), Victor Jara, Violeta Parra, Quilapayún (Chile), Roy Brown and El Topo (Puerto Rico), Amparo Ochoa (Mexico), Alí Primera and Soledad Bravo (Venezuela) and Tania Libertad (Peru). All these singers became the voices of the Spanish-speaking international left and practically all of them performed in Cuba to enthusiastic crowds. If the 1960s and part of the '70s generation in the West were brought up on the music of the Beatles, the Rolling Stones, Bob Dylan and Jimi Hendrix, to name some emblematic figures, in Latin America it was the New Song that defined their coming of age. This does not mean that Latin American youth did not also listen to the Beatles, Stones et al. They did, but New Song artists spoke more closely to their yearnings and dreams.

Emergence of Cuban Cinema with an International Presence

As with literature and music, Cuba showed a remarkable creativity and freedom of expression in film. The founding of the ICAIC (Cuban Institute of Cinematic and Industrial Art) in 1959, barely three months after the overthrow of Batista, was a statement of how important film was to the new revolutionary government. It was led by three central figures: Alfredo Guevara (1925–2013), Tomás Gutiérrez Alea (1928–1996) and Julio García Espinosa (1926–2016). Guevara headed the ICAIC (1959–83; 1991–2012), but was not a film director. In addition, he was the founder and president of the Latin American Film Festival from its inception (1979 and still running). His leadership was invaluable during the 1960s, a period some call the Golden Age of Cuban Cinema. The ICAIC was responsible for film production, technical assistance, financing and distribution, plus its international presence at festivals around the globe. The ICAIC initiated the Noticiero del ICAIC (ICAIC Newsreel) that would play weekly in theatres. The Newsreel, focused mainly on Cuba and Latin America, was usually under ten minutes long and aired for thirty years (1960–90), producing almost 1,500 documentaries. Santiago Álvarez (1919–1998) was the director of the project, as well as many of his own award-winning documentaries, including *79 Springtimes* (on Ho Chi Minh), *Hasta la Victoria Siempre* (on Che Guevara), *LBJ*, and *Ciclón* (on Hurricane Flora). Álvarez favoured what he called a collage technique (using stills, cut-outs, newspaper clippings and so on), avoiding the use of voice-over and talking heads. He sometimes used music in a jarring way. For example, in *79 Springtimes* he combines footage of Ho Chi Minh's funeral with Iron Butterfly's 'In a Gadda Da Vida' on the soundtrack. Though musically it seems out of place, the track is a love song that says, 'Oh, won't you come with me and walk this land', echoing the film walking us through Ho's life and Vietnam. Perhaps Álvarez's best-known film was *Now!*, a five-minute foray into committed cinema, about the U.S. civil rights movement, with dramatic stills and footage rhythmically edited to Lena Horne's rendition of the song. The short is a powerful statement on racism, and the dignity of black struggle, ending with bullets being fired spelling the word NOW. (Many of Álvarez's films are available on YouTube.)

Many Cuban film-makers began learning their craft by making documentaries and graduated to making features. Tomás Gutiérrez

Alea is probably Cuba's best-known director, having made over a dozen feature-length films, but his masterpiece is *Memories of Underdevelopment* (1968). Based on the 1965 novel of the same title by Edmundo Desnoes (b. 1930), it tells the story of the well-to-do Sergio, whose wife and family emigrate to the U.S. shortly after the Revolution (1961). He remains in Cuba, in part because he is curious about what will happen there, and in part because he wants to become a writer, his lifelong dream, postponed on account of taking over a family business. Relieved of family ties, Sergio revels in his new-found freedom, but there is an emptiness as well. The novel takes place between 1961 (after the Bay of Pigs) and 1962 (the Cuban Missile Crisis, where it ends), two crucial moments in Cuban history.

The film is structured according to diary-like entries that Sergio is making, which in the film are done through voice-over. As he reviews his life (marriage, relationships, work) he also makes observations about his current situation, street life, politics, culture and underdevelopment, all while pursuing amorous conquests as well. Sergio is a man between two worlds: he rejects the shallow materialism of pre-1959 Cuba, but cannot fully embrace the revolutionary changes happening all around him. When Sergio refers to underdevelopment, he not only means economics and politics, but also culture. In one scene he talks about how Cubans live in the moment, do not connect all the dots, and have others think for them, which he sees as typical of cultural underdevelopment. This kind of internalized colonized thinking, as Fanon would say, contributes to Sergio's elitist views, and keeps the island from being truly 'civilized' according to the protagonist. But he falls into the same trap as many in the upper classes in wanting to be and live like a European; at one point he says, 'I've always lived as if I were in Paris.' Gutiérrez Alea is sympathetic to Sergio's plight, but by no means agrees with him. Because of the first-person voice-over, the viewer tends to identify with Sergio (and mistakenly confuses his view with the director's), but Gutiérrez Alea actually has scenes where we are allowed to see Sergio from other people's points of view, which show him in an unflattering light. Gutiérrez Alea also effectively uses documentary footage, which invariably takes us away from Sergio's rarefied inner world and grounds the film in historical reality.

Memories as a film raises some of the issues that surrounded the *P.M.-Lunes* controversy, and handles them in a sophisticated and complex way. At one level, it is easy to dismiss Sergio as a bourgeois intellectual, a man of privilege (and sexist to boot), someone who cannot embrace the new society being built in Cuba. But he often says intelligent things, some of his criticisms are consistent with a socialist and decolonizing perspective, and he is not entirely hostile to the whirlwind of change around him, even if it often overwhelms him. The film also includes two scenes that deal with writers and/or underdevelopment: one is a visit to Finca Vigía, where Hemingway lived when he was in Cuba (and which is now a museum); the other a round-table discussion on literature and underdevelopment. The Hemingway scene is ironically titled 'An Adventure in the Tropics', perhaps playfully spoofing Hemingway's love of fishing and hunting in tropical climes. Sergio visits the museum with his lover Elena, whom he has recently met. They conduct the visit in the company of Czech and Russian tourists, the tour leader being René Villareal, who had been a majordomo to Hemingway for two decades. The American author had found him on the streets of San Francisco de Paula, the neighbourhood surrounding his estate. Villareal is both informative and courteous and almost reverential towards his boss, but Sergio's voice-over seems to undermine much of the guide's narrative. At one point Sergio looks at a photo of Hemingway with Villareal and says: 'He molded him to his needs. The faithful servant and the great lord. The colonialist and Gunga Din. Hemingway must have been unbearable.'[22]

A few shots later, Sergio is looking at the author's desk and quips: 'Boots for hunting in Africa, American furniture, Spanish photographs, magazines and books in English, a bullfight poster . . . Cuba never really interested him. Here he could find refuge, entertain his friends, write in English, and fish in the Gulf Stream.'[23] The remark about Cuba not interesting him is a bit of a simplification, but the idea behind the 'tropical adventure' is perhaps that foreign writers who come to Cuba – even when they live there for a while – are still skimming the surface of Cuban reality and can be condescending. Of course, the other issue alluded to but never spoken out loud is Hemingway's rather opulent lifestyle: a writer with three houses (in Idaho, Key West and Cuba) and, of course, a fishing boat. What Cuban author before 1959 was able to make a good living from their writing or lived that kind of life? Gutiérrez Alea is keenly aware that development (and underdevelopment) applies to writers as well, at least in the material sense of the word.

Right after the Hemingway house sequence in the film, Sergio attends a round-table discussion titled 'Literature and Underdevelopment'. Moderated by Cuban literary scholar Salvador Bueno (1917–2006), the panellists are Italian author and film-maker Gianni Toti (1924–2007), Argentinian writer David Viñas (1927–2011), Haitian poet and novelist René Depestre (b. 1926), and Edmundo Desnoes (b. 1930), author of the novel *Memories of Underdevelopment* and co-author of the script. In effect, they play themselves. After some abstract theorizing about underdevelopment and national liberation by Depestre and some personal remarks by Desnoes about racial discrimination against Latinos in the u.s., Toti decides to play devil's advocate. He claims that words like 'underdevelopment' 'are sick ... that these words are language traps, accomplices of an already wasted culture, a stratagem, a linguistic alibi, a linguistic-ideological entanglement that can lead us to the mental peace of clichés'.[24] Despite the ponderous language, Toti has a point: the binary of development–underdevelopment has implicit assumptions: poorer countries need to catch up, they need to modernize and become technologically savvy, create transparent political systems, all because they are 'backward' or 'inferior'.

Like other Third World countries at the time, Cuba's past had been colonial (or semi-colonial) and capitalist. When many former colonies became independent or had revolutions (or both) they looked for alternative modes of development and, of course, the USSR was an example of a poor country that had become a super-power in a little over thirty years. China, Vietnam and North Korea were also poor peasant economies embarking on socialist paths that seemed to offer positive examples in the 1960s. The panel discussion not only highlighted these elements but also the role writers had in this process. These issues would haunt Desnoes for decades: after *Memories*, his third novel, he would not publish another for almost forty years. The next, *Memories of Development*, was published in 2006 (English translation 2013). Desnoes left Cuba in 1979, and the protagonist-narrator of the more recent novel (who has the author's name), after having been a professor in western Massachusetts, moves to the New York area. If Sergio from the novel (and film) cannot adapt to socialism, Edmundo cannot adapt to either socialism or capitalism, recalling Sartre's comments to Cuban writers that 'intellectuals are not happy in any society'. Interestingly, this last novel was also made into a film by Miguel Coyula, a young director with an interest in science fiction.

Sam Spade as Anti-imperialist Socialist Detective and Espionage Fiction

As Cuba headed into the 1970s, there was an attempt, largely success-ful, to promote a literary genre that would be both entertaining and extol revolutionary values: detective and counter-espionage novels. The first Cuban socialist detective novel, *Enigma para un domingo* (An Enigma Made for Sunday; 1971), was by Ignacio Cárdenas Acuña. It sold sixty thousand copies, an impressive sum (the equivalent in the U.S. at the time would have been fourteen million copies). In 1972 the Ministry of the Interior (MININT) announced it would be giving an annual award for socialist detective fiction. Its purpose was 'to advance government ideology, promote conformity with revolutionary norms, and reinforce the unmasking and suppression of antisocial tendencies'.[25]

Most critics see the Cuban socialist detective novel as a variant of socialist realism, which to a degree is true. But, honestly, can we say that most detective fiction (or TV drama) in capitalist countries is anything but 'capitalist realism'? Do shows like *Law and Order, CSI: Las Vegas* or *Hill Street Blues* offer serious critiques of their societies? Sure, we might see episodes that show corruption, greed, decadence, sexual depravity, family dysfunction, addiction, deceit, mendacity, political chicanery (sometimes), economic disparities, racism, traumas of all sorts, but it all ends up being part of restoring the social status quo and protecting 'the way things are'. Even shows that are more innovative (*The Wire, Dexter, True Detective*) do not really stray far in terms of questioning the social contract. So why can't socialists have a little fun and indulge some guilty pleasures, especially when the bad guys are counter-revolutionaries, CIA agents, decadent bourgeois holdovers from capitalism or sociopathic individualists, all of whom are damaging the noble construction of a better society?

The detective novel is a product of modernity and capitalism, and particularly of urban settings, though not exclusively. The anonymity and alienation of a big city, the crowding and the pace of life, the passions that it unleashes are conducive to crime. An ordered world is disrupted by a crime, often violent (murder), and it is up to the detective (police or private) to find the killer and restore a degree of order. In a sense, crime fiction is both conservative and utopian; conservative because it is concerned with personal safety and restoring order, utopian in its belief that the detective will always catch the criminal.

Ernest Mandel admirably defines the genre:

> Nevertheless, the common ideology of the original and classical detective story in [Britain, the U.S., Europe] ... remains quintessentially bourgeois. Reified death; formalized crime-detection oriented toward proof acceptable in courts of justice operating according to strictly defined rules; the pursuit of the criminal by the hero depicted as a battle between brains;

human beings reduced to 'pure' analytical intelligence, partial, fragmented rationality elevated to the status of an absolute guiding principle of human behavior; individual conflicts used as a substitute for conflicts between social groups and layers – all this is bourgeois ideology par excellence, a striking synthesis of human alienation in bourgeois society.[26]

What Mandel means by reified death is death that is not presented as natural, but as accident or murder and the body is treated as a corpse, an object to be scientifically studied, not a unique human life to be fondly remembered or mourned. Mandel's definition does not cover all forms of the genre (for example, what is known as 'postmodern or metaphysical detection'), rather what one could call the more modern (if not hard-boiled) versions. And the modern sleuth – often a loner, prone to alcoholism or other addictions, someone who functions beyond the law, not afraid to use violence, awash in an atomistic social milieu – is somewhere between a misfit and an existentialist warrior, yet somehow committed to justice, even if they are cynical about the way the world works.

So how to take this archetype of the detective and make it function under socialism? One has to dispense with the lone wolf trope for a socialist detective, so revolutionary Cuban crime fiction would have to construct another model: a detective who is not at odds with his society, one who is not an individualist, and a public servant dedicated to not only solving crimes but also performing a type of ideological cleansing. In a socialist society a crime is not only morally reprehensible or an act of personal passion and/or wicked-ness, but equally an act with social and ideological implications. Murdering someone is not just a transgression of the ethical code about taking a human life, but a profoundly ideological and polit-ical act: in a society where human solidarity and the collective good is paramount, the violent death of a person is also a political and social crime that undermines the unity of such a society. A socialist Sam Spade, therefore, would embody traits that a new society would uphold: class solidarity, revolutionary morality, a commitment to the aims of socialism, rejection of bourgeois values like selfishness, individualism and social indifference. He fights against 'antisocial activities', the 'nonintegrated', 'individualists'. Non-integrated means that someone was not integrated into the revolutionary process, and shows signs of individualism, acquisitiveness, intellectualism, elitism, protecting their privacy, or insufficient enthusiasm for the projects and demands of the Revolution, like voluntary labour, attendance at meetings, participation in rallies. As literary critic Persephone Braham suggests: 'The socialist detective novel was part of a project of ideological retrenchment that is often referred to as the "consolidation" of the Revolution.'[27] This period was also called the institutionalization of the Revolution, where the more improvisatory (and sometimes slapdash) methods of the 1960s were refashioned and a more deliberate way of proceeding became the norm: Cuba joined the Soviet bloc common market COMECON (1972), factories were reorganized on a Soviet enterprise model, the Cuban Communist Party held its first congress (1975), and the country adopted a socialist constitution (1976).

Although crime fiction has changed in recent years, the archetype (or stereotype) of the detective as someone who is tough, rugged, brave, ethical and also a bit cynical, and able to navigate the violent world of criminality with resolution, if not panache, is still the most positive image. Traditionally, this meant the sleuth would be a male figure, and in the Cuban detective world the good guy is definitely male.

As we have seen, the ideal of the Cuban revolutionary is a *guerrillero*, a guerrilla fighter, and no one fits that image better than Che Guevara. So, the ideal is a man of physical courage, a warrior, and a man of the people. In the 1960s and '70s in Cuba, that meant that anything smacking of elitism, effeminacy, 'extravagant behaviour' or ultra-refinement was seen as unmanly and not revolutionary. In a 1965 interview, Fidel expressed his theory that homosexuality was incompatible with revolutionary morality. These views dominated the Cuban cultural scene until at least 1980, in part due to an East German textbook on sexuality used in Cuba that spoke of homosexuality as a variant of sexual behaviour, neither a sickness nor an example of 'ideological diversionism'. This textbook was widely distributed in the school system.

Among the novels that not only sold but were received with critical acclaim were Luis Rogelio Nogueras's (1944–1985) *Y si me muero mañana* (If I Die Tomorrow; 1977) and another novel by him co-authored with Guillermo Rodríguez Rivera, *El cuarto círculo* (The Fourth Circle; 1976), a counter-espionage novel that won the MININT prize. Nogueras was better known as a poet, winning the CASA Award in 1981, but these two novels made him a best-selling author.

Daniel Chavarría (b. 1933) is another author who works in both the detective and the espionage genres. Born in Uruguay, he has lived in Germany, France and Spain, and while living in Brazil (1964) the military coup led him to flee to Cuba, where he has lived ever since. Of Chavarría's more than a dozen novels, *Joy* (1977), *La sexta isla* (The Sixth Isle; 1984) and *Allá ellos* (That's Up to Them; 1991) are considered among the best of Cuba's espionage genre. He also co-authored *Completo Camagüey* (1982) and *Primero muerto* (You'll Catch Me Dead First; 1983) with Justo Vasco (1943–2006), each winning the MININT prize for their respective years. Chavarría won Cuba's National Prize for Literature in 2010. Chavarría, like Nogueras, can be innovative in his narrations, mixing up documentary, stream-of-consciousness, temporal jumps and the like, giving his narratives an experimental flavour, especially when compared to other works of the time, which were more conventional in their plotting, characters and so on. Politically, of course, his works adhered to revolutionary ideology; otherwise, how would they be able to win MININT prizes? And yet *Allá ellos*, written in 1980, was not published for eleven years.

The detective/espionage genre was popular among Cuban readers. Between 1971 and 1983 it accounted for 25 to 40 per cent of all titles published during that period. Print runs were large: from twenty thousand to 200,000 often going into several editions and sometimes selling out days after publication.[28] Even so, during the 1980s, close critical attention was paid to the quality of the work, and shortcomings were pointed out by critics (sometimes writers of the genre, themselves). There was worry that the good guys were too flat, and the bad guys were more richly portrayed, perhaps inducing an unwanted sympathy on the part of readers. Novelist Leonardo Padura wrote in 1988 that 'The Cuban detective novel of the 70s was apologist, schematic, permeated with ideas of a socialist realism that was all socialist but very little realist.'[29]

It was Padura himself who would transform the genre. Though he began as a journalist and critic, producing a book of interviews on salsa and another on the work of Alejo Carpentier, beginning in the early 1990s he created a police detective character who has become one of the most endearing (and enduring) personalities of Cuban fiction: Mario Conde (discussed earlier). Conde is a melancholic figure, sensitive, not at all like the hard-boiled, tough-as-nails detectives of the noir genre. He is a wannabe writer, is given to drink, does not have great fortune in love (he is luckier in sex) and is deeply loyal to a close circle of friends, among them El Flaco (Skinny), an Angola vet in a wheelchair, and his mother Josefina, who often cooks for this motley crew. He is interested in matters cultural and is disillusioned with Cuban society and the Revolution, but he is not entirely cynical about it. Padura refers to himself as part of a generation in Cuba that grew up with the Revolution, coming of age in the 1970s and '80s (he was born in 1955), a period of revolutionary fervour and utopian ideals, who later have seen their desires for that 'beautiful totality' dashed by the collapse of the USSR and Eastern European socialism. But Padura has elected to stay in Cuba, and though many foreign observers try and depict him as a 'dissident', a loaded word in Cuba, to be sure, the author is adamant in both making his important criticisms and remaining on the island. Padura is probably the best-known author on and off the island, and some would claim that his international reputation guarantees a degree of expressive leeway not available to all Cubans – authors or otherwise.

Padura has written seven novels featuring Mario Conde. The first four are considered a quartet, all taking place in 1989. The year is significant in that Cuba's fate would dramatically change with the fall of the Berlin Wall and the subsequent dissolution of the USSR. In that same year Cuba was also shaken by the Arnaldo Ochoa (1940–1989) trial, in which a high-ranking general and three other top officials faced charges of drug-trafficking, corruption and the smuggling of ivory, diamonds and hardwoods into Cuba. They were accused of links to the Medellín cartel and of engaging in money laundering. Ochoa had been decorated as a 'Hero of the Revolution' in 1984. He had fought with Castro's guerrillas as a teenager, at the Bay of Pigs, as well as leading Cuban troops in Ethiopia and Angola. He was arrested on 14 June, and on 13 July he and three other high-ranking officials from the military and the Ministry of Interior were executed. Scores of other military and MININT officials were jailed as well.

This background of uncertainty and change in both the Soviet bloc and Cuba underlies Padura's narratives of the quartet. In the first two novels he deals with issues of official and personal corruption (*Pasado Perfecto*, 1991, translated as *Havana Blue*, 2007), the second focusing on a 24-year-old teacher who is murdered, and whose locker reveals that she was living way beyond the means of an ordinary schoolteacher (*Vientos de cuaresma*, 1994, translated as *Havana Gold*, 2008). The third deals with the murder of a transvestite and allows Padura to delve into Havana's homosexual milieu (*Máscaras*, 1997, translated as *Havana Red*, 2005). The final novel of the quartet (*Paisaje de otoño*, 1998, translated as *Havana Black*, 2006) features an important government official who leaves for Miami but mysteriously returns to Cuba to retrieve something valuable, and is brutally murdered.

Máscaras, the third novel, deals with the murder of a young cross-dresser, Alexis Arayán, who turns out to be the son of a prominent Cuban diplomat. Conde's investigation leads him to Albert Marqués, aka el Marqués, an ageing gay writer and theatre director who had been ostracized in the 1970s. No doubt, the figure of Marqués is loosely based on Virgilio Piñera, and the epigraph at the beginning is a quote from Piñera's best-known play, *Electra Garrigó* (1943). It is worth quoting:

> Pedagogue: [...] No, there's no way out of this.
> Orestes: There's always sophistry.
> Pedagogue: That's true. In a city as conceited as this, on the basis of feats yet to be performed, monuments never erected, virtues nobody practices, sophistry is the supreme weapon. If any of the wise women tells you she is a prolific writer of tragedies, don't dare contradict her; if a man declares he is an accomplished critic, encourage him to believe his lie. We have here, and don't you forget it, a city in which everybody wants to be deceived.[30]

The title, *Máscaras*, literally means masks. This is intricately tied to the labyrinth that Conde must traverse to solve the crime, but also to the masking and unmasking that occurs throughout the novel. None of this is new to crime fiction, as often plots, motives and characters are unmasked by the detection process. It is a well-known trope of the genre that characters are not who they seem to be, motives are sometimes hidden or misleading (a murder made to look like suicide, robbery gone wrong, for example), a person has been living under an assumed name, someone has faked their own death and, of course, there is no shortage of characters who lie and deceive others. Every society wears its own masks, and crime fiction just highlights these tendencies or points out its more brutal extremes.

In the novel, murder victim Alexis Arayán turns out not to be a transvestite, though he is gay. The killer has dressed him up as a female character from *Electra Garrigó*, Electra herself. As Conde explores some of Havana's gay underworld, he has to face the reality of homosexuality in Cuba, and the memory of the worst of Cuba's homophobia of the

1960s and '70s, a period when many homosexuals in Cuba, particularly those in the arts, had to remain in the closet and also suffered ostracism by prudish authorities. Closeting is a form of masking as well.

Padura is critical of that treatment, as seen in the following passage, where he quotes from a report from the security services (from the 1970s) on Marqués:

> That very particular, diabolical Alberto Marqués, a hugely experienced, predatory homosexual, politically apathetic and ideologically deviant, a provocative, conflictive individual, lover of the foreign, hermetic, obscurantist, potential consumer of marijuana and other substances, protector of derailed queers, a man of dubious philosophical affiliations, steeped in class-based, petty-bourgeois prejudice, all annotated and classified with the precious help of a Muscovite manual of socialist-realist techniques and procedures . . .[31]

Padura takes all the rhetoric and prejudices of the period and compares them to socialist realist aesthetics. Even though Conde admits to being homophobic (he fears that Marqués will try and seduce him when he goes to the bathroom at the director's house; at a gay soirée he describes himself as a 'Macho-Stalinist'), during the course of the novel he develops a grudging respect for Marqués and what he has lived through. His aversion to homosexuals does not mean he wants to criminalize their sexuality or ideas. Despite his macho traits, Conde is still someone who wants to be a writer, and Marqués (Piñera) challenges the detective in terms of sexuality but equally as a model of artistic integrity. The queer author is a reminder to Conde that he has not fulfilled his artistic dreams. This tension between hyper-masculinity and being a writer runs throughout the Conde series, especially in the fifth novel, *Adiós Hemingway* (2001; same title in English, 2005), and conjures up a famous quip from Virgilio Piñera, cited by Cabrera Infante: 'Real men don't read books. Literature is for faggots and I am a pure faggot.'[32]

The theme of masking and unmasking is central to the novel: a possible suspect, Alberto Marqués, ends up aiding Conde, enjoying his role as a kind of sleuth; the murder victim, though not a transvestite, had been dressed up as a woman the night he was killed; Conde's writer friend Miki, though a bit cynical, is a hack who adheres to the Party's cultural policy line; his closer friend Candito (El Rojo) runs an illegal business and deals drugs; Poly, the young woman he beds, might be a transvestite (but is in fact just bisexual); his buddy on the force, el Gordo Contreras, who has been suspended, and is a person he totally trusts, turns out to be corrupt; and Alexis's father, a Cuban diplomat, turns out to be a fake revolutionary, and the killer to boot. The only people who are what they seem are his surrogate family: Skinny Carlos (the Angola vet in a wheelchair) and his mother Josefina, who often cooks for him, as he and Carlos drink industrial quantities of alcohol.

Transvestism, then, raises crucial issues about identity, desire and writing in Padura's novel, and for this he draws on another Cuban queer author, Severo Sarduy (1937–1993), who is quoted verbatim in some passages. Sarduy often used transvestite characters in his novels, and in some cases they changed gender or identity. Oscar Montero claims that more than gay or homosexual, Sarduy's more fluid notions of identity and desire were more fluid, or queer, arguing that the straight–gay binary still carried a heteronormative bias. He says: 'The history and politics of homosexuality are one thing; queer writing is something else', and

> Homosexuality is not the subversion of heterosexuality, a coded predictable mirroring. Sarduy's queer subjects laugh at such duplicity, aiming for a deviation of a different order. There is in his work neither negation nor affirmation of contraries but rather a queer subjective progression to the tune of a rumba.[33]

The oscillation between what Conde understands to be gay, or homosexual, and queerness is what leaves him perplexed. Homosexuality he has a grasp of, but queerness seems to elude him. He hasn't quite got the queer rumba beat.

In the novel, the character based on Sarduy is called Muscles, an understandable mistranslation of Recio, which is similar to *severo*, or severe, but the real Sarduy would not fit that description of being ripped. Alberto Marqués lends Conde a text written by Recio where transvestism is discussed. The real text is Sarduy's book of essays called *La simulación* (1982), where he borrows Roger Callois's ideas to talk about three aspects of transvestism: metamorphosis, camouflage and intimidation. Conde tries to use these concepts to aid him in his investigation, as he attempts to decode the world of Alexis Arayán and Alberto Marqués. As he enters that world, Conde feels he is on slippery ground, not only because he does not like gays, but because there are a series of codes, behaviours and meanings that he does not quite understand and that threaten his sense of reality.

One could see transvestism as challenging some of the Revolution's goals in that it asks whether one's identity as a revolutionary winds up being a mask. These notions of masking and unmasking go to the heart of Conde's perplexity and the kinds of role reversals he runs up against in his investigation. One could question this assumption: rejecting essentializing notions of the self does not necessarily mean rejecting all notions of self. What Padura is suggesting is that the self can be constructed and reconstructed or transformed. In the case of revolutionary Cuba an ambitious attempt to create a revolutionary self led to a hardening (a word with masculinist overtones) set of definitions about what it meant to be a revolutionary and a man, and being queer was not one of them. Masking (transvestism) also implies some notion of appearance and reality, if only to overturn them as well; it strikes at the revolutionary ideal of total transparency, where private and public self are in harmony. While this has been the goal of revolutionary socialism, the ideal goes back to Rousseau.

For Sarduy, transvestism and writing are analogous. I wrote the following about this relationship:

In a sense, then, Sarduy claims . . . that writing is a kind of transvestism. What does this mean? On an almost literal level, it means that writing is not what it appears to be, that it is a kind of linguistic makeup that hides a certain practice. This would be the equivalent of saying that writing is a kind of fetishism. Writing is a disavowal of a lack that is constantly affirmed and denied at the same time. In Freudian and Lacanian theory the lack fetishism tries to conquer is the absence of a maternal phallus. [For Lacan, the phallus is not always exactly the equivalent of the penis, but also a generator of language and meaning.] The child sees that nothingness and as a result makes substitutes for it, which simultaneously affirm and deny that lack (e.g. shoes, raincoats, gloves). Literature fetishizes desire itself (in part because it uses words, signs, that always point to, but *are not* what they designate, so it mimics the desiring process), and Sarduy takes this to an impossible extreme.[34]

Conde experiences this fetishization of desire in the novel, especially in his sexual encounter with Poly, a bisexual woman whom he thinks may be a transvestite, but also in his imaginary recreations of the crime scene and the stories Marqués tells him about his time in Paris.

All detective fiction is an exploration of interpretation or hermeneutics and *Máscaras* is no exception. Hermeneutics as applied to literature is the interpretation of signs, a wonderful analogy for how a detective or sleuth interprets clues to unravel the mysteries of a crime. The word comes from the Greek god Hermes, who was the messenger to all the other gods (Elegguá in Cuban Santería terms); but equally significant is that he led souls to the underworld after death. Both these traits are germane to detective fiction and Padura seems to embody them in his Conde series. Padura equates writing and detection, and Conde's character fervently desires to bring them together in a utopian synthesis of meaning and justice.

José Latour (b. 1940) is a Cuban writer of crime and espionage fiction. Born in Havana, he worked in different government ministries, ending up at the State Committee of Finance in 1977. In the 1980s he published three novels on the island, but his fourth novel, *The Fool* (1994), was rejected for publication, and earned him political ostracism. Its plot was too close to the events surrounding the Ochoa Affair, so he decided to begin writing his work in English, publishing *Outcast* in 1999, which was well received. In 2002 he and his family moved to Spain and since 2004 they have lived in Canada. Like Padura, Latour's fiction deals with masculinity and how Cubans interact with both state and societal pressures. He does not use a detective character like Conde, but Elliot Steil, born to a Cuban mother and American father, appears in at least three of his novels. Unlike Padura, Latour's antipathy towards the Cuban Revolution is evident and outspoken in his different works, but not an all-consuming concern.

In his English-language debut novel (*Outcast*), Steil works as an English teacher in Havana, where he meets a man who claims to be a friend of his deceased father. The man offers to take Steil to the U.S. where he can start a new life and claim his father's inheritance. They escape on the man's boat but on the way to Florida he is pushed off the vessel into the shark-infested waters of the Florida Straits. Fortunately, he is spotted by a group of *balseros* (rafters), who pick him up. This journey, and the one he must embark on to avenge his disinheritance, form the backbone of the novel. Although Steil is happy to have left Cuba, he has arrived in Miami under difficult circumstances: he has nothing to his name and must unravel the secrets of his attempted murder. Furthermore, his stepbrother, an FBI agent, is one of the villains of the novel. Latour's critical eye is not only focused on Havana but on Miami as well, as he witnesses criminal activity, violence and racism in his newly adopted home. Because of the treachery and deception he faces, Steil must often take extreme measures, committing several minor crimes and almost killing his stepmother and stepbrother. As Helen Oakley observes, 'Elliot Steil at different points of the text encompasses the role of the victim, villain, and detective.'[35] If Padura draws on the work of Piñera and

Sarduy in *Máscaras*, Latour borrows from Shakespeare's *The Tempest*. The novel's somewhat upbeat ending does not overshadow some of the issues related to immigration, criminality and intractable social problems in both Havana and Miami.

Latour's *Havana's Best Friends* (2002; also published as *Hidden in Havana* and in Spanish as *Mundos sucios*) focuses on an American couple coming to Cuba on behalf of a Cuban exile Carlos Consuegra. They are to retrieve a $10 million fortune hidden inside the apartment of a special needs teacher, Elena, and her brother Pablo. The loot is retrieved but not before a series of betrayals and deaths, which leaves Elena with Carlos, but with the eventual loss of her brother and somewhat unsure of how she will adapt to life in the U.S. The novel also has some interesting segments about Cuban tourism and how the island is becoming a marketable commodity.

Finally, we must turn to an important crime writer, with a female detective as protagonist. Carolina García-Aguilera (b. 1949) was born in Cuba and emigrated to the U.S. in 1959. Her detective, Lupe Solano, is featured in ten novels published from 1996 to 2013. The author actually ran a private investigative agency for ten years before deciding to become a writer. Lupe is a 28-year-old single woman and private investigator. She describes herself succinctly: 'I had established myself as an independent and successful woman in a notoriously macho field of work.'[36] As for men, she is not eager to become romantically involved nor very sanguine about their reliability: 'I couldn't deal with the male ego on a daily basis. If I wanted to deal with fragility, I could just as easily go out and have some children.'[37] Lupe comes from a wealthy family that lives in Coral Gables, but is adamant in pursuing her line of work, and as a woman seems to fit the definition of hard-boiled detective. Reluctant to use her weapon in the first novel, as the series progresses she engages more and more in violence (out of necessity, of course). Solano is a complex character, sometimes showing feminist attitudes, at other times showing more traditional traits (she likes bubble baths, men's cologne, having doors opened for her).

García-Aguilera's fictions focus more on Miami, although in some instances Detective Solano does wind up in Cuba to work on cases. Similarly to Latour, García-Aguilera's antipathy towards Fidel and the Revolution is obvious, but Miami and the Cuban exile experience are not painted in rosy images either. As with Padura and Latour, her 1990s work reflects some of the hardships in Cuba during the Special Period, when the Cuban economy dramatically declined after the collapse of the USSR. One of her more unusual narratives, *A Miracle in Paradise* (1999), centres around a religious miracle. An order of nuns has prophesied that the statue of the Virgin of Charity (in Miami), the patron saint of Cuba, will cry real tears on 10 October, Cuban Independence Day, marking the date when Carlos Manuel de Céspedes freed his slaves and proclaimed Cuban independence in 1868. Lupe's sister is a nun and helps her investigate the 'miracle'. As they dig deeper, an anti-Castro plot is revealed, bodies start to pile up and Solano begins to unravel some of the tensions within the Cuban exile community. The author has taken a prominent Cuban symbol – one that has religious, political and patriotic connotations – and crafted a compelling tale about Cuban cultural identity. The reason for the Virgin's tears is her dismay at how Cubans are divided, especially politically, and so 'if the Virgin was sad, it was our job to make her happy. It followed that we Cubans were supposed to find a way to come together, to set aside our political and social differences.'[38] These thoughts are not just about the differences between Cubans on the island and those abroad, but also about the sometimes bitter divisions between members of the exile community. Given the course of history up until now, those divisions – though far less poisoned and/or deadly than before – are still real, and in some cases open wounds.

Cuban crime fiction has gone from being a genre that was created to support a revolutionary cause to one that is much richer in political, social and aesthetic nuance, either on the island or abroad. Despite the political differences between Padura and Chavarría on the one side, and Latour and García-Aguilera on the other, all use the genre to examine Cuban or Cuban diasporic realities: the troubles of the Special Period, religion, sexuality, gender, race, class differences, issues of power and corruption, politics and history. And they have done so by taking one of the most formulaic of literary genres and using it with wit and insight.

FOUR

From Mariel to the Special Period
(1980–1990)

> To count as utopia, an imaginary place must be an
> expression of desire. To count as a dystopia it must be an
> expression of fear.
>
> John Carey, 1999

On 4 May 1980, a 37-year-old *campesino* (peasant) from Holguín left Cuba and eventually made it to Key West, Florida. He left on a boat called *San Lázaro* (St Lazarus), and it was part of the Mariel Boatlift, an event that began with a series of seemingly minor incidents in foreign embassies, then exploded into a full-blown diplomatic crisis that caused an exodus of some 130,000 Cubans in six months, and possibly cost Jimmy Carter's re-election. This peasant was one of the most gifted writers in Cuban history: Reinaldo Arenas.

The Mariel crisis was a major event for Cuba. First, it laid bare the unresolved issues of immigration (U.S.) and emigration (Cuba). While Fidel has always stated that those who have wanted to have been able to leave, the agreements with the U.S. on how to manage that flow has sometimes been haphazard. After a steady flow of émigrés from 1959 to 1962, there was a pause after the Cuban Missile Crisis in 1962. In order to have some orderly process for Cuban emigration, both Cuba and the U.S. agreed to the flights from Camarioca, initiated in 1965 and lasting until 1973. From 1973 to 1980 the only way to leave was illegally, and it was estimated that at least 100,000 Cubans were waiting to leave when the Camarioca airlift was terminated. On the U.S. side, because of Cold War tensions, any Cuban leaving the island was considered a refugee from Communism, and Cuban nationals were given special treatment unlike other immigrants from the Caribbean or Latin America. Because of these favourable immigration policies, Cuba has rightfully argued that the U.S. encourages illegal immigration from the island.

Second, Mariel revealed some fault lines within Cuban society: economic, political and ideological. Despite being a member of the Soviet economic bloc (CMEA or COMECON) and receiving Soviet largesse, the Cuban economy had had some difficult years just before 1980. Also, because of negotiations between the Carter administration and Cuba starting in 1977, many political prisoners were released (some 3,600); but additionally and for the first time since the Revolution, the Cuban community abroad was allowed to visit family back home. Some 100,000 exiles visited in late 1978 and 1979, providing an important influx of foreign reserves for the economy. However, the return of these émigrés, often laden with cash and other gifts, made many Cubans on the island see what the local economy was not providing. While some returning visitors often exaggerated how well they were doing in the U.S., any attempt to compare the Cuban and U.S. economies was bound to be unfavourable to Cuba. As Fidel has often said, Cuba is a poor Third World economy, but when Cubans compare themselves to other countries they do not think of Mexico, Argentina or Chile, but the United States, a comparison that is bound to create disappointment, at best. Added to the economic comparison were political and ideological concerns: Cuba's one-party system seemed restrictive (in terms of emigration) and concerning socialist ideology, Mariel brought out issues related to class and inequality.

Mariel was also a wake-up call for Cuban culture as far as opening it up to international currents was concerned. The Grey Five Years, which became a decade, had been a period of turning inward, but as the 1970s progressed the hardening in cultural policy began to slacken. A welcome step came in 1979 as Cuba hosted the Havana Latin American Film Festival, still held yearly at the beginning of December, followed by the 'Volumen 1' show in January 1981, to be discussed later.

Mariel also radically changed the image of the Cuban refugee in the U.S. Since a percentage of those who came to the U.S. through Mariel were criminals and/or mentally ill, the image of the Cuban exile as a successful white middle-class professional was overturned. Many *marielitos* were working class, black or mixed race, and also different from the early waves of immigrants who were not accompanied by their families (70 per cent of *marielitos* were male, some 20–30 per cent black or mixed race). The identification of 'criminal' for Mariel émigrés was vastly overestimated, since many of the crimes they might have been charged with in Cuba (black market activity, holding of dollars) would not be considered crimes in the U.S. or most other countries. Many *marielitos* were not only rejected by U.S. mainstream society, but by the Cuban community as well.

On the island, however, Mariel forced a reckoning with the exilic nature of Cuban history, one that went back to the nineteenth century, and at different historical moments would flare up. Since 1959 this had taken on a heated and more ideologically charged dimension. For example, if you chose to leave Cuba after the Revolution, the Cuban authorities would accuse you of abandoning the country (instead of leaving, emigrating, moving). To abandon is a more loaded expression. Those who were leaving were called *gusanos* (worms), which was not only an insult, but implied that leaving was seen as unpatriotic, a betrayal of revolutionary principles and embracing of the world and ideology of the enemy (given that most fled to the U.S.). This was certainly the most common epithet hurled at those who made it into the Peruvian embassy – the detonating event of the Mariel crisis – or applied to leave through Mariel. In his speeches Fidel thundered at the *gusanos*, further adding that they were *escoria* (scum), *lumpen* (from lumpen proletariat) and 'anti-social elements', and that Cuban society would be cleansed of these undesirable elements. Curiously, when Cuban exiles began to return to visit loaded with goodies in 1978 and 1979, with their customary humour locals said the *gusanos* had become *mariposas* (butterflies) since they were bringing desperately needed goods and cash. Even Fidel tempered his rhetoric, calling them 'members of the exiled community'. Finally, Mariel certainly influenced an upswing in the Cold War, especially after Reagan's election, which increased tensions between the U.S. and Cuba (guerrilla insurgencies in Central America; the invasion of Grenada; Radio and TV Martí;[1] and Cuba's military role in Africa).

What caused such an extraordinary and, at times, bizarre chain of events? The instigating event occurred on 1 April 1980, when a bus carrying five Cuban nationals crashed through the gates of the Peruvian embassy in Havana. There had been several incidents at different embassies in the previous months as well as the hijacking of vessels taken to the U.S.; in all cases the countries gave the Cubans asylum. What made the Peruvian embassy incident different was that, as the bus broke through the barrier, Cuban police drew their weapons and in the crossfire one of the guards was fatally wounded (it turns out, accidentally, by one of the other guards). The Cuban government at first thought the guard had been shot by the asylum seekers and demanded the Peruvians turn over the five, but the embassy did not comply. After several days of negotiations, the Cuban government decided on 4 April to retire any security personnel from the embassy, a highly unusual move, intended to put the embassies and the U.S. on the defensive. Cubans were not sure what this announcement meant, but the next day Fidel himself appeared near the embassy and reassured everybody of the statement's sincerity. The Cuban government imagined that several hundred people at most would take up the offer, but within 72 hours some 10,800 people had rushed into the compound. There was barely room to stand; people were in the trees, on the roof, even clinging to the fence (on the inside). Soon it became a logistical nightmare since people had to go the toilet, eat and sleep. The first few days were the worst, since there was little food, and portable toilets had not been delivered as arranged. The leaves of the trees in the compound were eaten, as well as the bark, and the ambassador's parrot was snatched and eaten. Eventually, little boxes of food began arriving, as well as portable toilets; passes were issued to people so they could go home, assured that they would be able to leave the country. In addition, the government said anyone who wanted to leave Cuba could do so, provided they had a visa from their country of destination.

Costa Rica offered to take in the Cubans and by 16 April planeloads of émigrés were landing at San José airport. With news teams showing the Cubans kissing Costa Rican soil, the media spectacle proved embarrassing for Cuba, and the flights were stopped two days later. By then the decision to switch to a boatlift had been made and the first vessels arrived on 21 April. The Mariel Boatlift was on, and would continue unabated for the next five months. Mariel is a small port city of 42,000, 25 miles (40 km) west of Havana. On 4 May, due to a bureaucratic mistake (a misspelling of his surname on his identity document), the *campesino* from Holguín was able to board the *San Lázaro* and make it to Key West.

The *campesino*, Reinaldo Arenas (1937–1990), had undergone extraordinary travails in Cuba (censorship, prison, persecution, confiscation of manuscripts), and was about to embark on a flurry of literary production over the next decade of his short life. Arenas had been able to publish his first novel in Cuba, *Celestino antes del alba*, in 1967 (*Singing from the Well*, 1987). It would also be the last book he published in Cuba. Nonetheless, he was able to smuggle out manuscripts of other works that were published abroad, which was considered a counter-revolutionary activity at the time. Through his friend Jorge Camacho (1934–2011), also Cuban, an excellent Surrealist painter who lived in Paris, other works were published in French and Spanish, particularly *Hallucinations* (French 1968, Spanish 1969, English 1971), perhaps his best-known novel, and *Con los ojos cerrados* (1972), a short story collection published in Uruguay.

Later, his *Palace of the White Skunks* (French 1975, Spanish 1980, English 1990) appeared in French before the Spanish original.

Arenas wrote a story about someone in the Peruvian embassy, heavily based on the testimony of his friend Lázaro Gómez Carriles (b. 1958), a writer-photographer. The unnamed narrator is inside the embassy compound with thousands of others amidst terrible over-crowding, the stench of faeces and urine, lack of food; he is waiting for his friend to join him inside. Given his hunger, he goes chasing after a lizard, which slithers through the mud, or climbs up a woman's skirt or down a man's shirt, seemingly just out of reach. Narrated at a feverish pitch, the stream of consciousness of the tale goes from the past to the present to the future as the narrator grows more anxious about the whereabouts of his friend and more eager to trap the lizard. We find out that the narrator has been in prison and is a writer who sees writing as a form of vengeance and lives in a place very similar to the rundown Hotel Montserrate (a semi-abandoned building) where Arenas lived before he left Cuba. Finally, he spots the friend but he is outside the embassy and is dressed in a uniform. Realizing he has been betrayed, he watches the soldiers – including his friend – passing out small boxes of food rations, which causes fights among the refugees since there is not enough to feed everyone. He refuses to take a box, claiming that it is shit, and the story ends with the narrator finally trapping the lizard. Arenas wrote the story in 1980 and it appeared as the ninth story in a collection he had previously published in 1972 (*Con los ojos cerrados*; With Eyes Closed). The ninth story, entitled 'Termina el desfile' (The Parade is Over), is a kind of sardonic reference to the first story in the collection, 'Comienza el desfile' (The Parade Begins), which describes happier times at the beginning of the Revolution. With the new story added, Arenas had the collection published in 1981 with the title changed to *The Parade is Over*. Clearly this choice reflected his disillusionment with the Cuban Revolution.

Events like the Mariel crisis, plus the travails he endured at the hands of Cuban authorities (harassment, prison, interrogations, confiscation or destruction of manuscripts, censorship) until he left are described in Arenas's autobiography, *Antes que anochezca* (1992; *Before Night Falls*, 1993), published posthumously. This controversial book, which reads like an adventure novel (he is not unlike the protagonist in his *Hallucinations*), has lyrical interludes about his childhood, moving descriptions of his adolescence and the early years of the Revolution, mixed in with bitter encounters with both the literary and political establishments of the time, harrowing accounts of his times in prison, racy descriptions of sexual encounters, plus biting anecdotes about Cuban literary and cultural figures. Arenas was a socio-political, sexual and literary outlaw and he wore that badge with great pride.

Before Night Falls might be the only Cuban book that has been turned into a major film and an opera. Surely, the breathless pace and unbelievable events in Arenas's life have an operatic flair to them. The film, by Julian Schnabel, was released in 2000, and starred Javier Bardem as Arenas, in a convincing and moving performance. Though Lázaro Gómez Carriles worked with Schnabel and others on the script, there are many liberties taken with the book and the chronology of Arenas's life, not to mention a superficial handling of the Padilla Affair, the publication dates of his books and the omission of his sometimes highly critical views of the United States. There is little contextual information on the Cuban Revolution, the UMAP camps (Arenas claims in his book they were founded around 1963, whereas most scholars say they began in 1965) or even the Mariel crisis. The film becomes a fairly traditional treatment of the persecuted artist under Communism (with homophobia thrown in), the symbol of personal and artistic freedom fighting the power of the state. None of this is meant to deny that Arenas was hounded by homophobes, censors, bureaucrats and informers (and even betrayed by a few 'friends'), but to read his autobiography and/or his work in such a narrow fashion yields a limited view of his life and creativity, as well as what was happening in the wider context of Cuban society and culture.

For example, in a chapter titled 'My Generation', he outlines a longer history of troubled relations between writers and those in power:

> Ours is a national history of betrayals, uprisings, desertions, conspiracies, riots, coup d'états, despair, false pride, and envy ... Two attitudes, two personalities, always seem to be in conflict throughout our history: on the one hand, the incurable rebels, lovers of freedom and therefore of creativity and experimentation; and on the other, the power-hungry opportunists and demagogues, and thus purveyors of dogma, crime, and the basest of ambitions.[2]

Arenas give three examples from Cuban history: General Tacón and the poet Heredia (1820s); Martínez Campos and Martí (1870s); and Fidel with Lezama and Piñera (1960s and '70s). While Arenas admirably captures the underlying violence in Cuban history and its effects on writers, the reference to Lezama and Piñera must be more nuanced. Though both writers died ostracized, by the early to mid-1980s their work was being published and re-evaluated positively and their important contributions to Cuban culture were recognized. Unfortunately, these events happened after the authors died. Arenas would probably see these changes as mere window dressing, as well as the fact that some of the authors singled out by Padilla in his confession (1971), after not being published for a decade, have subsequently gone on to win the National Prize for Literature: Miguel Barnet (1994), Pablo Armando Fernández (1996), César Lopez (1999) and Antón Arrufat (2000). If Arenas were alive, he would no doubt consider the awards a cynical move by the Cuban state. Since its inception in 1983, the prize has never been given to a Cuban writer living abroad.

Arenas takes up the dichotomy between rebels and opportunists to castigate certain well-known Cuban writers, claiming that once they showed their adherence to the Revolution their literary work became insignificant. Hence, Alejo Carpentier wrote nothing worthwhile after *El siglo de las luces* (Explosion in a Cathedral; 1962). But what of *El recurso del método* (Reasons of State; 1974), *Concierto barroco* (Baroque Concert; 1974) and *El arpa y la sombra* (The Harp and the Shadow; 1979)? Are these the works of a hack? Hardly. What about Guillén's *El Gran Zoo* (The Great Zoo; 1967) and his *El diario a diario* (Daily Daily; 1972)? The same holds true for Vitier, García Marruz and Diego, even if some of their later work might not always be as brilliant as some of their earlier material. Their literary essays maintained a high standard throughout their careers. One could argue that Guillermo Cabrera Infante never achieved the same level of quality after *Three Trapped Tigers*, when he had left Cuba and presumably had more freedom to write. One could also make a similar argument concerning Padilla's work post-1980, or that of other exiled writers. The point is that staying in Cuba as a writer and espousing the revolutionary line is no guarantee of mediocrity, nor is leaving the island and becoming an exiled author a guarantee of creative genius.

Another chapter of his memoir is entitled 'Superstalinism' and briefly recounts Cuban reactions to the Soviet invasion of Czechoslovakia, as well as the hardening policy in the cultural sphere that set in between Padilla's award (1968) and his incarceration in 1971. Again, Superstalinism sounds like a clever neologism, but does it truly have conceptual or explanatory rigour? Does Cuba merit the term Stalinist or Superstalinist? Stalinism has been associated with certain features that characterized Soviet society from 1929 until Stalin's death in 1953. These features include a revolution from above, a cult of personality, forced collectivization (especially in agriculture), a rigid centralized form of economic planning, the widespread use of terror and then labour camps to curb dissent, the imposition of philosophical orthodoxy (Marxism-Leninism plus key texts by Stalin), violent purges within the ruling party, and the adoption of socialist realism and strict ideological criteria in the area of culture. Does Cuba fit the bill?

Starting with culture, we have already seen that the Cuban Revolution never enforced a philosophy of socialist realism in the arts (recall Fidel's words to French reporter Claude Julien: 'Our fight is with imperialists, not abstract painters'). However, as we have seen, there was a hardening in policy that led to the Padilla Affair: the UMAP camps (closed by 1969, others say 1968 or 1967); the proscription of rock and jazz music (lifted or simply ignored by the 1970s); the censorship of certain writers (which changed in the 1980s and beyond); writers going into exile (Arenas, Cabrera Infante, Benítez Rojo, Lydia Cabrera, Sarduy, Baquero, Labrador Ruiz, Padilla, Montenegro, García Vega, Casey, among others). Still, this is a far cry from what happened to writers in the Soviet Union who were sent to do hard labour or even killed.

In terms of the other traits of Stalinism, the Cuban context is radically different. As for the cult of personality, despite the enormous presence of Fidel in Cuban society there is not a single statue of him in the country, though he is on political billboards and his photo is in many government offices, which is not entirely different from other countries, Communist or not. Che Guevara's image is far more prevalent in public spaces than Fidel's. Despite an official reverence towards Fidel, it is far less deifying than what occurred under Stalin, or in China under Mao or North Korea under Kim Il Sung. Cuba is not North Korea with palm trees. Did Cuba collectivize its economy? Certainly, but again this was nothing like what happened in the USSR in the 1930s or China under the Great Leap Forward (both producing famines); some 20 to 30 per cent of Cuban farmland remained in the hands of small private landowners, and this figure has grown in recent years. Did the Cuban Revolution use widespread terror and huge purges to consolidate its power and implement its policies? Again, without ignoring some of the more unsavoury aspects of Cuba's political system, which can be harsh on dissent, the Revolution did not engage in Great Purges à la USSR 1936–9, nor in the wholesale slaughter of its political opponents as did many Latin American regimes from the 1960s to '80s, with thousands executed or simply disappeared. Nor has Cuba had anything as convulsive and destructive as China's Cultural Revolution (1966–76), when many artists, scholars and intellectuals were jailed, sent for 're-education' or killed.

Arenas had great hopes that the Soviet invasion of Czechoslovakia would be rejected by Fidel and the Cuban leadership, leading the island away from 'Soviet-style socialism', and taking the Revolution on a more libertarian path, presumably away from a one-party government and towards a less restrictive policy on cultural affairs. But what were the choices Fidel truly had? Cuba's promotion of revolutionary movements in Latin America had produced considerable friction between the Kremlin and Havana, and the death of Che Guevara in Bolivia only underlined that tension. Fidel and other Cuban leaders had excoriated the lack of verve and revolutionary ardour of traditional Communist parties in Latin America during the 1960s. It took three days before Fidel gave a major speech on the Soviet invasion, and not surprisingly he came down on both sides of the issue. First, he admitted that the Warsaw Pact invasion (led by the USSR) of the country was a violation of Czechoslovak sovereignty and that, as a small Third World nation that has often had its sovereignty violated by imperial powers (Spain, U.S.), Cuba could only sympathize with the plight of the Czechoslovak people. But, at the same time, he shared the view that the Prague Spring, under the leadership of Alexander Dubček (1922–1992), had been led astray by reforms that were reintroducing capitalism to Czechoslovakia, and drawing the country closer to the West, into the imperialist camp (eventually). As such, the socialist brotherhood of nations could not afford to lose one of its members to the U.S. and/or NATO. This Cold War logic was not exceptional: both sides often saw political changes as a zero-sum game, be it in Europe, Asia, Africa or Latin America. One of the most poignant examples was China: from 1949 into the early 1950s, Western elites were still arguing about 'who lost China' (as if China were the property of some nation or nations, or the West in general).

In any event, Arenas was being politically naive, particularly given the circumstances of Cuba in 1968. Just months earlier (on 13 March), as part of a Revolutionary Offensive, the state had nationalized some 58,000 small businesses. One of the posters supporting the measures read, from top to bottom, 'More Revolution; War on: Weakness; Egoism; Individualism; Parasitism; Vice; Exploitation; More Revolution'. The move was towards economic radicalization, leaving small and cooperative farmers (about 30 per cent) as the only non-state-owned sector of the economy. It was a disastrous move in that many of these small firms conducted business with the state; and equally disastrous for Cuban musicians since among many of the nationalized (or closed) enterprises were restaurants and nightclubs. This period reflects a certain puritanical streak in the Revolution's policies, with homophobia becoming more pronounced, the existence of the UMAP camps, the banning of rock music and so on. A month before the Revolutionary Offensive, the Soviets had cut off oil supplies to Cuba, due to political differences on internal party politics as well as foreign policy (Cuba's support for armed revolutionary movements around the globe versus the Kremlin's policy of peaceful coexistence). These actions by the Soviets gave the Cuban leadership more than enough reasons to patch up their relationship with the USSR, which had been troubled since the Cuban Missile Crisis. And Fidel's speech supporting the invasion of Czechoslovakia was a way to begin mending the relationship. It was costly in international terms, as it tarnished Cuba's revolutionary credentials. A little more than a decade later Cuba would suffer again when supporting the Soviet invasion of Afghanistan in 1979, barely three months after Cuba had hosted the Non-aligned Movement Conference, which it headed.

Despite Arenas's severe assessment of post-revolutionary Cuba, he was no typical Miami exile, whatever that means. After the Mariel exodus, he lived in Miami for several months and found the city stifling, and the constant *cubaneo* not conducive to his writing. The great scholar of Afro-Cuban religions Lydia Cabrera warned him and suggested he move north. As an openly gay author he found that homophobia also characterized the exile community, and he was critical of the indifference to the arts shown in the city, as well as the rampant materialism of U.S. life. Politically, he did not find Miami welcoming either. In his novel *The Color of Summer*, he says, 'In Miami there is no dictatorship only because the peninsula has not been able to secede from the rest of the United States.'[3] The statement unequivocally suggests that if Florida were not part of the U.S., a Cuban-ruled Miami would be similar to typical Latin American right-wing dictatorships. Comments such as these did not endear Arenas to the Cuban exile community in southern Florida, and explains why he quickly moved on to New York, where he spent the rest of his life.

Arenas's work is undeniably harsh and relentless against the Revolution, and given the circumstances of his life, this is hardly surprising. However, to use his writings and ideas as a 'true lens' on Cuba would be as misleading as exclusively using interviews with Fidel Castro to discuss the merits or failures of the island's socialist experiment. Arenas would describe Cuba under Castro as a type of hell; Fidel would see it if not as paradise, at least on the way to constructing a type of promised land. As always, the reality lies somewhere in between.

The literary excellence of Arenas's oeuvre is beyond question: *Hallucinations*, *Farewell to the Sea* and *The Color of Summer* are canonical works of Cuban and Latin American literature. His belonging to the Mariel generation led him to found the magazine *Mariel* in 1983, which ushered in a new generation of Cuban artists who would have an unusually complex and critical relationship with Cuban culture, bringing a different perspective to the debate around intellectuals and the Cuban Revolution. One need not agree entirely with Arenas's ideas to see that some of the old paradigms about these issues were outdated. Arenas's life and oeuvre do bring up the exilic or diasporic nature of Cuban culture. One could argue that Arenas was already a kind of internal exile long before he left the island in 1980, and various testimonies by concerned foreign intellectuals who visited Cuba in the late 1970s and enquired about his whereabouts only to be told that no such person existed are beyond Kafkaesque. How could anyone expect that denial to be believed about someone who had published a novel in Cuba, two abroad, as well as a collection of short stories? This attempt to truly make Arenas a non-person would be comical if it were not horrifyingly true.

At the time Arenas was leaving Cuba, another Cuban artist, born in Cuba but raised in the United States, was travelling back to Cuba for the first time in almost twenty years. In terms of her social background, Ana Mendieta (1948–1985) could have not been more different to Arenas; her family had many members prominent in Cuban history and nationalism. A great-uncle had briefly been president in the 1930s; her father, a lawyer, was well connected to many political figures. Like Arenas, Mendieta was an exile, but as an adolescent, not as an adult, so the decision to leave was not entirely her own. She left Cuba in 1961, at the age of twelve, along with her sister Raquel, as part of Operation Peter Pan, which lasted from late 1960 until the Cuban Missile Crisis (October 1962). This operation, under the auspices of the Catholic Church, but also the U.S. State Department, brought over fourteen thousand Cuban children to the U.S. without their parents (the idea was that the parents would join them later). Most reunited but sometimes it took years or never happened. Mendieta's father was arrested in 1961 for working with anti-Castro forces during the Bay of Pigs invasion, and was not released from prison until 1979. Her mother and brother finally joined them in the U.S. in 1966.

Mendieta and her sister lived in various foster homes in Iowa and in 1965 she began her art studies, eventually obtaining a Master's degree in 1972 from the University of Iowa, and continuing in the Intermedia Program under the mentorship of Hans Breder. It was in this period that Mendieta began to move away from traditional artwork to earth-body work, performance, body art, installation, film and video. She began her *Silueta* (Silhouette) series, and travelled several times to Mexico to create works (documented either with photos or film). In 1980 and 1981 she returned to Cuba to create a series called *Rupestrian Sculptures* in the caves of Jaruco. After winning the Prix de Rome she spent time in Italy (1983–5) and married minimalist sculptor Carl André. Their marriage was brief: eight months later, on 8 September 1985, Ana Mendieta fell from the 34th floor of their New York apartment after a fight with her husband. Because of the discrepancy between the 911 call and physical marks on André at the scene, he was charged with second-degree murder. André opted for a trial without jury and was acquitted in 1988. (André claimed that his wife had committed suicide, even though she was about to file for divorce and had documented evidence of his infidelities.) Many artists (especially women artists) felt André was guilty, and the fact that many issues remain unresolved about what actually happened makes Ana's death a sober reminder about gendered violence. To make matters worse, the judge permanently resealed all documents related to the trial.

Despite her short yet incredibly productive career, Mendieta's work and legacy has been important for Cuban art and culture. She brings up issues about identity, culture, nature, exile and nationality that are still challenging us today. Perhaps her best-known work is the *Silueta* (Silhouette) series, which she performed in Iowa, Mexico, Pennsylvania, New York and Cuba, and which had different modalities, although all had to do with her own body and the earth. In the literal sense her own body (or a plywood silhouette of her) was imprinted on the earth and she often was covered with earth, mud, flowers, water, and so on. Despite the statement of her embracing the earth, and finding sustenance from it, these works were ephemeral and bound to disappear, hence, the need to document them through film or stills. Despite creating her art in (and with) something as timeless and solid as the earth, Mendieta's *Siluetas* are about disappearance; their impermanence makes them more haunting.

She described her artistic trajectory as follows:

My art is grounded in the belief of Universal Energy which runs through everything from insect to man, from man to specter, from specter to plant, from plant to galaxy. My works are the irrigation veins of the Universal fluid. Through them ascend the ancestral sap, the original beliefs, the primordial accumulations, the unconscious thoughts that animate the world.

There is no original past to redeem; there is the void, the orphanhood, the unbaptized earth of the beginning, the time that from within the earth looks upon us. There is above all the search for origin.[4]

It would be easy to interpret this statement in an earth goddess New Age way, but as we will see, Mendieta's work complicates matters on how she views the earth. Earth is obviously associated with nature and contrasted with nation, linked to culture. The former (nature) would be considered timeless, prehistorical, female, primitive, the body and as something that is essential, unified and natural. The latter (nation) is particular, contingent, historical, male, colonial (or post-colonial), the mind, and something that is constructed, multifarious and artificial. This dichotomy can seem arbitrary and part of previous binaries we have examined; but this does not imply that these differences are absolutely antithetical. For example, although every nation is a particular in the global scheme of things, within its own territory it creates a universal ('out of the many, one'); it tries to infuse a timelessness into its temporal horizon, and in terms of identity seeks to naturalize, essentialize and create a unified concept of national belonging. Although nationalism strives to naturalize and homogenize the national subject, countries are riven by social inequality, racial subjugation, ethnic tension, gender domination, sexual difference, various religious traditions and political-ideological discrepancies. While nationalism can trump some or even all of these differences at any given time, issues of difference can be seen not only as troubling, but as threatening. Think about what it means to belong to a society when one is a tin miner in Bolivia or a woman in Saudi Arabia, a Muslim in Myanmar or an African under apartheid in South Africa, an untouchable (*dalit*) in India or a gay man in Algeria, a Moroccan immigrant in France or an anti-Communist in North Korea.

In her work, Mendieta historicizes nature while also complicating notions of nationhood, citizenship and belonging. Many critics have pointed out that her fascination with creating earth-body works relates to the fact that she was an exile from her native land. These works focus on issues of displacement, absence and loss, and critics have suggested that each piece of land she worked on (Iowa, Mexico, Pennsylvania, New York) was a substitute for Cuba. These interpretations are useful, but they do not exhaust the richness of Mendieta's work. Despite her yearnings for her homeland, Mendieta also realized – at least given the situation of the 1970s and '80s – that one could return but not fully come home. To a degree, then, Mendieta cultivated several homes: Oaxaca, Iowa, Rome, Cuba and, to a lesser extent, New York, where she lived during the last years of her life. No doubt symbolically, emotionally and spiritually, Cuba loomed larger than the other homes, and yet Mendieta's art seems to go beyond either nostalgia or narrow definitions of *cubanía*, in that you do not have to live on the island to be Cuban, nor is your art any less Cuban if not created on Cuban soil. In this sense Mendieta's art underlines the diasporic history of Cuban culture: after all, the only 'true Cubans' were its indigenous Taíno inhabitants and everyone else has come from elsewhere (Spain, different parts of Africa, China, the Middle East, other parts of Europe).

From her *Silueta* series to other works, Mendieta has drawn on both indigenous sources (Mexican, but also Taíno) and Afro-Cuban, especially the religions of Regla de Ocha and Palo Mayombe. From the Ocha tradition she drew on the notion of *aché*, which definitely informs her earth-body sculptures. Where she speaks about the 'universal energy', this can be viewed as a synonym for *aché*, which is the cosmic energy that makes events happen, gives life, transforms things (similar to chi in Taoism). As we saw earlier, it is the orishas who are the conduits for *aché* from God to us mortals. The orisha of the earth, agriculture and crops is Orisha Oko, also known for being a hard worker, chaste and an arbiter in disputes. He is male, which differs from many other religious traditions, but the earth must work with water to be fruitful and so Ochún (sweet waters, fertility, sensuality) and Yemayá (the ocean, motherhood) are two important female orishas that Mendieta invokes in her works.

In the series she did when she returned to Cuba in 1981, *Rupestrian Sculptures*, she references many of the female spirits of the Taínos: Atabey (mother of the waters), Guanaroca (first woman), Guabancex (wind), Maroya (moon) and Itiba Cahubaba (Great Bleeding Mother). Itiba has been magnificently represented in a *cemí* (a clay or wooden figure with spiritual meaning, also *zemí*) currently housed at the National Museum of the American Indian: she is shown in the process of giving birth to twins, which she does not survive. Her giving birth is a sacrificial act. The *cemí* is an important object-concept in Taíno culture, one that is similar to the concept of *aché* in Regla de Ocha or the Taoist notion of qi (ch'i). A scholar of the Taíno says:

> The Taíno-language term cemí refers not to an artifact or object but to an immaterial, numinous, and vital force. Under particular conditions, beings, things, and other phenomena in nature can be imbued with cemí. Cemí is, therefore, a condition of being, not a thing. It is a numinous power, a driving or vital force that compels action; it is the power to cause, to effect, and also denotes a condition or state of being.[5]

Mendieta's work can be seen as a kind of artistic shamanism that channels *aché* or *cemí*. The sculptures done in the caves of Jaruco also evoke the Taíno beliefs that humankind emerged from caves, not to mention that the Taíno also used them as places of worship.

Mendieta goes beyond the spiritual in her Jaruco sculptures. The caves were used as a hideout by runaway slaves and also by the *mambises* who fought against the Spanish in the nineteenth century in favour of Cuban independence. The Jaruco work then brings together not only issues of identity and exile, but also the personal and the historical, as well as the spiritual and the political. The artist documented the work in both photography and film (Super 8 and once on 3/4-inch video), most often silent.

The one exception to her silent films is her last one, *Ochún*, a piece that opens with sounds of the ocean and seagulls. It was shot off Key Biscayne, Florida, in October 1981, and lasts a little over eight minutes. In it, we see her doing the usual silhouette of a body, but this time it is in the water, and unlike the others the form of the body is open at the 'head' and the 'feet' and so the ocean flows freely through the silhouette. Mendieta said she wanted to do this piece in (and with) the water because it was the ocean that linked Key Biscayne with Cuba, a way of expressing their connectedness (as well as the separation). In evoking the orishas related to water, the artist seems to recall Bachelard's phrase: 'Thus water will appear to us as complete being with body, soul, and voice.'[6]

To speak of body, soul and voice means personhood, and Mendieta's art, by invoking indigenous and Afro-Cuban beliefs, is putting forth a different concept of personhood to the customary one of individuality. José Oliver, a scholar of Taíno culture, draws on the work of Chris Fowler in which he speaks about individuals and 'dividuals'. Fowler defines the latter as a 'state of being in which the person is recognized as composite and multi-authored'.[7] By multi-authored he not only means social relations with others but that a person has a mind, soul and body, and that these three elements 'might not be fixed in the matter of the body but either enter into or emerge from the person during certain occasions'.[8] This definition not only includes the qualities of shamanistic experiences but also spiritual practices that involve a community of living worshippers as well as ancestral spirits, spirits of the dead, trance, rites of initiation, possession and other forms of interacting with the numinous. As Fowler underlines, personhood is 'contextual and shifting'.[9] These qualities associated with 'multi-authored personhood' will conflict with European notions of personhood and form a continuum with

Cuba's subsequent history and the arrival of African slaves and their similar, but not identical, notions of personhood.

Mendieta's vision of 'multi-authored personhood', in engaging earth, nation, history and memory, reminds us that 'Remembrance is a process, not a task to be completed; it is carried out through constant repetition and renewal.'[10] Perhaps this is why the *Silueta* series went on for so many years and occurred over so many geographical spaces.

During her first trip to Cuba, Mendieta met with a group of artists who exhibited together in a show titled 'Volumen I' (January 1981) and became close to several of them. The group included Flavio Garciandía, Tomás Sánchez, José Bedia, Gustavo Pérez Monzón, Ricardo Rodríguez Brey, Leandro Soto, José Manuel Fors, Israel León Viera, Juan Francisco Elso, Rubén Torres Llorca and Rogelio López Marín (Gory). They were contemporaries, born within three to four years of each other (from 1953 to 1957), except Sánchez, who was born in 1948, the same year as Mendieta. All the artists were professionally trained in Cuban art schools, and after the 'Volumen I' show they became well known not only on the island but internationally as well. One of the most gifted of the group, Elso, died at 31, and Gustavo Pérez Monzón stopped creating work, but still teaches art (in Mexico). Interestingly, only one artist of the group (Fors) still lives in Cuba; the others are in Mexico, the U.S. and Europe.

The 'Volumen I' show did not cause a scandal like Angel Delgado's 'bio-sculpture' of 1990, but it did break new ground. Organized by the artists themselves, there was no overarching theme to the exhibit, nor stylistic unity, and it has been described as a 'fresh, eclectic mix of pop, minimalism, conceptualism, performance, graffiti, and arte povera.'[11] The show was popular, drawing some ten thousand visitors during its two weeks. The artists stayed away from the overtly political or patriotic themes that were more the norm at the time. Although the exhibition was a critical success, more traditional critics called it 'cosmopolitan', 'ideologically weak' and an expression of a 'rootless vanguardism', out of touch with Cuban reality.

Flavio Garciandía (b. 1954), one of the featured artists, was already known for his hyper-realist painting *All You Need is Love* (1975), considered a critique of the mandatory optimism of socialist realism. Its title is a sly reference to the fact that the music of the Beatles had been banned in Cuba from 1964 to 1966. The painting shows a young woman in a flowery dress lying in the grass turned towards the viewer with a rapturous smile. Decades later, in 2000, the Cuban government would commission a statue of John Lennon in Menocal Park, now John Lennon Park, on the twentieth anniversary of his death. In 2011, a club called Yellow Submarine opened next to the park, and is completely dedicated to the Beatles, although live bands that play there don't necessarily play Beatles music.

Garciandía's work is an ongoing conversation with the artistic tradition (as well as taking on the nature of kitsch and art), whether playful parody, respectful but irreverent homage or outright provocation. In the 1980s he produced work on Cuban popular sayings, which reflected his interests in bridging the divide between high art and popular culture, or between kitsch and art. Towards the end of the 1980s he worked on a series of works/installations called *Tropicalia I* and *Tropicalia II*. In these Garciandía used recognizable forms that were silhouetted on colourful backgrounds, as well as plants, usually arranged between the different paintings. The forms were bodies, hammer and sickle, machetes, palm trees, penises, flamingos and so on. In some instances, the border around the silhouettes was filled in with gold-coloured glitter. The backgrounds had an action-painting look to them. By stylizing the hammer and sickle, as well as the other forms, the work takes on an edgy dynamism, like the Futurist paintings that extolled machines.[12]

Garciandía's use of palm trees, glitter and political icons in repetition evokes what Kundera called 'Communist kitsch'. In his novel *The Unbearable Lightness of Being* (1984), Kundera speaks of the relationship or the need for kitsch under Communism, even if he also points out that all political-ideological-religious systems (democracy, fascism, Catholicism, Protestantism, Judaism, feminism,

Europeanism, nationalism, internationalism) have their own kitsch.[13] Sabina, the main female protagonist, objects to Communism not on political or even ethical grounds, but on aesthetic criteria:

> What repelled her was not so much the ugliness of the Communist world (ruined castles transformed into cow sheds) as the mask of beauty it tried to wear – in other words, Communist kitsch. The model of Communist kitsch is the ceremony called May Day.[14]

Of course there are other examples, though perhaps May Day is the most spectacular. In Cuba 26 July is also an important date and day of public spectacle (this one moved around and celebrated in different cities, while May Day is always staged in Revolution Plaza, with many local celebrations in the interior). Kundera even argues that the unwritten slogan of May Day parades was not 'Long live Communism!' but 'Long live life!'. This observation is based on the fact that the ceremony drew from 'the deep well of the categorical agreement with being'.[15] Kundera attributes this to the cunning and power of Communist systems in being able to manipulate the latter slogan, convincing even those who were indifferent to Marxist-Leninist ideology.

One need not agree entirely with Kundera to see how kitsch can play a role in buttressing ideological positions, and in the case of socialist societies how kitsch can dovetail not only with socialist realism, but with all types of political messaging ('Kitsch is the aesthetic ideal of all politicians and all political parties and movements').[16] Why does Kundera make this assertion? Kitsch has been described as predictable, easy to understand, cheesy, sentimental, of low quality and evincing bad taste. From these traits one can see how it would appeal to anyone with a political message, because kitsch is accessible, immediately perceived and understood. No one delivering a political message wants it to be obscure, confusing or unintelligible.

In aesthetic terms, kitsch is often seen in terms of deception, self-deception or even a form of aesthetic lying. Hence Garciandía's

All You Need is Love, of the young girl in the grass, evoking the sweet kitsch of French academic painting like that of Adolph Bouguereau (1825–1905), whose portraits of little girls are exemplary as kitsch. And because of its appeal, kitsch is seen as a 'pleasurable escape from the drabness of modern quotidian life'.[17] This escapism of hyper-optimistic Communist kitsch is what Garciandía is contesting in *Tropicalia I* and *Tropicalia II*, where the hammer and sickle are shown in repetitive fashion, somewhat like pop art, but also in subverting their symbolic power, as when the hammer is shaped like a penis, and where the sickle is going up someone's behind. (Had the artist done this work in 1977, it would probably never have been shown publicly.)

Garciandía is trying to take the obvious and immediate (or kitsch-like) aspects of an important Communist symbol and make it, say, more complicated. The hammer and sickle is usually placed in/ on certain objects or places: banners, flags, buttons, pins, uniforms, medals, party insignias, certain buildings, statues and propaganda (print and visual). The artist has the ultimate Communist symbol placed against an action-painting background, with silhouetted bodies that are not in a May Day rally, with plants (referencing the tropics and perhaps tourism?), and the ever-present glitter. The added sexual or erotic elements mentioned earlier only complicate matters further (evoking Slavoj Žižek's notion of politics as enjoyment?). The artist has ventured into delicate territory, especially with such a universally recognizable symbol, but alternatively, he might be giving it more meaning in offering new (or different) interpretations.

Gillo Dorfles writes: 'Perhaps politics is always kitsch. Which would prove that there can be no agreement between politics and art ... Nowadays, whenever art has to bow to politics – or generally speaking to some ideology, even a religious one – it immediately becomes kitsch.'[18] Dorfles seems to be suggesting that the relationship between kitsch and politics makes it an equivalent (or analogue) of propaganda. No doubt, propaganda and kitsch share some traits: accessibility, a direct message, a lack of ambiguity, an appeal to one's instincts. But they are not exactly the same because kitsch usually elicits an emotion (sentimentality), whereas propaganda – which also can draw on emotions – wants you to act, whether it is to buy something, support a political idea (voting, activism) or practise a desired behaviour (wear condoms, get inoculated, go to college).

Kitsch is often discussed in terms of mass production and consumption, especially in reference to capitalism. It is a commodity subject to the laws of supply and demand and because it can be easily (and usually cheaply) manufactured, it is more affordable than art. But what about kitsch and commodities under socialism?

Régis Debray claims that ceremony is the typical commodity of actually existing socialism and that the overabundance of ceremony compensates for the lack (or shortages) of goods.[19] He provides an extensive (if not exhausting) list of ceremonies that propel the life of state socialist societies:

> In the heartlands of 'real socialism', collective life expresses itself and exhausts itself in the repetitive enthusiasm of endless popular processions, military parades, corteges, anniversaries, inaugurations, closures, festivals, congresses, tributes, funerals, visits (artists, athletes, foreign dignitaries), meetings, galas, exhibitions, receptions, speeches, oath-taking ceremonies, presentations of medals, flags, trophies, diplomas, pennants, and so on . . . The ornamental becomes the basic fabric, decorum becomes the substance of the drama.[20]

This is an accurate description of what we could call the Communist spectacle, where the spectacle is not the proliferation and display of commodities, but the spectacle of ideology. And given the above list, the ceremonies are involved with the production of meaning: military parades (preparedness against imperialism), diplomas (not only party-mindedness but academic achievement), exhibitions (cultural vitality), medals (patriotism or athletic excellence). Clearly some of these ceremonies also take place in capitalist societies; what Debray argues is that because of the lack of commodities (shortages, shoddy products, lack of advertising and visual understimulation), socialism seeks to fill the vacuum with ceremonies.

In light of Debray's comments, one could argue that this is how state socialism keeps the citizenry engaged in the construction of a purportedly new society. In this manner the state recognizes its obligation to its citizens, the existence of an unwritten contract. The state says you must participate in the parades, processions, tributes, congresses, mass organizations (women, students, workers, block committees) but don't mess with elite (party) politics or the media. In exchange, we'll give you employment, education, culture, health care, housing, sports, utilities and food at subsidized prices. It is not the worst socio-political arrangement in the world, especially for a Third World country, even though it comes with a price, as all such 'contracts' do, be it, for example, neo-liberal, social democratic or authoritarian.

Cuban Arts Heading Into the Special Period

Cuba's milieu of performance art had its most delicate moment on 4 May 1990, when a 24-year-old artist named Angel Delgado, as part of a show called 'The Sculptured Object', defecated on the gallery floor, surrounded by a series of prints of bones that he had placed in a circle. He squatted within the circle onto a copy of the government's official newspaper *Granma* that had a hole cut in the middle so that his excrement did not fall directly onto the newspaper. His biologically made sculpture remained on the floor for a full day, photographed by the police and other authorities. The show was closed and six days later Delgado was arrested and served a six-month prison sentence. While in prison he learned from the prisoners about carving (using soap) and drawing on handkerchiefs, a technique he has used over the years.

Much has been said of Delgado's performance, from its being a commentary on the Cuban art world by introducing a taboo substance into the gallery space, to more political statements about Cuban society at large. Naturally, critics have pointed out how Delgado's work drew on Cuban vernacular speech, not uncommon in Cuban art of the 1980s and beyond. In Cuban Spanish, the phrase 'Me cago en' ('I shit on' plus the noun of your choice) is a way of expressing extreme displeasure or rejection, the equivalent in English of 'I don't give a shit'. In this sense Delgado's act was a harsh indictment of the arts establishment in Cuba, and he must have known that despite all the tolerance for new artistic currents during the 1980s, his scatological gesture was going to be more than controversial. No doubt some Cuban artists were hopeful that the policies of perestroika and glasnost would reverberate on the island, but from Fidel's speeches of the period there was no ambiguity: Cuba was not going for the kind of changes being called for by Gorbachev. Delgado must have been cognizant of this because despite his 'statement'; he was careful not to defecate directly on the *Granma* newspaper. *Granma* is the official organ of the Cuban Communist Party and is named after the boat that Fidel, Che, Raúl and other rebels came on from Mexico to initiate the guerrilla struggle against Batista. Despite the mediocre quality of the paper, Delgado knew that a direct hit on it would be considered a desecration of a publication sponsored by a 'holy institution', the Communist Party of Cuba. However, what remains unsaid but understood by most Cubans is that *Granma* often gets used as toilet paper in a country where this item is almost always in short supply.

Delgado continued to give performances and show art after his release, and much of his subsequent work is profoundly marked by that experience. Many of his performances (live and filmed) have dealt with physical limitations: being buried and disinterred, or walking about handcuffed and with chains on his feet, as in his performance in Puerto Vallarta, Mexico. In another, titled *Digesting the News*, he takes several different Mexican newspapers and puts them in a blender, then pours them into a plastic glass for people to try. At the end, he finally prepares one for himself, almost gulps it down and then vomits off camera, but you can still hear it.[21] To a degree Delgado's bio-sculpture was the culmination of the work of the artists of the 1980s, many of whom left in the 1980s or '90s.

As the Cuban art and literary world was changing, the imminent collapse of the Soviet bloc would be devastating to the Cuban economy. However, it continued to further open the island to global artistic currents, which we see reflected in not only the Havana Biennial, but also the International Film School (created in 1985), the continuation of the Havana Film Festival and the ability for Cuban artists to go (or work) abroad. If the Mariel crisis shook up Cuban society, the Special Period would be a full-blown storm.

FIVE

From the Special Period to Obama
(1990–2014)

We make out of the quarrel with others, rhetoric, but out of
the quarrel with ourselves, poetry.

W. B. Yeats, 1924

History has already been made, but it has to be made anew.

José Lezama Lima, 1960

In 1994 Carlos Varela released a CD, *Como los peces* (Like the fish).
One of the songs is among his signature compositions, 'La política
no cabe en la azucarera' (Politics doesn't fit in a sugar bowl). It is
wry, funny, sardonic and defiant. He begins by referencing a friend
who has bought a '59 Chevy but is reluctant to change the parts and
now the car doesn't move. Aside from alluding to the simple reality of
old American cars kept running by the ingenuity of Cuban mechanics
in inventing new parts, Varela might be invoking time and mobility.

It is tempting to equate the '59 Chevy with the Cuban economy,
which after the Soviet collapse in 1991 and the subsequent withdrawal
first of direct aid and then of favoured trading status, was taking a
beating and chugging on, with a leaky radiator, doors that needed to
be opened from outside and a coughing engine. Next, he sings, 'The
people are waiting for something, but here nothing happens,' unequivocally stating a need for change, but observing how that change
is slow, if not crawling.[1] Cuba in 1994 was living through what has

been called the Special Period in Times of Peace (usually just Special Period). 'Special' because conditions of wartime-level rationing and lack of energy or transportation overwhelmed Cuban society with 35 per cent reductions in GDP. Cuba had to reinvent itself under dire economic circumstances, made even more precarious because the U.S. reckoned that without Soviet largesse Cuba would go under, and so tightened the blockade and imposed additional restrictions on family travel and remittances.

The 'Special Period' was regarded throughout Cuba as a collective disaster to be survived through the generosity of family and friends and the ingenuity of *el invento*, the wily inventiveness that makes every single precious resource count. While memories of hunger from the Special Period still haunt many Cubans, others remember with pride the supreme creativity with which they traded and foraged for food or recycled and repurposed precious material goods, their survival representing a victory over the forces of history. In this chapter, a wide range of creative arts of the period, including music, feature and short films, sculpture, novels and dystopian science fiction, 'ruinology' and performance art present this period of Cuban history as both a crushing challenge and an expanded political opening to define the Cuban socialist project on Cuban grounds and in Cuban terms.

The Special Period: Cuba All Alone and *El Invento*

The collapse of the Soviet Union was disastrous for Cuba. The island conducted 85 per cent of its foreign trade with the Soviet bloc. The USSR provided all of its wheat, 65 per cent of its powdered milk, 50 per cent of its fertilizers, 40 per cent of its rice and almost all of its oil.[2] In five years GDP shrank by 35 per cent. Many schools and factories had to close down, blackouts became more common, many workplaces operated with a reduced staff, and nutritional levels suffered. Cuba was on its own and needed cash desperately. It began to revitalize its biotech industry, but the biggest change came in tourism, the quickest way to bring in desperately needed foreign exchange. The holding of U.S. dollars was decriminalized, and stores were set up where purchases could be made in dollars either earned in the tourism sector or sent from family abroad. These changes that inserted Cuba into a globalized economy were not measures that the Cuban government would have chosen to undertake. However, it was a matter of urgency and national security to revive the economy, which happened, albeit slowly. It did, however, exacerbate issues of inequality on the island. The GINI coefficient, which measures inequality (*lower* means *more* equality, *higher* means *less* equality) in 1986 was .22, one of the lowest in the world, and by 1999 it was .41. A recent *Economist* report says it is now probably close to .50, which places it more along the lines of other Latin American countries. This is a dramatic change for Cuban society in a short period of time.

Let us return to Varela's song. In it, he lays out some of the ways Cubans tried to cope with the Special Period: *invento*, individualism ('Save yourself if you can!'), immigration (the Rafter Crisis of 1994, where tens of thousands fled on makeshift rafts), hustling tourists, prostitution, a yearning for celebrity status. There is no doubt that the Special Period produced not only an economic crisis, but social and spiritual ones as well. The newer generation of *Nueva Trova* singers, like Varela and Frank Delgado, started to focus their lyrics on these crucial issues brought on by the Special Period. Before 1991 the Cuban state provided almost everything for Cubans: education, health, housing, employment, food, sport, transportation, water, electricity and so on either free of charge or at a heavily subsidized rate. The Special Period marked the beginning of the state's inability to provide these services free of charge. As Cubans were increasingly left to their own devices, they also began to seek alternative methods of employment, especially those where they could earn dollars. Ideologically and spiritually, matters became more fluid. In the spiritual realm, Cubans turned to religion, whether Catholicism, Evangelical Christianity, Afro-Cuban religions, even Judaism, Buddhism and Rastafarianism. This should come as no surprise, given the severity of the Special Period. Even the government acknowledged it by amending the constitution (1992) and party statutes to allow believers to become Party members, something inconceivable ten years earlier.

Ideologically, the regime moved from an emphasis on Marxist-Leninist thought and drew on home-grown thinkers who were instrumental in constructing Cuban nationalist and anti-imperialist doctrine: Martí, Maceo, Gómez, Varela, Céspedes, Ortiz, Marinello, Guiteras, Mella, de la Torriente Brau, Vitier, among others. The overarching narrative became one of patriotism and nationalism as central to the Revolution, with the latter representing the culmination of these values. The leadership, Fidel included, recognized that, given the devastation of the Special Period, the further building of socialism was on hold, and that most important was national unity, ensuring some degree of economic revival through greater use of the market, and defending the major gains of the Revolution (health and education, particularly).

Let us return to the title (and refrain) of the song: 'Politics doesn't fit in the sugar bowl'. At one level, Varela has gone to the heart of the crucial issues of political economy and one can see these words as a criticism of the dangers of over-politicization. Politics is what the government is responsible for; the sugar bowl is a symbol of the population's daily struggle to feed itself, not to mention a reminder of how important sugar has been in Cuba's history. One could argue that in a socialist economy like Cuba's there is a disconnect between politics (ideology) and kitchen-table issues, and Varela's lyric would support that interpretation. Is Varela suggesting he agrees with the neo-liberal doctrine of keeping politics separate from economics?

Not exactly. Further on in the song he says: 'In school they taught me that in Apartheid/ Not everyone is equal and the law didn't matter./ That's why the things I see bother me/ Listen to me brother: fuck your blockade.'[3] The first three verses are a clear reference to the economic changes in Cuba that have accentuated inequality, but could equally be a reference to the growing inequality unleashed by globalization on a world scale (a kind of economic apartheid). That these lines are followed by a rejection of the block-ade (the term Cubans use for the embargo) is also a reminder that the Cuban economy is under permanent assault by the U.S.

Back to the Future: Sci Fi or Semper Fi (for the Revolution?)

One of the harshest depictions of the Special Period is captured in *Planet for Rent* (2015), written by Jose Miguel Sánchez Gómez, who assumed the pen name Yoss in 1988. First published in Spain in 2001, the novel is set in 2024 and tells the story of an impoverished Earth's occupation and colonization by humanoid and non-humanoid aliens from powerful planets across the galaxy, who have turned the whole planet into a popular, affordable tourist destination. All of planet Earth faces the dilemmas experienced by Cuba during the Special Period, resorting to desperate measures to ensure basic survival while subjected to the contempt and oppression of a colourful, vicious and inconsider-ate array of alien exploiters. The book presents fourteen chapters, each a short story, vignette, or historical narrative, focused on interconnected human characters with different social roles. There is a 'World Human Parliament', paternalistically structured and completely for show, when the real power is with the 'Planetary Tourism Agency'. The book opens with Buca, a 'social worker' and prostitute, whose few years of highly paid work at the side of an insect-like, chitin-armoured Grodo will culminate with her death as an incubator for his brood. She provides a panoramic overview of the many forms of exploitation grounded in the Cuban experience during the Special Period, particularly with the expansion of tourism. Non-humanoid aliens who find Earth's atmos-phere and they are incompatible are able to purchase a person, termed 'Body Parts', whose body they can appropriate to safely experience all that the Planet for Rent can afford. 'Mounting' their 'Body Parts' human as they would a horse (using a term from Santería, where an orisha mounts a human), they possess the body for the duration of the visit. However, this role is so undesirable that it has become a mandated sentence for criminal transgressions, not only because the human body is terribly abused but also because the 'mounted' person is likely to be conscious of this abuse, finding the experience body- and soul-destroying. Moy, a performance artist working on the planet Colossa, has an agent, whom he names 'Ettubrute', whose small stature relative to others of his species forces him into this low-status but highly-paid work, and with whom he shares a complex relationship of sexuality and mutual dependence. Moy produces self-annihilating 'art' while suspended on a cross. Relying on drugs and futuristic medical procedures, he narrates to his audience a discourse on art and 'deconstruction', while destroying his own body piece-by-piece through dramatic well-timed explosions, culminating in his death and rebirth through cloning. Daniel, a Voxl athlete who nearly leads the Earth's team to defeat the undefeatable Legion planetary team, first strives to be a patriot and demonstrate the equality of humans but then sells out for a well-paid position on the Legion team. Mestizos, the offspring of human and alien procreation, are described as highly attractive and artistic, filled with hybrid vigour, but also sterile and emotionally unstable. One security guard narrates the 'Rules of the Game', describing the elaborate strategies by which those with even lowly official positions can trade their authority and knowledge to acquire money and power. The desire to leave the planet is so great that a security force must constantly monitor small home-made pirated spacecraft, the equivalent of Cuba's *balsas* (rafts). The 'queered' Colossus Ettubrute returns in a final story, as someone who is both an appreciator and patron of human art but also a punishing 'angel' whose intercourse with both men and women artists whom he promotes infects them with a deadly virus carried by his species. This view of Ettubrute, provided through a letter he writes to a young girl he has provided for after the death of her mother in an escape attempt, discloses both his great love of Moy and the vindictive power with which he expresses his self-hatred. The novel explores, reworks, satirizes and subverts many of the binaries we have examined during the course of this book, as well as being a sobering reminder of the rapacious nature of globalization.

Spiritual Questioning and the Special Period

Fernando Pérez's *Life is to Whistle* (1998) gives us a more whimsical and surreal portrait of the Special Period. A comical allegory, it features three characters, Elpidio, Mariana and Julia, plus an unusual narrator, Bebé, who is intricately involved with the fate of the three protagonists. All three are 'orphaned' in one way or another and their unhappiness is manifested through their bodies. Mariana is a sensuous ballerina who is sexually active but aspires to have the leading role in *Giselle* and, as a result, prays to the Virgin of Charity that, if given the role, she will give up men. Elpidio, a hustler, musician and someone involved in the 'informal economy', has decided to tattoo on his back right shoulder, 'There is no love like a mother's love' because of his mother's abandonment. Julia, a social worker for the elderly, suffers from narcolepsy and faints when she hears the word 'sex' due to the trauma of having given up her child for adoption. All seek individual happiness, revealing the interpersonal dynamics of the Special Period. Two use religion (Mariana, Elpidio), the other a psychologist (Julia), to help them overcome obstacles to their happiness. In Pérez's allegory the three are also linked to the orishas.

Mariana, the passionate dancer, also linked to sensuality and pleasure, evokes associations with Ochún, the orisha of marriage, sensuality and fertility. Ochún is also known as a seductive dancer, all traits that define Mariana. Ochún is linked to the Virgin of Charity in the Catholic pantheon, and is the patron saint of Cuba. Elpidio is linked to Changó and even has an unusual statue of St Barbara (the Catholic equivalent) in his apartment. He wears a red and white bandana, is a musician and flaunts his virility, all traits associated with Changó. Julia, the social worker, is associated with Ochosi, the earth, game animals, and is tethered to the earth. Finally, the narrator, Bebé, is a combination of two orishas: Yemayá (motherhood, the ocean) and Orula, who deals with fate and divination.

One of the curious features of the film is the whistling, and hence the title. Cuba is a notoriously oral culture, which finds expression in many ways: conversation (humour, storytelling, sharing, friendship), pleasures (food, drink, sexuality), creativity (music, singing, theatre, dance) and spirituality (particularly, but not exclusively, Afro-Cuban religions). Language is paramount in the film: verbal, body language, music and, of course, whistling. Pérez effectively uses street slang, the language of art (particularly dance), therapeutic language (the talking cure), the language of seduction and love (verbal and non-verbal), confessional language, political discourse and ritual language. The director is convinced by the power of words. For example, Julia faints when she hears the word 'sex', presumably because it conjures up the trauma of the child she abandoned. When she finally begins her sessions with Dr Fernando, the psychologist, he takes her out to the balcony, where they watch people on the Malecón (Havana's famed boardwalk) also faint in the street upon hearing certain words. He says that this is a common modern malady: a fear of not only words, but of ideas too. The doctor then accompanies Julia through the streets pronouncing certain words that make people fall off ladders, collapse on stairs or simply drop to the sidewalk. Despite the seriousness of the topic, director Pérez shoots the scene humorously, as if folks were becoming zombies or simply swooning. The words spoken by Dr Fernando are freedom, opportunism, fear of the truth and dual morality. Pérez has carefully selected words that can have a personal and political meaning. Even when he uses the word 'opportunism', which often has political connotations, the person who faints on the steps is Settimio, a hunky assistant to Mme Garcés, the artistic director of the ballet and Mariana's coach. Settimio is probably thirty years younger than Garcés, but is sleeping with her to climb up through the administrative hierarchy of the ballet. Dual morality, or *doble moral* in Cuba, refers to the nature of Cuban life, where one can lead a model revolutionary life in public, but do otherwise in private. Words like freedom and fear of truth can have both personal and political connotations. Perez's emphasis on words (and ideas) perhaps touches on one of the key issues of the film with regard to the Special Period: the delicate balance between collective and individual happiness.

To a degree, Cuban society up to the Special Period focused on its collective needs, but because the Cuban state could not deliver on all of these needs post-1989, Cubans as individuals began seeking their own journeys to ensure that their personal needs were fulfilled (through alternative employment, religion, family ties or remittances). One could argue that this remains a delicate dialectic to the present and a key to Cuba's future.

Whistling is often called a paralanguage, a non-verbal means of communication. It has been associated with music (as in whistling tunes), emotions (contentment or disapproval), customs (its inappropriateness in certain circumstances), coping with uncertainty (whistling in the dark), signalling (especially at a distance, or to communicate with animals), sexual advances (wolf whistles) and with magic and superstition. In the latter case, different cultures see whistling and spirits in two distinct ways: it either attracts spirits or drives them away. For example, there was a taboo among British miners about whistling underground.

At the beginning of the film, a young orphan, Bebé (our future narrator), is chided for whistling in class instead of speaking like her classmates. The teacher is teaching them the word *igualdad* (equality), certainly a key word in Cuba's revolutionary discourse. Is Pérez suggesting by having Bebé whistle the word instead of pronouncing it that equality doesn't mean everyone has to be the same? Interestingly, whistling and music are linked when the teacher, Cuba Valdés (Elpidio's mother), has the children dancing to the music of Ignacio Vila, aka Bola de Nieve (1911–1971), one of Cuba's most popular singers, who as a black Cuban was also a *santero*, gay and a supporter of the Revolution (Bebé is not present yet). The next time we see the class they are dancing to the music of the great Benny Moré (1919–1963), his famous 'Son Maracaibo'. Bebé whistles while she dances, and seeing her do so, young Elpidio joins her. Afterwards, she is removed from the school for continuing to whistle. As she is carried away by the headmistress, Bebé's crucifix falls to the ground, whereupon it is picked up by Mariana.

One could argue that all three main characters are whistling in the dark, so to speak, because of their unhappiness. As the plot evolves, all three are asked to go to Revolution Plaza at 4.44 p.m. on 4 December because something decisive about their fate will de determined. (4 December is the feast day of Changó (St Barbara).) There they are supposed to be met by the people who made the request: for Mariana this is Ismael Cienfuegos, a dancer she has fallen in love with; for Julia, Dr Fernando, for Elpidio, Crissy, his gringa Greenpeace activist girlfriend. The only three who show up are Elpidio, Mariana and Julia. They stare at each other in the vastness of the Plaza, the monument to Martí slightly out of focus in the background. Elpidio realizes that their respective fates have been intertwined all along, since Mariana had been a child in Elpidio's class (and still had Bebé's crucifix), along with Bebé, the child that Julia had abandoned. At this moment of recognition, Elpidio begins to whistle. As the camera goes to his face in medium close-up, there is a dissolve to the last scene, where Bebé, as narrator, declares that she is God and that all the people of Havana will achieve happiness by 2020. She says the solution is simple: 'Life is to whistle'. She begins to whistle, then the camera pans to Cubans along the Malecón, either walking or skating, who are also whistling. As well as the whistling, we hear Bola de Nieve's version of 'La vie en rose' by Piaf, sung in French, which continues as the credits roll.

The issue of fate or one's destiny evokes one of the most important orishas, Elegguá, linked to the crossroads, fate, the unexpected, and who is messenger to all the other orishas. Hence, in all significant ceremonies Elegguá is invoked first. We see that invocation to Elegguá when Elpidio has his shells read by an *oriaté* (*santero*) whom he has sought to find out what course to take regarding his mother, who has abandoned him. Fate, however, is not something that functions as an impersonal force, passively accepted by the characters. On the contrary, each is faced with certain dilemmas concerning their unhappiness, but must act, in effect, shape their own fate. This recalls a well-known Cuban song by Gema y Pavel that speaks about Elegguá (Elewá) in very similar terms:

'Bangán' by Pavel Urquiza/Gema Corredora

> Elewá shows you the path
> But not how to walk
> Fate is made day by day
> Fortune does not sit by waiting
> ... and light a candle to the saints
> but don't lie down and sleep
> if you don't lay it on the line
> no one will do it for you.[4]

It is not difficult to read the fate (and happiness) of the three main characters as an analogy for Cuba at large. Take, for example, Elpidio, our ne'er-do-well hustler. Pérez has given him the name of Cuba's most famous cartoon character, Elpidio Valdés, created by Juan Padrón in 1970 for a comic book, and subsequently the subject of three animated features and many shorts. Elpidio is a *mambí*, a nineteenth-century warrior for independence (against Spain), so presumably Elpidio's mother (appropriately named Cuba) expected her son to embody the spirit of the *mambí*: courage, selflessness, a willingness to sacrifice oneself for the *patria*. In a post-revolutionary Cuba that evokes Che Guevara's concept of the New Man (previously discussed), Elpidio falls short, according to his mother. There is a moment in the film when Elpidio discusses his mother's expectation that he should be exemplary, a 'vanguard worker', a model citizen, and equally her great disappointment in that he is a musician, hustler, gambler and thief. Elpidio might be a lovable rogue, but he's a rogue, albeit one with a conscience. There are moments in the film when Elpidio faces ethical quandaries, and each time Pérez gives us a brief clip of the faces of either Bola de Nieve or Benny Moré. It is a curious way to represent Elpidio's conscience but perhaps it harks back to his mother, who after all is the one who played their music for the children at the beginning of the film. Elpidio's mother wears an *idé*, a bracelet on her left wrist that indicates she has at least done Ifá (similar but not identical to Regla de Ocha). Either way Pérez has given us a layered cultural approach to Elpidio as a character that goes back to the nineteenth century, the island's Afro-Cuban legacy (music and religions), and continues into the present. Pérez presents Cuban resilience and ingenuity as a product of its rich culture, also embodied in the character of Mariana, the ballerina.

Mariana represents the more European aspect of Cuban culture: she is white (not mixed race like Elpidio), performs classical ballet and sports a Catholic cross. When she decides to give up having sex with men in order to obtain the role of Giselle, she prays to the Virgin of Charity, who, apparently, responds. Ecstatic that she has received the part, Mariana then meets her male counterpart, Ismael, and is totally smitten. A new happiness (artistic) is met by unhappiness in the romantic sense, not to mention breaking a promise to God. Must the sacrifice of becoming a great artist mean forfeiting love? In a dramatic scene, which Pérez also plays for laughs, Ismael tells Mariana that she can have it all and that he, the ballet and God all love her equally. Ballet is highly regarded in Cuba and the island's National Ballet is world renowned, even if its repertoire tends towards the traditional. It was the revolutionary government's commitment to ballet that has made it so popular and central to Cuban culture. It was Fidel himself who suggested that Alicia Alonso, a star with the American Ballet Theater in New York during the 1940s and '50s, return to Cuba to found the National Ballet of Cuba. She accepted, receiving a large grant, and she is still running it at the age of 94!

Musically, the Pérez film reflects all of these cosmopolitan strands of Cuban culture. There are four songs by Bola de Nieve and two by Benny Moré, strongly rooted in Afro-Cuban traditions; there are classical idioms (*Giselle*, *Swan Lake* and Paganini's Violin Concerto no. 1 in D major); as well as original music composed by Edesio Alejandro (b. 1958), an electronic score strong on atmospherics. Alejandro has done over forty film scores and worked on every feature film of Fernando Pérez.

In the same vein we might add that the film uses two quotes, repeated at key moments in the film – one by John Lennon, the other by Ho Chi Minh. From Lennon, Pérez quotes from 'Beautiful Boy': 'Life is what happens when you are busy making other plans.' From Ho, the following: 'Never is the dawn closer than when the night is at its darkest.' Both quotes truly relate to the lives of the three protagonists. The Ho quote clearly refers to a more overtly political situation, but Pérez works it into the fabric of the film beautifully and with a certain humour in one scene. Ho's words resonate at a personal and public level: as a Cuban, one can certainly see the 'darkness' of the Special Period (sometimes, literally, given the ubiquitous blackouts) as a harsh challenge to be overcome by Cuba's commitment to make things better, even under dire circumstances.

Because of the allegorical nature of the film, some claim that it did not address some of the grittier aspects of the Special Period. While this is certainly true, it was not Pérez's intention to make a documentary-style film; instead he focused on the spiritual malaise of that period, every bit as significant as its material counterpart. The Special Period did open up Cuban society, by starting a conversation about how to rebuild the nation after the Soviet collapse. Culturally this was reflected in songs, literature, the visual arts and film.

Pérez's loving and poetic *Suite Habana* (2003) is perhaps a warning on how (or how not) to speak about and represent everyday Cuba. Mixing a documentary approach with fictional devices (use of certain camera angles, sound overlapping into different scenes, music), he offers both individual portraits of a day in the life of Havana and a collective portrait of a city. There is virtually no dialogue in the film and no voice-over narration. Pérez structures the characters and their daily routines around one day: getting up in the morning, having breakfast, going to work (or school), lunch, afternoon and return home, dinner and evening leisure time. There are many memorable 'characters': Francisquito, a ten-year-old boy with Down's syndrome; Iván Carbonell, who works at a hospital, cross-dresses at night and performs in a club; Juan Carlos Roque, a doctor who also works as a clown; and 79-year-old Amanda Gautier, a peanut vendor who works along the Paseo del Prado. In their everyday activities we see coffee-makers, pressure cookers, the chopping of onions, people getting dressed, beds being made, TVs, people combing their hair, meals being served and eaten, the bustling rhythms of life on the streets, people in transit, whether on foot, bicycle, taxi (or in one case, aeroplane). After showing their daily routines we find out about their dreams: Carbonell wants to perform on a grand stage; Heriberto, who plays sax, wants to be in an orchestra; Roque the clown wants to be an actor; Ernesto, who is fixing his mother's house, wants to be a ballet dancer.

Pérez's acclaimed film was seen and widely discussed throughout Cuba and all over the world, as it depicts the dignity, hardship and beauty of one ordinary day in the lives of twelve Cubans as they strive to survive, keep a roof over their heads and food on the table, and fulfil their dreams for themselves and their families. Pérez's film shows us the often limited material resources and abundant sense of loving regard and shared responsibility with which Cubans, their families and neighbours confront dilemmas and strive to actualize their dreams. They do so through webs of relationships extending through family, neighbourhood, workplace and beyond to the transnational diaspora. The ordinary and extraordinary Cubans at the centre of this film demonstrate the complex configurations of governmental resources, personal initiative and mutual exchange with which Cubans solve daily problems: housing, food, transportation and coping with an intergenerational household. These ordinary Cubans dream of lives requiring less drudgery to secure food, housing and daily survival, enriched by opportunities to travel, to reunite families separated by diaspora, or to fulfil artistic talents. Stepping outside highly ideological arguments regarding state and personal responsibilities, and without a single reference to the health care system (except as a workplace for several protagonists), these people show us how Cuban families protect and promote shared well-being and health. Pérez's haunting images and unforgettable protagonists make the heated and politicized discussions about the Cuban paradox (they 'live like the poor but die like the rich') come alive.

The New Man Goes Queer

The Special Period also created a climate for looking at the past, but seeing it in a critical sense that would be useful for dealing with current problems. *Strawberry and Chocolate*, from 1993, directed by Tomás Gutiérez Alea and Juan Carlos Tabío, dealt with important issues of intolerance, homosexuality, art, propaganda and Cuban cultural identity. The only Cuban film ever to have been nominated for an Oscar (it didn't win, losing out to *Cinema Paradiso*), it was made during the worst moment of the Special Period, but is actually set in 1979, just as Cuba was emerging from its grey decade. The film was based on a short story by Senel Paz, 'El lobo, el bosque y el hombre nuevo' (The Wolf, the Forest and the New Man), winner of the Juan Rulfo Short Story Prize (1990). Its two main protagonists enter into a complicated but heartwarming friendship that involves politics, queerness, revolutionary commitment and art, all issues still relevant in 1994. David is a university student and member of the Communist Youth (UJC), with an interest in culture (he has acted in plays and written some short stories). He meets Diego, almost a generation older than him, an art critic, curator and cultural promoter who is openly gay. At first Diego is interested in seducing David, but the latter is suspicious and utterly heterosexual. However, Diego has books by authors that have been proscribed in Cuba because of their politics (Vargas Llosa, Juan Goytisolo, Severo Sarduy). With the lure of this forbidden fruit and the fact that Diego has photos of David's performance as Torvald in Ibsen's *Doll's House*, he goes to Diego's apartment. This first visit will be the first of several in which both David and Diego pour their hearts out on matters related to politics, religion, art and sexual preference.

At first David is visibly uncomfortable with Diego's gayness, about which Diego is upfront. In addition, Diego confesses that he is a believer, has had problems at work and is viewed as ideologically suspect (he has contacts at foreign embassies). In 1979 Cuba was still living through a period of official homophobia and also rejection of believers. So to be a revolutionary meant having to be straight, a non-believer and adhering to the tenets of the Party. To David, then, all the things that Diego embodied were considered counter-revolutionary. David's fellow student at the university, Miguel, is intrigued by Diego and enlists David to gather more information on him, fearing he 'might be up to something'.

So David continues to visit Diego in order to dig up possible incriminating evidence. Diego is negotiating a possible art show for Germán, a fellow artist and friend/lover, with the help of a foreign embassy. Germán's sculptures combine religious iconography with political symbols: one of his sculptures is a Jesus with a hammer and sickle in the back of his head; another is a bust of Karl Marx with a halo. The sculptures evoke the issues about kitsch, propaganda and art that we examined in the previous chapter. But as time goes on, David becomes more and more curious, and engages in more intense conversations with Diego, who lends him books by Cuban authors like Lezama Lima, but also John Donne, and yes, Vargas Llosa. Diego is a lover of opera and even plays Maria Callas for David. We see David later in his dorm room relaxing and turning the dials of his radio until he finds a station playing opera.

David's curiosity is only equalled by his ignorance, and Diego embarks on providing a crash course on Cuban culture, from a distinct, queer-inflected perspective. The directors very astutely use Diego's walls to create his cultural world: on one he has a huge painting by Servando Cabrera (1923–1981), who painted lush depictions of human bodies. Cabrera was gay. On another wall he has photos, figures, necklaces and so on. Some of the prominent photos are of José Lezama Lima, Lydia Cabrera, Bola de Nieve and Julián del Casal, all queer. To be sure, Diego also has photos of non-queer writers and artists: Rita Montaner, Fernando Ortiz, Martí, as well as when he plays the music of Ignacio Cervantes for David. Diego clearly wants David to see that queer artists and intellectuals have made important contributions to Cuban culture, but in a wider context he is arguing that their contributions go beyond sexual difference to include spirituality, various political ideologies, views on race and so forth. To a degree, the film harks back to some of the debates about the revolutionary intellectual in the 1960s discussed earlier, except that being a film of the 1990s it tries to reflect the changes in Cuban society (greater acceptance of believers, a willingness to deal with homophobia, a desire to look at the relationship of art and politics with greater nuance, more comprehension about the dual lives that people engage in, and an understanding of why people might want to emigrate). One of the fascinating aspects of the film is that the closest thing to a villain in it is Miguel, the hardline Communist who convinces David to spy on Diego. This would have been unthinkable in a Cuban film a decade earlier. Despite the growing friendship between Diego and David, Diego feels his life in Cuba has no future, and decides to leave, which is how the film ends.

One can argue that the film, despite its anti-homophobia, is still very much a heterosexual vision of gayness, and that Diego's character is stereotypically portrayed: his gestures, voice and body language are flamboyantly femmie, he loves opera and he wears a kimono indoors. All this is true, but that did not prevent the film from being a hit, viewed by millions and discussed vigorously in the street and in the press. Despite all the attention and polemic – something not seen since the discussion about women from *Portrait of Teresa* (1979) – the film did not air on Cuban television until seven years later. And yet it surely influenced thought in Cuba about LGBT rights that would lead to CENESEX (an organization dedicated to promoting healthy sex and sexual rights for all Cubans, regardless of sexual orientation) and legislation in the last decade that make the island a leader on these issues. Transgender surgery is not only legal in Cuba, but free. This is a far cry from the times of the UMAP.

Senel Paz, on whose story the film was based, also wrote the script. From the title one sees the allusions to issues from the 1960s and Che Guevara's call for a New Man. The film title refers to Diego's preference for strawberry over chocolate ice cream, featured in the meeting between the two at Coppelia, a famous ice cream palace in Havana. For Paz and for the film-makers, the New Man is not embodied by Diego or by David, but by the dialogue between them, it would be the Cuban born of their strengths and weaknesses that would be a possible model of socialist citizenship.

Author and photographer Orlando Luis Pardo Lazo (aka OLPL), includes a story from his book *Boring Home* (2013) that imagines Diego's return to Cuba after a twenty-year absence. Sardonically titled 'The Man, the Wolf and the New Forest', Diego's return has him meet up with artist and former lover, Germán, Nancy (his next-door neighbour in the film, absent from the original story) and David, now a middle-aged successful writer. Unlike the original story, which was told from David's point of view, the Pardo Lazo narration is from Diego's perspective, and his view of Cuba is not a positive one, nor are his comments about Germán, Nancy or David.

Ruins: Life, Revolution and the City

Nothing could be further from the Pérez allegory in *Life is to Whistle* or Gutiérrez-Alea's comedy than the work of Pedro Juan Gutiérrez (b. 1950), a journalist-turned-author whose work has been described as 'realismo sucio' (dirty realism). Although he has been compared to Bukowksi and Henry Miller, Gutiérrez had not read them when he began publishing his Centro Habana Cycle of five novels that appeared between 1998 and 2003. A native of Matanzas, he moved to Havana and lived in a gritty neighbourhood that experienced great travails during the Special Period. He documents the life of vagrants, hustlers, prostitutes, transvestites, criminals and ordinary folk with a keen, unsentimental eye as they struggle in the squalor of their surroundings. Told in a semi-autobiographical voice (the narrator's name is Pedro Juan, and he is an ex-journalist), Gutiérrez strings together short narratives of intense sexuality, depravity, filth, desperation and abjection that are often moving and sometimes humorous (*Trilogía sucia de La Habana*, 1998; translated as *Dirty Havana Trilogy*, 2002). Sandwiched between the formerly well-to-do neighbourhood of El Vedado and Old Havana (colonial architecture, tourism), Centro Habana, despite having some architectural landmarks, is mostly working class and poor, with a large black population. Many of its buildings are in a precarious condition. Gutiérrez's apartment is on San Lázaro, which is a block away from the Malecón (boardwalk), so on the higher floors (or the roof) there is a view of the ocean. Centro Habana is close to areas of tourism but is not exactly an area that tourists, unless they are adventurous, would find attractive. Although the author reads and admires some of the great writers of Cuba (Carpentier, Lezama Lima, Piñera and Arenas), his view of literature and style is quite different. He shares with Arenas his vision of chronicling the not-so-sunny side of Cuban history or reality, even if he stays away from his anti-revolutionary politics. Gutiérrez, however bitter and sardonic his worldview, through a stoic and dark humour somehow manages to express a defiant resilience, one that never shies away from humiliation, despair, hunger and the scatological. The narrator is wracked by loneliness, doubt, cynicism and a fairly constant state of horniness (sex, along with alcohol and weed, being one of the few means of escape from the harshness of his life).

At one point in his *Dirty Havana Trilogy* (DHT) the narrator lays out his existential plight as follows:

> At the age of forty, there's still time to abandon routines, fruitless and boring worries, and find another way to live. It's just that hardly anybody dares. It's safer to stick to your rut until the bitter end. I was getting tougher. I had three choices: I could either toughen up, go crazy or commit suicide. So it was easy to decide: I had to be tough.[5]

Other characters seek out the other options (or attempt to leave the country). Despite this toughening up, there are moments in DHT where our picaresque narrator softens up, either because he has genuine feelings for a lover, or because a friend is in need, or because someone's plight makes him feel something close to compassion. None of this takes away from the grim situations that the narrator and those he comes across have to navigate.

The narrator describes his vocation as a writer as follows:

> I am a shitraker. And it's not as if I were searching for something hidden in the shit. Usually I find nothing . . . I just do what children do: they shit and then they play with their shit, smelling it, eating it, and having fun until mom comes along, picks them up out of it, bathes them, powders them, and warns them that a person doesn't do things like that . . . I'm not interested in the decorative, or the beautiful, or the sweet, or the delicious . . . Art only matters if it's irreverent, tormented, full of nightmares and desperation. Only an angry, obscene, violent, offensive art can show us the other side of the world, the side we never see so as to avoid troubling our consciences. So. No peace or quiet. Whoever achieves balance is too close to God to be an artist.[6]

Gutierrez's view of art is clearly one of provocation, which conjures up writers such as Sade, Bukowski, Burroughs, Bataille and, closer to home, the likes of Virgilio Piñera and Reinaldo Arenas. He likes to wallow in filth, in the dark side of reality, sinking slowly without completely drowning.

It is easy to attribute metaphorical aspects to Gutierrez's fiction: it would seem that it represents the demise of the Revolution, that his chronicles are merely an autopsy, someone playing around with a corpse that is clearly decaying, and that his writing gives us an excruciating portrait of that unravelling. Gutierrez's apparent nihilism doesn't help. Some critics have pointed out the zoological references in his fiction, comparing Cubans to a species in a post-socialist limbo. In many of his descriptions the author focuses on smells and odours (rancid, putrid, sweaty bodies, excrement, urine). Smell is considered the lowliest of our five senses, and the one most closely aligned with animals.

Analogously, Gutiérrez and other writers, particularly Antonio José Ponte (b. 1964), have remarked on and analysed the proliferation of ruins in Havana, given the deteriorated state of many buildings in the capital. This has become a source of fascination for tourists and foreign photographers, some of whom have documented these structures in great detail. Along with this fascination with Havana's ruins is an accompanying nostalgia that delves into pre-revolutionary times (and had its musical equivalent with the Buena Vista Social Club craze), but also calls attention to post-revolutionary neglect, along with its own nostalgia of the 1960s, '70s and '80s, when Cuba's socialist experiment was on firmer footing (a nostalgia of the future that never quite arrived?).

Ponte calls himself a *ruinólogo* (a ruinologist) and, drawing on a seminal essay by Georg Simmel, he seeks to explain the uniqueness of Cuban ruins. The word traditionally is applied to spaces that are no longer inhabited, stimulating our curiosity to reconstruct the lives and/or history of the abandoned structure. In Cuba, Ponte argues, people still live in these ruins, which creates a different dynamic and forestalls an overly nostalgic approach. Or perhaps we can follow Svetlana Boym's two types of nostalgia – restorative and reflexive:

> Restorative nostalgia does not think of itself as nostalgia, but rather as truth and tradition. Reflexive dwells on the ambivalences of human longing and belonging and does not shy away from the contradictions of modernity. Restorative nostalgia projects the absolute truth, while reflective nostalgia calls it into doubt.[7]

Ponte's meditations on ruins would seem to dovetail with Boym's reflexive nostalgia, one that calls into question the certainties of traditional ruins. Since Cuban ruins are inhabited, one is forced to deal not only with the building itself but also with those who live in it; it is not only a living history, but a lived-in history too. In a German documentary based on his work, Ponte quotes Cocteau: 'ruins are like an accident in slow motion.'[8] In this he is emphasizing the ruin as a vengeance of nature – it is nature's forces that eventually turn buildings into ruins. However, Ponte points out that the disrepair and decay of these buildings is also a wilful policy of 'urban neglect' that was part of the government's strategy to promote construction in rural Cuba and other parts of the country outside Havana. He also claims that these buildings are the result of a war that was never fought. Because of the possibility of a U.S. invasion (which did happen in 1961, with the infamous Bay of Pigs fiasco), the island has been waiting for the next one, and so Havana's buildings have been put on hold for decades, the argument being why repair buildings if they are going to be devastated by a war at any moment? Except the war never came. Some observers have pointed out that 'the war of time' has taken its toll, and no doubt decades of neglect (and salt air) have made large chunks of Havana one of the world's great future projects for repair and restoration.[9]

None of this is new to Cuban thinkers and writers. We can see in the work of Carpentier and Lezama the ruin as a type of refuge or marker of historical and cultural continuity, especially with regard to twentieth-century Americanization – all the way from the early decades of the twentieth century to the Special Period. Scholars such as Odette Casamayor have pointed out how different authors approached this urban phenomenon, 'as a place to safeguard one's need for secrecy (Abilio Estévez), a statement of a defiant and absurdist resignation (Gutiérrez), or a symbol of ideological inertia (Ena Lucía Portela)'.[10] To this we add Ponte's anti-nostalgic or 'reflexive nostalgia' that disrupts a naïve search for truth and instead invites us to take a more rhizomatic approach:

> Reflexive nostalgia . . . loves details, not symbols . . . This typology of nostalgia allows us to distinguish between national memory that is based on a single plot of national identity, and social memory, which consists of collective frameworks that mark but do not define the individual memory.[11]

In effect, all of the more recent authors like Ponte, Gutiérrez, Portela, Estévez, among others, are vigorously seeking those multiple or collective frameworks that offer a thicker, more complex, multifaceted narrative where private and public memory coincide, diverge and sometimes contradict each other.

Many journalists and scholars make 'natural' associations between Havana's decaying (sometimes collapsing) buildings and the ideological inertia of the regime. I put natural in quotes because buildings and societies are often associated with each other, whether under capitalism or socialism. Even the trite expressions 'building the future' or 'on a solid foundation' evoke construction or architectural metaphors; when we say an economy or a political system is not doing well we often use expressions like 'shaky foundations' or 'the roof is about to fall in'. So it is not surprising that photographers, scholars, writers and journalists have linked these images. Perhaps it is a bit facile, but it is tempting.

Carlos Garaicoa (b. 1967) is an artist, photographer and installation artist whose work specifically deals with buildings, architecture and urban space. A 1991 graduate of the Institute Superior de Arte (ISA), his work ingeniously blends drawing, sculpture, photography, architecture, installation and text to make insightful observations on the urban textures and landscapes of Havana. In one series, *Continuity of Somebody Else's Architecture*, which was done for Documenta 11 in Kassel (2002), Garaicoa uses either finished or unfinished buildings or sites. In one case he took a building by architects Garrido, Alarcón and Pérez, which only has some columns and half-built walls, and reworking the original plans designed an apartment complex of eighteen units in which the interior walls are transparent, sort of blurring the difference between private and public. Called *Public Building as Greek Agora*, here is how Garaicoa describes it: 'This project requires absolute indifference to an outsider's gaze. We may observe the other's lifestyle, but they also have the right to see ours. We may watch but we don't. We may be seen but we are not.'[12]

The agora was the centre of an ancient Greek city, where different activities (artistic, political, commercial, spiritual, athletic) took place. Many of these activities (including the courts!) were held out in the open and the idea is that they were carried out as transparently as possible, where one could see or be seen. Garaicoa seems to be satirically playing with the idea of the Greek agora, since presumably an apartment is a place where the dweller safeguards their privacy. In the model built to display his project there are open spaces in front of the building that hint at the agora of the wide-open public space, but it is modest in size. This regime of total visibility suggested by the artist is in some ways the ideal of Communism, where there is total transparency between the private soul and the public citizen. As Rousseau said, 'If I could change my nature and become a living eye, I would do so willingly . . . while not concerned about being seen, I need to see [my fellow man].'[13] One can read more dire possibilities into the implications of this visibility. However, the visibility, according to Byung-Chul Han, can become coercive: 'The imperative of transparency suspects everything that does not submit to visibility. Therein lies its violence.'[14]

Garaicoa is commenting on that violence (of neglect, time, social policy) that affects the built environment of the city. As part of the same project, Garaicoa references the micro-brigade movement, an initiative begun by Fidel in 1970 to stimulate construction of housing as a supplement to state initiatives (though funds and materials were provided by the state). The movement consisted of brigades of some thirty-odd workers who would build five-storey prefab apartments, which the brigade members were entitled to inhabit. One of the major efforts was Alamar, just east of Havana, where some 100,000 people currently live. Intended to take pressure off the housing shortage in Havana proper, it was meant to be a mini-city with its own stores, businesses, schools, clinics and community and cultural centres. It didn't quite turn out that way, as most residents still commute to Havana to work, and many of the support structures to create a sense of community were not built. There is also no centre to Alamar, giving the site a sense of endless sprawl. Much of the construction was shoddy, the workers cutting corners to meet deadlines. The prefab housing and design do not work well at that specific site, and aesthetically the buildings are ugly. Socially and politically, Alamar was a commitment to and an example of egalitarian housing principles, but the voluntaristic excesses of the micro-brigades turned out to be costly in terms of money and time. Since the Special Period, Alamar has deteriorated substantially: the buildings need painting and repairs, garbage is strewn about in open spaces, the salt air is corroding the metal fixtures and the sense of social isolation, particularly among youth, is palpable.

Garaicoa did several pieces that used images of the micro-brigade projects that were not finished. He described them as follows:

> In Havana, as in other cities of the country, idyllic and nostalgic ruins of the colonial era and the first republic coexist with ruins of a social and political project that has lost its luster. Hundreds of unfinished, disregarded buildings exist in a momentary oblivion. It seems like everyone had gone to lunch and remained in a post-prandial lethargy. The encounter with these places evokes a strange sensation; they are not the ruins of a luminous past, but of a present of inability. We are faced with an architecture that has not come to fruition, poor in its incompletion, proclaimed a Ruin before existing. It is a true image of ruin by abandonment; I would call it ruins of the future.[15]

This notion of 'ruins of the future' is doubly suggestive: on the one hand its conception (and supposed realization) is supposed to embody the socialist city of the future (forever postponed), but on the other it has become a ruin before coming into existence, a kind of reversal in time, a historical backflip. Garaicoa plays with the temporal paradoxes of twentieth-century state socialism: despite the proclivity towards building the future, they were societies immersed in a kind of amber, somehow stuck in time, living in a heroic eternity (hence slogans like 'Men are mortal, only the Party is eternal').

Critic Okwui Enwezor has described Garaicoa's work using Giorgio Agamben's notion of apparatus (from the French *dispositif*, drawing on Michel Foucault). Agamben quotes Foucault:

> [Apparatus is] a thoroughly heterogeneous set consisting of discourses, institutions, architectural forms, regulatory decisions, laws, administrative measures, scientific statements, philosophical, moral, and philanthropic propositions – in short, the said as much as the unsaid. Such are the elements of the apparatus. The apparatus itself is the network that can be established between these elements.[16]

Garaicoa's works examine these networks of laws, regulatory decisions and architecture by creating 'maps of desire'. In this he follows Calvino's *Invisible Cities* with headings such as 'Cities and memory', 'Cities and desire', 'Cities and signs', 'Cities and the sky', 'Hidden cities' and so forth. Consider the micro-brigade project: clearly the traces of governmental policy, socialist philosophy, scientific calculations, housing law, along with the issues of time and ruins discussed above come into play. Garaicoa designs a new hidden or invisible city that somehow completes or adds to the original structure; it does not seek to erase it.

In a way, he offers small works of reconstruction (or reimagining) that go building by building, block by block, rather than coming up with a master utopian plan. His vision is a corrective to the grandiosity of architects like Le Corbusier or Niemeyer who seek to remake the world through their architecture. His modesty is revealed in a 2001 installation where he designed a model of a city with buildings made of wax that are lit like candles. The piece is titled, appropriately, *Now Let's Play to Disappear*.

In 2009 Garaicoa did a series called *The Crown Jewels*, which overtly deals with the more ominous aspects of the apparatus: he sculpted eight pieces in silver of different sites around the world that deal with militarism, violence, torture and repression. The pieces are tiny – most can fit on the palm and fingers of an open hand. The eight structures are the Pentagon, the Guantánamo Naval Base, the KGB headquarters, the Stasi complex (former East Germany), the National Stadium (Santiago, Chile), the Naval School (Buenos Aires), Villa Marista (where Cuban political dissidents are taken) and the DGI (National Intelligence Headquarters in Havana). Garaicoa's ironic title is meant to mislead momentarily since from afar each piece, on a wooden stand with a Plexiglas cover, does look like a jewel, the polished silver gleaming under the light. He also plays with the scale of these structures and what they represent. The sculptures are almost miniatures but the individuals unlucky enough to be taken to these buildings in real life are literally swallowed up in their overwhelming proliferation of interrogation rooms, surveillance equipment, corridors, prisons or torture chambers. This disruptive use of scale and surface only underlines the horror that one must imagine going on within. As Agamben says, 'I shall call an apparatus anything that has in some way the capacity to capture, orient, determine, intercept, model, control, or secure the gestures, behaviors, opinions, or discourses of living beings.'[17] Here we see the apparatus at its most sinister.

In another piece from 2009 Garaicoa has an installation on a wall that consists of a photograph of a building next to a scroll with the design of a tower. The photo shows a building of pre-1959 construction overgrown with vines and moss. On the wall of the building is a slogan: 'De por vida con Fidel' (For Life with Fidel). The V of vida is formed by the two fingers of a hand giving a peace sign, and the E in Fidel is a Cuban flag. In the foreground are two signs pointing right, and towards the left part of the frame there are pedestrians on either side of the street. Given that the photo was taken after Fidel's illness and subsequent stepping down from the day-to-day running of the country, one can certainly see the shot as ironic to say the least (we don't know when the slogan was painted). Despite the triumphal nature of the slogan, it is a reminder about human mortality – our own and Fidel's. But Garaicoa also suggests that buildings have their own life, albeit inextricably linked to human lives, and that both are equally linked to nature since the top of the building is overgrown with vegetation. The scroll to the right of the photograph is an architectural drawing of a tower with totemic features coming out of the top of the building, also laden with vegetation. Garaicoa recognizes the building as on its way to ruin, and makes a design to make the existing structure both recognize this and also take on a new form (a new life?). In cleverly taking on the many dimensions of the apparatus (architecture, life, political slogans, signs, city traffic, mortality, nature) Garaicoa humorously reimagines the building's future while capturing its past, its history.[18]

Performing the Special Period, Performing Cuba, Performing Politics

One of the most important artists to have emerged from the Special Period was Tania Bruguera (1968–), born in Havana, and who since the 1990s has made her home between Cuba, Chicago, New York and Paris. Bruguera was deeply influenced by Ana Mendieta, although her work is more overtly political than her predecessor's. Her first works are devoted to recreating some of Mendieta's work, a project that lasted over a decade (*Tribute to Ana Mendieta*, 1985–96). Her work could best be described as a hybrid form between installation and performance, and like Mendieta she uses her own body in many (but not all) of her performances. Her early work consisted of publishing a newspaper called *Memorias de la posguerra* (Memoirs of the Postwar), which sounds similar to the words of Ponte about Cuba having lived through a war that was never fought. Of course, the title could be an ironic reference to the Cold War ending, which, of course, it did not between Cuba and the U.S. (maybe now, after 2014?). Many prominent artists and critics wrote for it, even if did not have a long life. It made a brief comeback in 2003 as a broadsheet filled with revolutionary catchphrases: 'Moving onward is our slogan'; 'We will struggle to the end'; 'We will always choose sacrifice' (if made to choose between indignity and sacrifice); 'What does it matter the dangers or sacrifices of a man or a people, when the destiny of humanity is a stake!'; and the top headline, with the first line, in bold red letters, saying, 'No more need for changes!', and the second line, 'Or socialist revolution or a caricature of revolution'.[19] Most of these were taken from slogans on billboards or in newspapers, or speeches by Castro.

Bruguera's *Table of Salvation* (1994), part of her *Memoirs of the Postwar* series, is an installation piece that is a kind of memorial to the *balseros*, whose crisis erupted in 1994 when over 35,000 Cubans made their way to the U.S. on rickety makeshift rafts. It is a remarkably minimalist piece with black marble slabs leaning against a wall, punctuated by wooden ribs that suggest the hull of a ship. The small spaces between the slabs are tampered with cotton and from them the wooden ribs curve out and up. The piece is both stark and sleek, with reflections in the marble having a ghostly or spectral quality. Bruguera is not the only Cuban artist to take on the theme of *balseros*: Luis Cruz Azaceta (b. 1948), Kcho (b. 1970; pronounced Kah-cho, his real name is Alexis Leyva Machado) and Carlos Estévez (b. 1969), among many others, have explored this painful part of the Cuban experience in highly creative ways. Cruz Azaceta's interpretations function on the unknown dimensions of fleeing on a raft, the loneliness and existential despair; Kcho's sculptures use boats, inner tubes, oars, bottles and debris, focusing on the grim material world of the *balseros* that both reflects vulnerability and a reckless determination. Estévez's approach is more philosophical and based on launching bottles into the ocean with a message and a drawing inside; most were launched from Norway and Havana, but also from Venice, France, Brazil, New Orleans, Malibu, Lisbon, Key West and Veracruz.

Bruguera continued working on projects that dealt with issues of symbolic, political or historic concern for Cubans. Her *Statistics* (1996–8) consisted of a 3.66 × 1.83 m Cuban flag made of human hair (on cloth and cardboard). The flag's colours are altered: instead of three blue stripes that alternate with two white ones, we have three white stripes alternating with two black stripes. The triangle is red, but the star is a yellowish brown (instead of white). It took five months to make, with many people working to sew it together. This collaborative process echoed the way flags were made in the nineteenth century, with women coming together and sewing a symbol of conspiracy, solidarity and independence. Given that the work was done during a period of economic crisis (Special Period), with people wanting to emigrate, this collective gesture tried to reinvent a sense of national belonging. However, the piece was more than that: in using a title like *Statistics*, and using human hair to make the piece, she was ironically trying to stay away from a demographic notion of nationhood, and emphasize the individuality of Cuban-ness, not a mere agglomeration of bodies as 'the people'. Hair is such an intimate part of a person, and it is this association, linked to national pride, that gives the work so much power.[20]

Bruguera used the flag as a backdrop to another piece called *The Burden of Guilt* (1997–9), described by critic Gerardo Mosquera as one of the most memorable and moving performance artworks he has ever witnessed.[21] Bruguera gave the performance from her house and opened the door so that people could come off the street, which immediately made a statement about public and private spaces, as well as how art is perceived in the gallery and in the street:

> The artist stood in front, facing the street, dressed in white jumpers, with an open lamb carcass hanging from her neck, and two ceramic bowls before her. In a state of concentration [and kneeling], Bruguera took soil from the bigger bowl, moistened in the smaller one that contained fresh water with salt, made small balls of dirt, and ate them.[22]

Bruguera's performance has layered meanings: eating dirt refers to the indigenous population of Cuba (Taínos, Ciboneyes) who did so as a form of resistance to the Spanish conquest (through suicide). Even to do this day, the expression 'comer tierra' (eat dirt) in Cuba means to be going through extremely difficult times, certainly an expression that would resonate with Cubans undergoing the travails endured during the Special Period. The open lamb carcass is dramatic and has biblical references dealing with sacrifice that are consistent with the eating of dirt, a kind of sacrificial ritual where one ends one's life. Mosquera aptly sums it up: 'The artist's body was her own subjective body, but it was simultaneously ritualized into a social body.'[23] Much of Bruguera's work begins with the subjectivity of her own body and then becomes intertwined with the social body. Her use of the body enacts, comments on and resists the way body is embedded in power relationships, and nothing could be truer of this than Spanish colonialism, which literally destroyed millions of indigenous lives in the Americas through overwork, mistreatment and, mostly, disease. But, as we have seen, the piece is not just about the conquest of the Americas, but also Cuba in the Special Period.

In 2009 she did another piece called *Tatlin's Whisper #6* for the tenth Havana Biennial, the island's most important art event, with international prestige. The set-up was a stage with a podium and single microphone, and a curtain behind the podium. It was made to look like the setting of an official event, where a prominent leader might speak. On each side of the podium was a person dressed up in *miliciano* uniform, one female, the other male. People were invited to go to the podium and speak freely for a minute. Two hundred disposable cameras were also handed out so that people could document what they were seeing. As each speaker went to the podium, a dove was placed by them. Again, Bruguera is drawing on the history of the country, but also its art history. In the first days of the Revolution, Fidel gave a speech where doves had been let loose. While he was speaking, one had come down to the podium and another settled on his shoulder (this photo was mentioned earlier, and is an iconic moment from the first days of the Revolution with a spiritual resonance). From the visual arts, the staged area reminds one of a painting by Antonia Eiriz, *A Tribune for Democratic Peace* (1968), which shows a podium with five microphones, a crowd of people in the background whose faces are unrecognizable, and a string of small banners with PCV on them and below, in smaller letters, 'for a democratic peace'. No one is at the podium. The painting has Eiriz's typical expressionistic and hallucinatory quality and its satire is achieved through absence: the absence of a speaker, the absence of recognizable faces, even the absence of hope.

Bruguera's hope was that the piece would not only be a performance, but one in which the audience *was the performance*, the effect being somewhat improvisatory. It would also be an act of social activism, and a means of empowering the audience. In most settings, a performance piece like this would not be a big deal, but this was Cuba, where open and non-supervised expressions of ideas were not the norm. (I am not saying that Cubans have never had a chance to express themselves openly since 1959, but that the circumstances for unfettered expression in public have been circumscribed.) If this kind of event seemed threatening to the authorities, why did they let it happen?

There are several reasons: first, the event took place at the Wifredo Lam Center, an artistic space, not a venue where huge crowds would necessarily turn up; second, *Tatlin's Whisper #6* was being shown at the Havana Biennal, and the international spotlight made it wise not to try to cancel the performance, which would tarnish Cuba's image in the international art world; finally, perhaps, the authorities imagined that people would speak up, but exercise some degree of self-censorship and not create a scandal or turn the event into a public demonstration. The first speaker was Guadalupe Álvarez, a Cuban art critic who had been supportive of the new trends in Cuban art, for which she eventually lost her job and emigrated to Ecuador. For her minute at the podium Álvarez wept loudly and was then accompanied off the stage. Many other people took the microphone, including Yoani Sánchez, a well-known blogger, as well as artists, writers and other interested attendees. Perhaps the most poignant was a young woman who only spoke one sentence: 'I hope that one day freedom of speech in Cuba is not just a performance.'[24]

This comment deserves more attention. Of course, the statement was meant to be both hopeful and ironic. No doubt she was referring to a wider societal issue about censorship in Cuba, but what makes the statement doubly revealing is that freedom of expression is not merely a concept but must be performed (enacted) in the true sense of the word. The performance was a first instance of this but, given the reduced area of the event (an art space), at best it could only be seen as a social(ist?) lab experiment. A 2007 film on censorship called *Zone of Silence* by Karel Ducasses Manzano examines the issue with some of Cuba's top writers and scholars: Antón Arrufat (novelist, playwright, poet), Gustavo Arcos (film historian), Frank Delgado (singer and songwriter), Fernando Pérez (film-maker) and Pedro Juan Gutiérrez (writer). They discuss not only issues of censorship, but self-censorship, and also contextualize censorship in terms of power. All those interviewed understand that all systems of government practise some degree of censorship, and that religions have also condemned certain forms of expression (witness the Catholic Church's index of prohibited books that lasted for centuries). The film was shown through independent circuits in Cuba, but it was never broadcast on Cuban television, nor in major festivals. More significant, though, is that nothing has happened to any of the people who appeared in it, and all of them are still living in Cuba.

The fate of Bruguera has been a little different. The reaction to her 2009 performance at the Havana Biennal was swift and unequivocal. The day after *Tatlin's Whisper # 6* was presented it was strongly criticized in the Cuban press and for several years she was not welcome back in Cuba. But she did return in December 2014, after President Obama announced a new change in U.S.-Cuba relations (17 December). Seeing that Obama and Raúl Castro had agreed to make relations between the two countries a true dialogue, Bruguera flew back to Cuba at the request of local artists to do a kind of update of her *Tatlin's Whisper #6*. However, this time she wanted to have the microphone outdoors, at Revolution Plaza. Ministry of Culture officials tried to negotiate to have the event indoors (at a gallery), but she insisted that the event be held outdoors. Revolution Plaza is a symbolically loaded space, as we have seen, both politically and in terms of nationalist sentiment, and one can understand why the authorities were somewhat nervous. After several attempts at negotiation, Bruguera insisted on going ahead with the performance, slated to happen at 3 p.m. on 30 December. Early in the morning of the 30th, security agents knocked on her door. She refused to open it. Finally, as the hour of the performance drew closer, she exited the apartment where she was staying and was taken into custody. Thanks to her sister, news of her detention spread quickly and Bruguera was released, but only after she insisted that others who had been detained in conjunction with her performance also be released. Bruguera's passport was in the control of the authorities, and she was not allowed to leave Cuba until her case was 'resolved'. She spent almost eight months under strict surveillance (although she could move about relatively freely) and finally was allowed to leave in late summer 2015. On 22 May 2015 she decided to enact another performance, a 100-hour reading of Hannah Arendt's *The Origins of Totalitarianism* (1951). Despite some interference by the state (at one point workers were drilling in the street with a jackhammer to drown out her reading), she completed the reading, but once finished she was again detained by the authorities, then released a few hours later. Arendt's book is long (almost five hundred pages) and if Bruguera read the entire book it would have required about eight hours per day for three days to finish it. Before the section on totalitarianism, there are two sections on anti-Semitism and imperialism that run to three hundred pages. The third section, 'Totalitarianism', runs for about 180 pages. On the book's publication date, the Soviet Union was still under the rule of Stalin, and the Third Reich had only been defeated six years earlier. Arendt's book was influential and led many to conflate fascism and Communism as equal evils from the right and left. Over time, our understanding of fascism and Communism has become more nuanced and Arendt's analysis has become dated in some significant ways. Totalitarianism became a key political word during the Cold War – often used to paint a broad picture of Soviet-style regimes – that did not account for the diversity of state socialist regimes. To view Cuba in 2015 as a totalitarian regime seems politically reductive, and to see acts of censorship as totalitarian is also problematic. If that were the case, then many countries in the world could be considered 'totalitarian', from Saudi Arabia to Guatemala, or even Mexico, where dozens of journalists have been murdered over the past few years. Has a Cuban journalist been murdered in the last several decades? Perhaps Bruguera chose Arendt's classic book because she was unflinching in discussing right- and left-wing variants of totalitarianism; but she also had plenty of other examples to choose from: *We* by Zamyatin, Huxley's *Brave New World*, Orwell's *1984*, or *Fahrenheit 451* by Ray Bradbury. Maybe Bruguera felt strongly about Arendt as a woman and political thinker who weighed in about major issues in twentieth-century history, and not only about totalitarianism, but also genocide, violence, democracy and the dynamics of power and domination.

The label totalitarian has often led to the facile equivalence of fascist and Communist regimes, obscuring their differences. Despite some similarities (one-party states, political repression, state control of the media), state socialist regimes were quite unique in their configurations: a new economic system that tried to go beyond (or abolish) the market, a concerted effort to ensure certain social rights (housing, health, education), an internationalist philosophy (despite Stalin's eventual insistence on 'socialism in one country'), and a vision of a classless society (and not one based on a superior race, as was the case with Nazism). Totalitarian also conjures up the notion of a society in which the government (or the state, which can be seen as synonymous) controls everything, and clearly this is not the case with Cuba, or certainly not in the last 35 years or so. It might be more useful to circumscribe the word to a certain period in a country's history (the USSR between 1929 and 1953, Cambodia under the Khmer Rouge (1975–9), China from 1958 to 1976, and perhaps North Korea since its inception until the present). Eastern Europe would have to be examined on a case-by-case basis.

Perhaps Bruguera is consciously using the Arendt book to pose the question of whether Cuba (and its relationship with the U.S.) has really moved past the antagonisms of the Cold War. How much have things really changed? She also encouraged people from the neighbourhood to read passages from the book and described their reaction:

> My neighbors were calling me crazy because the book was so clearly so critical of the Cuban government, but that moment I saw that they understood. I knew then that this was exactly what I should be doing in a sustainable and long term way. A one day performance doesn't change anything – I want to do it all the time.[25]

In this sense, she was right on the mark (Marx?), but she had to know that giving her performance in Revolution Square was going to come up against government intransigence. Now Bruguera has raised $100,000 to begin an Institute of Art Activism Hannah Arendt (or INSTAR) in Havana, where the Russian feminist punk collective Pussy Riot was invited to do a residency in September 2016. They will be followed by Palestinian artist Khaled Jarrar (who was denied permission to travel to the U.S. by Israeli authorities) and surveillance artist/cultural geographer Trevor Paglen. At the time of writing, none of these have happened as the Institute has not been allowed to open. This is an impressive line-up and what is interesting is that while they all address issues of freedom, artistic expression, surveillance, systems of repression and so on, none of them works directly with Cuba. This holds true for Bruguera's work as well: she has done work exploring U.S. politics with former cadres of Weather people and installations on immigration; she has done other talks or performances in Colombia, Europe and London, highlighting political issues in those specific national contexts. Whether INSTAR will open remains uncertain: the authorities are notoriously skittish about foreign foundations functioning on Cuban soil, especially with money collected in the U.S. (the money was raised via Kickstarter, with apparently no government contributions).

When we look at performance artists, writers, rappers, musicians who are giving their visions of Cuban reality – often at odds with official versions – we must be careful to avoid what Richard Curt Kraus calls the 'Bambi Meets Godzilla metaphor that the West adopts for understanding the politics of culture in China'.[26] (In the following two quotes I will replace the word China with Cuba.) The short animated film 'Bambi Meets Godzilla' (available on YouTube), barely a minute and a half long, shows Bambi grazing in the woods among flowers, a pastoral interlude punctuated by a Rossini overture as a warning, before a huge foot descends and utterly squashes the deer. With Bambi's legs sticking out from under Godzilla's monstrous foot, he wiggles his toes slightly. Kraus draws out the implications: 'Sweet and innocent artists merely seek joyful self-expression through the creation of beauty, when they encounter the heavy, clumsy, and dangerous foot of the monster, labelled in this version [Cuban] "Communist Party".[27] But how can we not sympathize with the plight of an imprisoned poet like Padilla, or censored artists like Delgado or Bruguera, or harassed musicians like Frank Delgado and Gorki Ávila? How can we not be critical of a political force (party) that seeks to maintain its grip on power in an arbitrary and sometimes unscrupulous manner? Again, Kraus warns us,

> [Cuba's] artists are sometimes not very Bambi-like, and while Godzilla has been known to stomp really hard, it turns out that he can tread rather lightly, and sometimes there are others dressed up in the monster suit besides the Communist Party.[28]

These cautionary words by Kraus are useful in understanding the complex relationship between artists, the state and cultural politics in Cuba.

In some cases the Cuban state has acknowledged mistakes and sought to correct them: writers like Lezama and Piñera, after being ostracized in the late 1960s until their death, are now not only published but widely discussed, with conferences sponsored for the centenaries of their birth. The same is true for others such as Antón Arrufat, César López, Pablo Armando Fernández and Miguel Barnet. Even some Cuban authors who left after the Revolution are being published: Lydia Cabrera, Lino Novás Calvo, Severo Sarduy, Padilla (although not with Cabrera Infante and only some texts by Arenas). The same has happened with the homophobic policies of the past, although much still needs to be done.

Musicians and visual artists have worked out a different sort of arrangement. Artists who have left did not necessarily do so as political exiles, but to work, and travel back and forth between Cuba and their adopted countries. Musicians, for example, will go back to Cuba to play in a festival or other venues. This is particularly true of the new wave of Cuban jazz musicians, many of them trained on the island, including the likes of Dafnis Prieto, Aruán Ortiz, David Vireilles, Yosvany Terry, Francisco Mela, Arturo Stable, Elio Villafranca, not to mention the 'older generation' of Gonzalo Rubalcaba, Omar Sosa, Hilario Durán and others.

Visual artists are in a similar situation, and many have returned to Cuba to have shows or be part of the Havana Biennal. In the 1990s, with the difficulties of the Special Period, the Cuban government actually encouraged Cuban artists to get grants or residencies abroad, since the economic situation at home was so dire. For painters, materials such as paint, canvas and brushes were difficult to obtain or too expensive. During this period, visual artists were also allowed to sell their work abroad (or at home), which gave them an important source of income. Many of the artists who went abroad during the Special Period decided to live in different places, such as Mexico, the u.s., Spain and Puerto Rico. Artists such as Flavio Garciandía, Marta María Pérez Bravo, Magda Campos Pons, José Bedia, Tomás Esson, Tonel (Antonio Eligio Fernández), Williams Carmona and Tania Bruguera (to some extent) have emigrated but maintained a close relationship with the art world on the island.

Nicanor: A Cuban Everyman Who Subverts Binaries and is Earnest in his *Choteo*

Film-makers (some already discussed) like Gutiérrez Alea, Fernando Pérez, Miguel Coyula, Jorge Molina and Eduardo del Llano have made films that have made very pointed comments on Cuban life. The case of del Llano is quite intriguing: over the last decade or so he has created a series of twelve shorts featuring a Cuban everyman character named Nicanor O'Donnell (drawn from short stories he wrote in the 1990s) that address some important issues in Cuban society. Played brilliantly by a well-known actor (Luis Alberto García, the male lead in *Life is to Whistle*), Nicanor assumes different roles according to the particular theme that del Llano wants to explore. He plays an obsequious husband who wants to rejuvenate his marital sex life, a party cadre, a journalist, a concerned father, an ordinary citizen, an interested son-in-law, an artist, a dreadlocked revolutionary who likes to do graffiti, a factory worker and a jaded revolutionary who resembles Che Guevara; Nicanor has time-travelled to 1960 from 2015. All the shorts are admirably acted (Nestor Jiménez, a well-known character actor, often plays a great foil to García), shot in a minimalist and realist style, but capturing the often absurd contradictions of Cuban daily life. The director often seems to use stereotypes (the ne'er-do-well husband, the jealous wife, the insensitive bureaucrat, the snoopy neighbour, the over-zealous party cadre), but always ends up humanizing them with sensitivity and humour. In *Pravda* (2010), for example, a young man with dreadlocks, who paints revolutionary graffiti on walls, has been brought in to be interrogated by someone from state security. Shot in an atmospheric basement office made to look 'sinister', the interrogation room looks like the archetypal 'despotic dungeon'. However, the conversation between the captain of state security and Nicanor is intelligent, candid and often humorous. Finally, the captain decides to let Nicanor go free, but Nicanor tells him that at 3 a.m. on Saturday he is going to do some graffiti. The short ends with the captain entering a note on Nicanor's dossier about his next action. What makes the film so poignant is that

Nicanor's graffiti extols the 26th of July Movement and the Cuban Revolution, and the reaction by state security is to see this as possibly subversive or even 'counter-revolutionary'. The short underlines not only generational differences, but also how revolutionary systems can become conservative over time.

Monte Rouge (2004), the first in the Nicanor series, is perhaps the most politically sensitive, because it deals with state surveillance. It begins with Nicanor preparing some coffee, when there is a knock at the door. He opens it and is greeted by two men who identify themselves openly as being from state security (a senior official, Rodríguez, played by Nestor Jiménez, the other, the tech person, by del Llano himself). They are cordial, almost friendly, and they ask him – since he voices very intelligent criticisms of the government – where would be the best spot to place a couple of microphones. At first, Nicanor is alarmed but the senior official asks, 'Would you prefer that we sneak into your apartment while you are out at work so that we can install the mics?' After a discussion about the relative merits of the different rooms of the house, they finally settle on the bathroom, which upsets Nicanor. He says that when he criticizes the government it is usually with friends present and that it would be awkward to be receiving his friends in the bathroom. Rodríguez says, 'Well, maybe we can arrange to have a mini-bar set up in the bathroom', but Nicanor is not receptive to the idea. Finally they conduct a sound check and the tech asks Nicanor to say something. He obliges with the usual 'One, two, three, testing.' No, no, they insist, say something 'subversive' so you can start practising. Nicanor speaks in a slightly raised voice: 'I would love to have a satellite dish', which at the time (and still) is illegal. The short ends with the senior official using the bathroom (to pee) while Nicanor and the tech chat by his front door. The tech says, 'Listen, if you want a satellite dish I can get that for you, but don't tell Rodríguez, he's a bit strict about that.' Fade to black.

Clearly the short brings up issues of state intrusion in the lives of Cuban citizens. With a typical Cuban *choteo*, del Llano highlights the absurdity of the situation that seems contradictory: if you are going to eavesdrop on someone you don't go to them directly and ask them where to place the microphones. This also raises the question of how they found out about Nicanor's conversations in the first place. Were they listening in somewhere else? Did someone inform on him? The latter seems possible, since at one point Rodríguez advises him, don't waste your time saying good things about the system, we just want to hear the bad, the criticisms. He reminds Nicanor about when he went on for fifteen minutes explaining good things about the government to a singer when he was riding the bus the other day. In subtle and not so subtle ways, the agents are letting Nicanor know that he has been under surveillance for a while, so he might as well be a good sport and play along. The somewhat chummy attitude taken by the agents is reciprocated on Nicanor's side when he offers them a *cafecito*, a strong black demitasse hit of caffeine that Cubans usually offer guests at any hour of the day. The informality underlines the intimacy and closeness of human relationships in Cuba, even amongst ordinary citizens and state security.

Has the Nicanor series made del Llano an 'underground persecuted artist'? Not exactly. While these shorts don't get shown on Cuban television, they have played in festivals (inside and outside Cuba) to acclaim, and he has continued to write scripts for features as well as direct a couple of features himself. The director was lucky that by the time the second Nicanor film came out (*High Tech*, 2005), YouTube existed, and since then the entire series has been made available on it. Cubans do not have the kind of Internet access that people in the u.s. or Europe have (or even in Mexico or Brazil, for that matter), but many have managed to access the Nicanor shorts or download them and pass them around on memory sticks. So they have been seen by a significant audience, although any precise numbers are hard to come by. If anything, Cubans are avid in their search for information, as well as for creative voices offering a refreshing look at their own situation.

Each short takes on a particular aspect of Cuban society: a lack of economic realism (*High Tech*), the nature of the press (*Brainstorm*), the trivialization of history (*Photoshop*), double standards (*Aché*), bureaucracy (*Pas de Quatre*), the vice of unanimity in political matters (*Intermezzo*) and the infantilization of the media (*Homo Sapiens*). Eduardo del Llano's Nicanor series is a great example of how the arts in Cuba deal with social issues in more complex ways (and with considerably more humour) than official media.

Being Black in Cuba: Cuban Hip Hop

Since the early 1990s hip hop/rap has taken root in Cuba. I have described Afro-Cuban cultural forms as part of an Afro-Diasporic dialogue using 'Black Atlantic aesthetic' defined by Paul Gilroy as a 'vast African dialogue born of enslavement, diaspora, dispersion, and dispossession'.[29] This Afro-Diasporic dialogue is also an ongoing ensemble of voices and invention that have resisted and countered these traumas to create unique cultures, especially in the Americas. Cuban hip hop came via American radio stations (from Miami) and then visitors to the island. In the 1980s it focused more on DJs, B-boys and breakdancing, but in the 1990s rappers came to the fore. It grew mostly out of the public housing area of Alamar, which back in the 1990s was supposed to be the model of a new socialist urban environment, but through lack of planning and neglect has become an urban/architectural eyesore for working-class families, as we have seen when looking at the work of Garaicoa.

The creators and promoters of the movement were from mostly poor families and predominantly black or mixed race. Seeing their conditions worsen during the Special Period – and not having family abroad to send them remittances – these youths realized that as black and brown Cubans they were suffering more because of discrimination (although during the Special Period all Cubans suffered from the tanking economy). This discrimination led many rappers to examine their identities as non-white Cubans. The traditional notion about race in Cuba is that the island is a racial democracy and through *mestizaje* (race-mixing) the nation has basically resolved the racial tensions that existed pre-1959, since the legal and public barriers to discrimination (in the workplace, on beaches, in schools, in health care) have been put in place. The reality is a bit more complex, even if the country has made enormous strides in dealing with racial disparities. Rappers also began to re-examine Afro-Cuban identity, and many have proudly embraced Afro-Cuban religions or Rastafari, even if they are not necessarily members or initiates. They went into Cuban history to rescue the PIC leaders of the early republic, and other prominent black intellectual figures such as Juan René Betancourt, Gustavo Urrutia, Guillén, Walterio Carbonell, as well as the likes of Martin Luther King, Malcolm X, Bob Marley and Nelson Mandela.

Racism was a key issue that many groups brought up, whether in 'Loma y machete' and 'Guapo como Mandela' by Anónimo Consejo, 'Tengo' and 'Lágrimas Negras' by Hermanos de Causa, 'La muralla' by Cuarta Imagen, 'Quién tiró la tiza' by Clan 537 or 'Pelo' by Obsesión, to name only some of the more memorable ones. In their song 'Tengo', Hermanos de Causa draw on a famous poem by Nicolás Guillén called 'Tengo' (I Have), which examines the distinction between life before and after the Revolution using a Juan-with-nothing and a Juan-with-everything. Soandry del Río of Hermanos de Causa skilfully uses the 'tengo' in his version to indicate what he *does not* have. He says:

> Nobody cares about jack
> Discriminated 'cause I'm black
> Got a job with big demands and no pay.
> Got so much that I can't touch
> Got all these places I can't go in
> Got freedom in a parenthesis of steel.[30]

The song becomes a long meditation on the promise and reality of the Cuban Revolution without necessarily disavowing its principles. Later in the song, for example, he attacks materialism and selfishness.

In 'Lágrimas negras', the group again quotes and samples a previous and well-known cultural artefact, the *bolero-son*, written by Miguel Matamaros in 1928. The original is a song about a jilted lover who cries 'lágrimas negras' (black tears). The rap version samples a salsa version of the song for about thirty seconds and then launches into a heartfelt denunciation of racism. Again, using the imagery of the original love song, the refrain reads: 'I feel profound hatred for your racism/ your irony no longer confuses me/ and I cry without you knowing that my sobbing/ is made of black tears like my life.'[31] The third and fourth lines are a direct quote from the original song, but when juxtaposed with the two previous lines, they of course take on another, heartbreaking meaning. The black tears of love have become the black tears of racial hostility and incomprehension. The poignancy of the sampling is more than mere borrowing or citation: it is also a reworking of what we could call Cuba's national romance of *mestizaje* – *mestizaje* as a kind of racially untroubled 'love affair' of Cuba's self-definition as a nation. And yet at the end of the song we hear: 'Black Tears against racism/ for all of my people: white, Chinese, black, *jabao*, albino/ all types, one people, one heart.'[32] (*Jabao* means mixed race with light skin and chestnut or blond hair but with other 'black' features.)

Cuban rappers brought up the issue of racism when few people in Cuba were willing to discuss it. Revolutionary ideology, heavily influenced by Enlightenment philosophy, tended to be colour-blind and universalist. For many in Cuba, bringing up issues of race was seen as divisive. Grudgingly, and over the years, things have changed and in the last decade and a half many local scholars and researchers have studied the issue with greater sensitivity and objectivity.

To a degree, rappers are in the tradition of the *Nueva Trova* movement in that their lyrics deal with important social issues that beset Cuban society as it tried to steady itself and get back on its feet after the Special Period: growing social inequality, lack of good jobs for young people, prostitution, dual morality, social marginality, racism, growing violence in poor neighbourhoods (though nothing comparable to the *favelas* of Brazil), the dual currency, lack of basic goods, political hypocrisy, the growing materialism in part sparked by tourism and a slackening of social cohesion and solidarity. To its credit the government has recognized how important some of the rappers' critiques are in that it is an outlet for Cuban youth to express themselves in a context that does not amount to open dissidence.

When rap first came on the scene, the government's reaction was not positive. They felt that rap in Cuba was merely an uncritical import from the u.s., or that it was American rap with Spanish lyrics. But Cuba's rap scene was quite different from that of the u.s. in many respects: no gangsta rap or glorification of violence, little reference to bling, less misogynistic lyrics, very little use of swear words (otherwise it wouldn't get air time), use of Cuban musical traditions like the guaracha, *son*, rumba, salsa and even the *batá* drums. Grudgingly, the cultural authorities began to relent and allowed annual festivals to be held, founded a magazine, *Movimiento* (published between 2003 and 2014), and created the Cuban Rap Agency (CRA). The latter, founded in late 2002, was created to promote Cuban hip hop through concerts, recordings, musical training, and so on. When it was founded, there were over five hundred rap groups in Cuba, but only a handful belonged to the agency, and many groups felt marginal to the process. Over time, more reggaetón groups formed part of the CRA and many rappers felt this was a betrayal of the agency's mission, since reggaetón was understood by them (and others) as dance music, materialistically flaunting bling and treating women like sex objects. The problem was that the dividing line between rappers and *reggaetoneros* was porous: some groups did rap, but to earn money performed reggaetón as well.

The Cuban rap scene has been hit hard by the commercial success of reggaetón, and also by the fact that many rappers, producers and DJs have gone abroad. One of the dilemmas faced by rappers is the ability to earn a living and maintain artistic integrity. Unlike in the u.s., where rappers can become millionaires or moguls, there is no domestic market in Cuba that makes this possible. For example, most rappers self-produce their recordings and need to sell their CDs from

5 to 15 CUC (Cuban Convertible Pesos) apiece so that they can not only recoup their expenses but actually earn enough to live on. For a Cuban, 5 CUC is no small thing; 15 CUC is an exorbitant sum (this would be charged to foreigners). When the rap festivals were held, which attracted many guests from abroad, rappers were able to have their work available (and sold).

For rappers who have emigrated, opportunities are greater than back home. However, those who emigrate to the U.S. are faced with a predominantly English-speaking audience, and breaking into the U.S. market is not easily guaranteed. For every Pit Bull (and he was born in the U.S. and sings predominantly in English) there are dozens of Cuban rappers struggling to get by. Perhaps one of the few Cuban rappers to be successful in both languages and cultures was Ulpiano Sergio Reyes (aka Mellow Man Ace), who recorded solo albums (*Brother with Two Tongues*) as well as being part of Cypress Hill. This bilingualism and biculturalism is a delicate balancing act.

The most successful Cuban hip hop group is Orishas, whose first album *A lo Cubano* (2000) sold over 400,000 copies. No other group has got anywhere near that figure. Originally formed in Cuba and first called Amenaza (Threat), they changed their name when they emigrated to France and recorded *A lo Cubano*. This first album begins with an 'Intro' that features Yoruba chants and stunning percussion and then flows into their best-known song, 'Represent', a homage to Cuban music (son, rumba) and culture, particularly Ocha. The catchy beat, lyrics and voices, particularly Roldán's soaring interpretations, are magnificent. All the members of the group are *santeros*, and one of the most beautiful compositions on the album is 'Canto para Elewá y Changó', which skilfully combines imagery of the orishas with a hip hop beat. Another composition samples the bass line of 'Chan-Chan' by Compay Segundo, and is a nostalgic evocation of Cuba: appropriately it is titled '537 C.U.B.A.', the numbers representing the country code (53) and Havana (7) when dialling from abroad. Because they were living abroad and had access to better equipment, their albums have a richer, more layered sound than many of the recordings from the island. So far, their four albums, plus a compilation album that includes some excellent music videos (available on YouTube), have resonated with audiences, particularly in Europe. Their albums include an interesting combination of songs with social commentary (immigration, the disappeared, violence, street life), interspersed with songs that talk about having fun, partying or relationships. It has been a winning combination. Even though it has been several years since the group has recorded an album, they still tour together. The three members live in Madrid, Milan and Paris respectively, but there are reports that they have reunited to do new material in 2016. So far, no album has been released but they did record a song, 'Cuba Isla Bella' (2016), which features Isaac Delgado, Gente de Zona and Descemer Bueno. The music video uses fairly standard imagery of Cuba and despite the beauty of the singing is entirely mired in nostalgia (available on YouTube).

Because of the uncertain future for rappers/producers/DJs, many have left the island, like Las Krudas (a militant feminist lesbian and afro-centric trio), Ariel Fernández, Pablo Herrera, Alexis Cantero (half of Hermanos de Causa), Randy Acosta (half of Los Paisanos) and the Aldeanos. But some have stayed: Obsesión (Magia López and Alexey Rodríguez), Doble Filo, Anónimo Consejo, Papa Humbertico and others. Still others have shifted to reggaetón, such as Alto Voltaje, Eddy-K and what used to be the rap group Primera Base, now baptized into reggaetón as Cubanitos 2002.

The reggaetón scene in Cuba has been criticized by both the government and by sectors of the hip hop movement. Influenced by dance hall, both musically and in its bawdy lyrics, the Cuban government banned it from the public airways in December 2012, but slowly that has eroded and through the *paquete* (a memory stick of music, TV shows and movies purchased weekly) Cubans are gaining more and more access to reggaetón, listening to Baby Lores, Gente de Zona, El Micha, El Chacal and El Insurrecto, among many others. Of course, one of the most prominent *reggaetoneros*, Candyman, from Santiago de Cuba, is still around and popular.

Though reggaetón has a reputation for sexism, frivolity and bling, some of its practitioners are capable of writing songs dealing with serious issues. Candyman's 'No me pongas en lo oscuro' (Don't leave me in the dark) is a strong statement about the disconnect between government and people, and his 'Señor oficial' is directed at the official attitudes towards reggaetón. Mucho Manolo, who has a good voice, has written songs about police harassment ('Policía no me molestes'), people who collaborate with the surveillance authorities ('Tu estás colaborando') and about the lack of goods and food items ('Abajo quien tu sabe'). In this last song the refrain is 'Down with you-know-who', a not very oblique reference to those in power, although certainly not as openly confrontational as Gorki Ávila, a rocker and bandleader of Porno para Ricardo who has openly insulted Fidel Castro in some of his songs ('El comandante'). (All these music videos are available on YouTube.)

And then there are artists like singer Danay Suárez, born in 1985, who seem to be able to move between hip hop, r'n'b, jazz, reggae-reggaetón and old and new *trova* with amazing ease. Her songs are about love and friendship, but also war and violence, about the struggles of daily life in Cuba. Her sultry voice can be ethereal and lyrical, and hard as nails, tender and relentless. She started with X Alfonso, another Cuban artist who mixes genres effortlessly, and performed with different groups before recording two solo albums (*Polvo de la humedad* in 2014 and *Havana Cultura Sessions* in 2015).

All That's Ideology Melts into Flesh: *Juan of the Dead*

Cubans are avid consumers of Western pop culture and films, and that includes zombies. As Gilles Deleuze and Felix Gauttari have said, 'Zombies are the only modern myth.'[33] Cuba is no exception to the myth, with Alejandro Brugués's film *Juan de los muertos* (*Juan of the Dead*; 2011), an irreverent and 'splatstick' view of contemporary Cuba that weighs in on various themes: family tensions, tourism, ideology, cynicism and mistrust, plus a sardonic glance at certain institutions like the CDRs, the police and the press. As far as I know, *Juan of the Dead* is the first zombie film ever made in a socialist country (*Kung Fu Zombie*, from 1982, was made in Hong Kong).

As a comedy, the film quotes or satirizes other zombie films (comedies or not) like *Shaun of the Dead* (2004), *Dawn of the Dead* (1978), *28 Days Later* (2002) and *Zombie Flesh Eaters* (1979), the latter by Lucio Fulci, featuring underwater zombies, with the added chutzpah of a zombie attacking a shark. Brugués also quotes from Cuban films: *Memories of Underdevelopment*, *Life is to Whistle*, *Guantanamera* and *Vampires in Havana*. Ultimately, however, the film has a somewhat standard approach to the genre: how to survive a zombie apocalypse. Fortunately, Juan and his sidekick Lázaro are the ultimate survivors. At the beginning of the film, while they are fishing in Havana harbour, Lázaro asks Juan, 'Do you ever feel like you should just keep going and row all the way to Miami?' Juan calmly responds:

> What for, man, I'd have to work there. Besides, I'm a survivor. I survived Mariel. I survived Angola. I survived the Special Period and that thing that came after. Here we are like the *taínos* [indigenous inhabitants of the island] waiting for the fruit to fall out of the tree. This is paradise and nothing will change that.

Straight afterwards Juan fishes a zombie out of the water and Lázaro finishes him off with a harpoon shot to the forehead.

Soon, the zombie plague will spread throughout Havana, testing the skills and ingenuity of Juan and Lázaro, who, with a mix of *guapería* (Cuban street-smarts with a hint of intimidation) and entrepreneurial zeal, set up a business for hunting zombies, charging Cubans in pesos and tourists or foreigners in CUC. The zombie extermination team also includes La China (a gay cross-dressing mulatto), el Primo (a hulk of a man with rippling muscles who must work blindfold because he faints at the sight of blood), Vladi California

(Lázaro's ne'er-do-well son) and Camila (Juan's daughter, distrustful of her father, who becomes an acrobatically expert killer of zombies).

Juan of the Dead also draws on Cuban bufo theatre. Here it borrows from *Vampires in Havana*, an animated film set in the 1930s that is a vampire comedy with touches of the gangster genre. Influenced by Spanish theatre, the *zarzuela* (light opera) and the *tonadilla* (a satirical musical comedy popular in eighteenth-century Spain), bufo theatre relied on a series of stereotypes: the *negrito*, a comic black character usually played by a white actor in black face; the *gallego*, a Spaniard of Galician origin, who is a bumbling, clumsy character unable to resist the sexual allure of the *mulatta*; the *mulatta*, a mixed-race woman who is a temptress, usually of the *gallego*; the *negra*, a black woman, often older, usually associated with sorcery and witchcraft but not sexually attractive; and *el chino*, a Chinese man, hardworking and industrious, but always made fun of for the way he speaks Spanish. Despite these stereotypical portrayals, Cuban bufo theatre was an attempt to envision Cuban identity and nationality on stage. In an ever-changing nineteenth century, with Cuban nationalism asserting itself in one of Spain's last colonies with slavery still in existence, bufo theatre represented an entertaining and deeply flawed attempt to negotiate Cuba's growing sense of uniqueness and nationhood within the parameters of a colonial, racist and sexist society.

Juan of the Dead evokes some of those stereotypes, with some interesting variants: the negrito figure is bifurcated into two characters, La China (Jazz Vilá) and El Primo (Eliecer Ramírez). The first, La China, with a sharp tongue, is a mix of *el chino* and the *negro catedrático* (a black bufo figure who pretended to be eloquent and erudite but stumbled over words). However, La China is male, flamboyantly gay, and not at all clumsy with words; in a sense he is a *catedrático* who is eloquent and a mulatta, since his sexuality is open, flirtatious and even hilarious at times, even if at another level s/he is a stereotype. With a bit of imagination one could argue that s/he represents a queering of the *mulatta* figure. El Primo, a hulking body-builder type, is certainly the stereotype of the physically potent black male, except that he faints when he sees blood. He barely speaks three lines in the film, again alluding to his physical prowess but non-existent verbal skills (evoking the *negro bozal*, the African slave who speaks a broken Spanish or none at all). Both he and La China are killed off fairly early in the film, following the all-too-familiar convention of eliminating black characters before many of the others.

One could also argue that the mulatta figure of bufo theatre is represented by Sara and Lucía, both white, as they symbolize desire and sexuality, at least to the main protagonists, Juan and Lázaro. Both, however, die fairly early on. The *gallego* figure is literally represented by Spanish male tourists who are with Cuban *jineteras* (*mulattas*, or paid escorts). Their brief scene culminates with a 'splatstick' battle with the lights out. In this case the *gallego* figure does not seem to have evolved much from the nineteenth century.

In the bufo spirit, if not the character stereotype of its time, both Juan and Lázaro play the wily and *pícaro criollo* (Creole picaresque hustler) figures, Juan being the *mulatto* and Lázaro the white Sancho Panza sidekick. They are people who survive by their wits, not to mention occasional petty crime, and are completely uninterested in conventional life or employment. They are likeable rogues, Juan a little more mature, Lázaro rather adolescent in his humour (often homophobic) and sexuality.

Being set in a Caribbean country, does *Juan of the Dead* represent a return to the roots of zombie lore? The word zombie supposedly derives from the Kikongo words *nzumbi* or *nzambi*, which refer to spirits or God. Both Haitian Vodou and Cuban Regla de Palo Monte have deep roots in Congolese religion and culture. In Vodou, the idea of the zombie is rooted in slavery, the concept of controlling a person's soul (*ti bon ange*) so that they can be under your power, a perfect analogy of the relationship between master and slave. As many have pointed out, Haitians do not fear zombies (they are harmless, and not the flesh-eating creatures created by Western cinema), they fear becoming one, since it is a horrific reminder of what it meant to be a slave. In Vodou, these Congolese roots are reflected in what is known as Petwo (or Petro) rites, as opposed to the more 'benevolent' Rada rites.

Cuban Palo Monte combines what in Haiti would be known as the Rada and Petwo rites, and in some instances includes some elements of the Yoruba-based practices of Regla de Ocha. In the case of Cuban Palo Monte, the practice is based on the initiate's relationship to a spirit that resides in an *nganga* or *prenda*. The spirit in the *nganga* works for its owner, bringing good fortune and blessings, or, conversely, can cause harm. The *nganga* is a large iron receptacle that contains many elements: earth, water, blood, sticks and other wooden objects, herbs, bones (animal and sometimes human), metal, dolls and so on. It is considered a kind of microcosm of the world that guides the *palero/a* through their life path. Joel James, perhaps referring to that wide mix of elements residing in the *prenda*, has called Cuba a 'Great Nganga'. *Juan of the Dead* might be read, perhaps, as an *nganga* that has toppled over and released its *muerto*, except that in the case of the film we might see it as *los muertos de la nación* (all the dead of the nation).

Palo is a religion and a practice that is profoundly linked with the dead, not surprisingly considering that most West African religions (and particularly those that made it to Cuba) have deep roots with the ancestral world. Although all of the major Afro-Cuban religions (Ocha, Palo, Abakuá, Arará) exhibit intimate ties with the world of the ancestors, Palo above the other three privileges this relationship. The spirit that resides within an *nganga* and works on behalf of the *palero* is that of someone who died, so one could argue that Palo is founded on a constant conversation with the dead. In his study of Palo, Todd Ramón Ochoa's informant Isidra links the world of the dead with Mama Kalunga, the 'deity' of the ocean within the Congolese cosmos, which is consistent with the Bakongo belief systems. Brugués's shot of zombies underwater has eerie associations with these Palo beliefs, even though the film does not make any overt references to Palo.

Ochoa describes how Isidra sees Kalunga: 'Kalunga is ambient: Kalunga surrounds, Kalunga saturates, Kalunga generates, and Kalunga dissipates.'[34] This ubiquity of the dead linked to the ubiquity of the ocean works powerfully in the film. There are many scenes shot near or on the water that reinforce this: the opening and closing scenes of the film, other scenes shot along the Malecón, still many others where the ocean is seen in the background, Sara's attempted escape from the Malecón, the image of the Virgin of Charity on the getaway car turned into a raft, Lázaro's harpoon as ideal weapon to vanquish zombies, the ebb and flow of the undead in the streets in their shuffling tides of attack.

Ochoa also mentions an aesthetic that *paleros* adhere to in the practice of their craft: 'the volatility of substances, speed of decision, the use of force against adversaries, and unsentimental action taken to transform fate.'[35] This is a perfect description of the group that Juan and Lázaro form to be hired out to kill zombies (for a fee, of course). Juan and Lázaro embody the *ndoki*, the dead spirit of the *nganga* who work to protect the *palero/a*, in their case hired to 'use force against their adversaries', and unsentimentally take action 'to transform [the] fate' of those around them.

In very Cuban fashion, Juan and Lázaro use the instruments at hand to do the job; remarkably absent are firearms, so prevalent in Western zombie films. In *Juan of the Dead*, the weapons of attack are low-tech: oars, machetes, baseball bats, slingshots, TV antennae and, of course, Lázaro's speargun. In Spanish we would describe their actions as *darle palo a los zombis* (beating the zombies with a stick), making everyone a *palero* of sorts. Machetes, the weapon of choice in the film, are very prevalent in the making of *ngangas* and, of course, evoke the machete-wielding *mambises* of the Cuban wars for independence, as well as the great hero-warriors who fought for Cuban sovereignty: Maceo, Gómez, Agramonte Céspedes, Martí, Moncada and Quintín Banderas.

Given these historical antecedents, one might wonder if these *muertos* of Cuban history still weigh too heavily on the living. In this they evoke the famous words of Karl Marx in his *Eighteenth Brumaire*:

> The tradition of all dead generations weighs like a nightmare on the brains of the living. And just as they seem to be occupied with revolutionizing themselves and things, creating something that did not exist before, precisely in such epochs of revolutionary crisis they anxiously conjure up the spirits of the past to their service, borrowing from them names, battle slogans, and costumes in order to present this new scene in world history in time-honoured disguise and borrowed language.[36]

Is Brugués, albeit indirectly, suggesting that Cuba has been crushed by this 'nightmare of the dead generations' as embodied by the presence of the zombies? What do these zombies infer in terms of conjuring the 'spirits of the past', and what might they say about the present or the future?

Marx's well-known *Eighteenth Brumaire* text begins as follows: 'Hegel remarks somewhere that all great world-historic facts and personages appear, so to speak, twice. He forgot to add: the first time as tragedy, the second time as farce.'[37] Brugués's film is certainly a farce in many ways, but is it a farce disguised as tragedy, or one that tries to laugh away the tragedy? Or put another way: is the bufo theatre distracting us from some of the tragic consequences of Cuban socialism? Are the reactions of both Juan and his cohorts, not to mention the government, 'borrowing slogans, names, costumes and language' from the past or merely reaffirming their roots in resistance and struggle that go back to the nineteenth century?

Zombie films lend themselves to metaphor and social allegory. Can this be said about *Juan of the Dead*? As a film made in a socialist society, what are the social ills being highlighted? A pessimistic and anti-socialist view would say that the zombies represent a kind of return of the repressed of socialism: an out-of-control bureaucracy, the rigidity of one-party rule, the vapid repetition of Marxist-Leninist dogma, the inefficiency of centralized economies, the fossilized ritual of five-year plans, the suppression of individual liberties, a dull, lifeless and censored press, stifling norms in the arts, the stultifying spectacles of party congresses, and the numbing vehemence of ideological discourse. Others would argue that as a society Cuba has been zombified by Fidel and the Cuban state. One could see the interminable wait concerning Fidel's health as a metaphor that permeates the film: poised between life and death, he is analogous to the undead, who are also in-between figures. In a short story by Cuban science fiction author Erick J. Mota, the narrator says:

> According to Panchito, all the people *up there* must be zombies too. The directors, the generals, the Council of State, the ministers – everyone. That's why they say Fidel is ill. He can't give speeches that last more than a hour because he's a zombie.[38]

Even as a zombie Fidel is exceptional: who ever heard of a zombie speaking at all, let alone for an hour?

But is this what we see in the film? There are certainly barbs at many Cuban institutions, from the CDRs (which seem more concerned about theft of cassette players from cars than the zombie outbreak) to the press, which claims the unleashing of the undead is due to the U.S. and its desire to infiltrate dissidents into Cuban society. The film plays this claim for laughs, and its satire on the press is consistent with many zombie films, where the press is often wrong, misleading or gives incorrect information on how to battle zombies. Where is the well-known Cuban solidarity and organization in dealing with catastrophes like hurricanes or other natural disasters? How about the ever-present Cuban police? Earnest, but ineffectual. The government? The best they can do is organize a mass demonstration in front of the U.S. Interest Section (now an embassy), but the zombies keep coming. If we understand the zombie menace as external threat, then Cuba's preparedness and defensive capabilities should be unquestionable in quelling the chaos, but such is not the case. Hence we must read the zombies not as 'other' but as internal (the zombies are us).

One could interpret the zombie hordes as representing Cuba's uncertain future, overwhelmed by the forces of globalization in a free market frenzy that leads to a capitalist playground with a stampede of tourists, foreign investors and multinational corporations primed to make the island a source of profits. Is that what Juan is referring to when he says at one moment 'Que en el final el capitalismo nos va a pasar la cuenta' (When all is said and done, capitalism is going to make us pay for it)? Perhaps, but either one of these interpretations is a reminder that *Juan of the Dead* does not lend itself to scoring easy ideological points, negative or positive.

Chris Boehm, in discussing the hit TV series *The Walking Dead*, argues that the apocalyptic tenor of zombie massive destruction has an unexpected utopian side to it, which he poetically labels 'apocalyptic utopia'. A zombie apocalypse destroys life as we know it, providing a kind of 'clean slate' to begin all over again – although it is not an entirely 'clean slate', since zombies still represent an existential menace to the survivors. What shows like *The Walking Dead* offer is a view of how we as humans react to these end times, and how we try and reconstruct a sense of order, justice and society from the ashes (and carnage) of the zombie onslaught. What the catastrophe teaches us is that the utopian project functions on the fantasy that once the mythic threat to its realization is eliminated (class enemies, social divisions, imperialism) then social harmony will automatically ensue. But this misses the point about schisms and differences within all societies. One must reconstruct things from the point of view of exclusion, from otherness, embrace what the disaster has wrought: our society's divisions (and otherness) are internal, not external. To try and make these divisions vanish will only unleash more destructive 'monsters.'[39] As David Beisecker says, 'A zombie apocalypse is thus not your garden variety apocalypse; it's one in which we are brought down from within, a battle *royale* in which what we have been fights to contain "what we have become".'[40]

The film's ending, for all its wise-ass humour, seems to validate a fidelity to the event à la Alain Badiou. The French philosopher defines an event in politics as something that opens up new possibilities and shatters old ways of seeing the world, allowing us to create change in unprecedented ways. In addition, it unleashes a truth process that creates a political subject that did not exist before the event. In Cuba's case the event is the Revolution. At the end of the film, Juan is supposed to board a kind of automobile/boat that will take him, Lázaro, Camila and Vladi California to Miami. But he intervenes to save a young boy from his zombie father and, instead, puts the boy in the car/boat and decides to stay. He returns to the Malecón with his trusty oar (his preferred weapon for bashing the undead) and, challenging the approaching zombie horde, leaps into the air to beat them back while the soundtrack plays the Sid Vicious version of 'My Way'. As Juan leaps, the ending turns to animation (quite effectively done), and gleefully he uses the oar to maim and decapitate zombies. The final shot is of a zombie with a hole through his torso, wearing a jacket that reads 'Hasta la victoria siempre' (Ever onward to victory), perhaps an unwitting reference to Lacan's notion that truth processes punch a hole in our sense of conventional knowledge. The quote, from Che Guevara's letter to Fidel when he left Cuba to pursue revolution in Bolivia, has become a key slogan of the Revolution. Is Juan's way Che's way?

Juan's decision to stay is 'heroic', if a little suicidal, and exemplifies the words of the national anthem 'Morir por la patria es vivir' (To die for the fatherland is to live), which is sung earlier in the film. Has Juan maintained a fidelity to the event (Revolution)? What about the zombie onslaught? Is that not an event as well, especially if we understand it as an 'apocalyptic utopia', mentioned earlier? Earlier in the film Lázaro says 'hay que irnos, alzarnos a la sierra' (we have to go, up into the mountains). The reference to guerrilla warfare here is metaphorical since they are in Havana, but the sentiment is definitely one of fidelity to the event. Badiou says that political subjects are always between two events; that subject is not to be confused with a psychological subject and is created by the event itself:

> I call the subject the bearer of a fidelity, the one who bears a process of truth. The subject, therefore, in no way pre-exists the process. He is absolutely nonexistent in the situation 'before' the event. We might say that the process of truth *induces* a subject.[41]

In *Juan of the Dead* the coming event has happened. We are poised at the unfolding of the new event, where new possibilities (and catastrophes) await. In the final shot one can see through the hole in the zombie surrounded by other undead and the horizon where Mama Kalunga dwells, in the ocean. Bufo and Palo, Juan and Che, Marx and his ghosts, zombies and the living: Cuba wobbles into the future echoing Beckett's words: 'Try again. Fail again. Fail better.'[42] Simon Critchley says that philosophy does not begin in wonder as Aristotle would have it, but in disappointment. So do revolutions.

SIX

Concluding Remarks
(2014–2016)

When President Obama announced a new relationship with Cuba on 17 December 2014, most Cubans recognized that it came on an important date in the Cuban calendar: the feast of St Lazarus. This saint is syncretized in Ocha with the orisha Babalú-Ayé, who is responsible for the curing of illness. Babalú-Ayé is usually depicted with crutches and two dogs licking wounds on his legs. Every year Cubans go on a pilgrimage to the town of Rincón to pray to San Lázaro, many on their knees, dragging heavy objects, in penance. Certainly if something needed healing it was relations between the two countries. In March 2016 President Obama visited Cuba. And three days after he left, the Rolling Stones performed before an open-air crowd of 500,000. By all accounts both events were a great success, although after Obama's departure the Cuban ideological counter-attack was in full force. In his speech to the Cuban people Obama spoke respectfully about Cuba, quoted Martí in Spanish and recognized that historically the relationship between the two countries had been that of a superpower over a protectorate (Cubans would say neo-colony), but he added that it was time to leave the past and construct a new and prosperous future between the two countries. Obama underlined that Cuba's future was to be decided by Cubans and not the U.S., and even spoke of the strengths and uncertainties of American democracy (portending the election of Trump), but he did not lecture, scold or talk down to his Cuban audience.

The official press castigated the speech, saying it was trying to sow ideological divisions within Cuba, and that Obama was a kind of Pied Piper playing the flute of capitalism, luring his audience with the melodies (illusions) of market plenty and regime change. Fidel himself responded with an article in *Granma* on 28 March, after Obama had left, and after the Stones concert. It appealed to the spirit of sacrifice and discipline of Cuba's revolutionary tradition, doubting that the U.S. sincerely meant to turn a new leaf after 57 years of hostility, military operations, acts of terrorism and sabotage, as well as an economic blockade. He finished defiantly: 'We do not need any gifts from the Empire. Our efforts will be legal and peaceful, because our commitment is with the peace and fraternity of all us humans that live on this planet.'[1]

Barely a month after Obama's visit the 7th Congress of the Cuban Communist Party took place (16–18 April). Many hoped that the Congress, perhaps building on the enthusiasm for Obama's visit, and the cultural opening of the Stones concert, would inaugurate important changes in Cuban society, both economic and political. Raúl spoke of the slow pace of economic change, saying that state payrolls had to be trimmed further (the overall percentage of state employees in the whole economy has declined to 70 per cent from 81 per cent since 2011). Foreign investment laws are still cumbersome; tourism – though on the rise – might reach a breaking point since Cuba cannot handle millions of extra tourists per year; and the recent political changes and low oil prices in Venezuela are hurting one of Cuba's most important economic benefactors. Still, the economy has grown modestly since the last Party Congress (2011), somewhere between 2 and 3 per cent per annum, but some economists say Cuba needs a higher growth rate to truly lift the economy from the beating it took after the collapse of the USSR, from which it has not yet truly recovered.

As for political reform (not a word Cubans use) the recent Party Congress ridiculed what it called U.S.-type democracy, and rejected any notion of a multi-party system, along with Western notions of civil society, and political and human rights. This is consistent with the Party's view of human rights: Cuba emphasizes social rights (housing, health, education, culture, sport) over individual rights (property, political pluralism, press freedoms, right of assembly and so on). The Politburo stayed the same and there was no major shake-up on the Central Committee either. Despite pledges to promote younger leadership, the two top figures, Raúl Castro and Machado Ventura, are 85 and 86, respectively. In this Cuba seems to have repeated the gerontocratic patterns of other Communist governments (witness the USSR and China in the 1970s and '80s); not to mention a bureaucratic stubbornness and inertia that reveals an innate conservatism of these types of regimes over time. Cuba, of course, is different in some ways. Even though he is no longer a major player (and recently died), the Revolution's historical leader lived over fifty years of revolutionary history. In a sense, Cuba's Lenin and Stalin are found in one figure, Fidel, and its Trotsky was perhaps Che Guevara (if you go with the idea of permanent revolution) or Raúl Castro (if you go with Trotsky as head of the Red Army). Lenin died very early in the Russian Revolution, and both Stalin and Mao were superseded by major changes after their respective deaths. Many of those changes represented a repudiation of some of their policies, as was the case with de-Stalinization in the Soviet bloc and the four modernizations undertaken by Deng Xiaoping, ushering in the era of 'Leninist capitalism' in China. None of this has quite happened in Cuba, where Fidel's authority and legitimacy still remain quite high, despite his passing.

Fidel appeared and gave a brief speech at the end of the Party Congress where he spoke of his mortality and, to a degree, gave a kind of farewell speech. He certainly didn't expect to be around for the next Congress (which will be in 2021), indicating he did not expect to reach 95. Fidel was right, as he passed away seven months later, on 25 November 2016. But true to his beliefs he also stated, 'The ideas of Cuban Communists will remain as proof that on this planet if you work hard and with dignity, you can produce the material and cultural goods human beings need.'² One, of course, can take this statement, à la Alain Badiou, as a remarkable expression of fidelity to the Event (Revolution, Communism), or, in a less generous view, as a stubborn refusal to face reality, a delusional belief in a failed system.

It has been 27 years since the fall of the Berlin Wall, a quarter of a century since the dissolution of the USSR. Almost everyone predicted that after those two momentous events, 'Cuba was next'. And yet, battered and bruised, staggering into the howling winds of global capitalism, Cuba has somehow managed to survive. This alone is remarkable, but survival is not thriving and that is the challenge that Cuba faces for the future.

Cuba's Future: Some Scenarios

When Cuba's future is discussed, different scenarios are presented, some bordering on science fiction. Let's focus on some of the more plausible ones. First is the Soviet (or Eastern European) denouement with a collapse of the ruling party and shock therapy economics leading to a full-throttle embrace of open markets. This seems highly unlikely, given the uneventful passing of the torch to Raúl Castro (2006–8) and his subsequent two terms as president (2008–18). He announced that that is all he will serve, in line with the previous law passed limiting presidential terms of five years to two. The Cuban Communist Party (CCP) is the institutional glue of the country, and there is nothing to indicate it will not remain so for the near future, buttressed by high officials in the FAR (Revolutionary Armed Forces), many of whom are on the Central Committee or the Politburo and who run many of the important state enterprises.

Despite the overweening presence of the CCP, it has been a considerable source of political stability in Cuban life. From its founding in 1925, the Partido Socialist Popular (PSP) was a respected party in Cuba, with prominent intellectual figures like Carlos Rafael Rodríguez, Juan Marinello and Ruben Martínez Villena. Some members of the revolutionary left found it too reformist, underlined by its virulent denunciation of the Moncada Barracks attack (1953) led by Fidel Castro, and what would become the 26th of July Movement (M-26-7).

The PSP was a party that had a powerful presence in the trade union movement, was the most vocal political voice around issues of racial discrimination in the Republican era and had a popular news-paper (*Hoy*) and radio station (1010). Naturally, after the Revolution they were supportive of the Fidelistas, and the PSP, along with other revolutionary organizations (the Directorio, M-26-7), finally merged into the PCC in 1965.

Cuba under the Republic had lived under considerable political instability that led to U.S. military intervention three times, a civilian dictatorship under Machado (1928–33), a turbulent period of uncertainty (1934–40) and a military coup in 1952, followed by a guerrilla war (1956–9), ending in the triumph of the Revolution. Since 1959 Cuba has had a degree of political stability unlike most countries in Latin America. The country has undergone different crises but they can nearly all be attributed to external factors: the Bay of Pigs invasion, the Missile Crisis and the Special Period (the collapse of the USSR). The exception is Mariel, although the latter can in part be explained by a lack of a solid immigration agreement between Cuba and the U.S. During all these crises, the country rallied around its leaders and the government (in the first two the PCC didn't yet exist), always providing coherence to a potentially destabilizing conjuncture. This is certainly true of the Special Period (1989–2004), when the loss of Soviet aid had many observers predicting the downfall of the regime. The CCP handled this period skilfully, as did Fidel, who always went on the offensive in steering the country forwards, somehow manag-ing to resurrect a sense of pride in Cubans who now had to look to themselves and their own resources to overcome the adversities of economic collapse (a 40 per cent downturn in five years).

Cuba sees the end of the USSR as an unmitigated disaster for the former Soviet people, with high unemployment, the ravaging of state enterprises by greedy apparatchiks, the deterioration of social benefits, especially health care, the unleashing of even greater corruption than before (in part because more money is involved), and the creation of mafias that have contributed to social decay and social violence. If Russia has been able to prosper, it is because it at least has an industrial base to build on, bountiful amounts of oil (and natural gas) and a weapons industry, none of which Cuba can claim. (To Cuba's advantage, it is not faced with the nationalist challenges that the Soviet Republics represented under Russian hegemony.)[3]

The second scenario is the path taken by China or Vietnam, both countries with which Cuba has had (or still has) good relations. Their approach to change is gradualist, which appeals to Cuba, since in both cases the ruling Communist party has not given up power. Raúl Castro has visited China several times and has closely examined its policies over the decades. He admires the way in which the Chinese state makes important investments in infrastructure and business (whether private, state or mixed), its impressive commitment to R&D, the expansion of the manufacturing base and its booming export sector. The China that has emerged since 1976 (the death of Mao) would be unrecognizable to the Great Helmsman, but this 'new' China entails some elements the Cubans are not thrilled about: unemployment, abandonment of universal health care, an increasingly two-tiered educational system based on privilege, an inconsistent if not dismal record on workers' rights (and exploitation wages), environmental degradation, rising inequality and staggering levels of corruption.

Despite the political attractiveness of the Chinese model for Cuba, it is doubtful the latter would unequivocally adopt all the elements of the former's economic path (becoming a source of cheap labour, abandoning health care, alarming levels of social inequality). This inequality is likely to happen under most scenarios (and, indeed, is already happening), but so far Cuba does not seem willing to entertain Chinese levels of inequality. Up to now there is no Cuban Deng Xiaoping saying, 'Poverty is not socialism. To be rich is glorious,' or 'Socialism does not mean shared poverty.' The Cuban Communist elite have perhaps focused only on the 'to be rich is glorious' part of Deng's remarks (although not stating this sentiment publicly).

What Deng's words allude to is one of the major economic flaws of centrally planned economies and their concept of investment. Soviet-style socialism clearly made major investments in the areas of education, heavy industry, health, culture and the sciences. But in terms of the production of all types of goods (not just heavy industry) most socialist experiments of the twentieth century were notoriously weak in sustaining an economic system that could not only grow in a self-propelling way but also innovate. The most flagrant example from the USSR was its ability to send a man into space, and its inability to make a good ballpoint pen. As a result, most socialist economies 'lived off' the infrastructure and investments previously made under capitalism, and Cuba has certainly exemplified this tendency to an extreme: witness the decaying pavements, potholed streets, collapsing water and sewage facilities, frayed communication systems and crumbling architecture throughout the country. This will be a major challenge for the future, and a brake on a smooth economic transformation for the coming decades, unless there is a major infusion of capital for rebuilding this infrastructure.

In the film *Memories of Underdevelopment* (1968), Sergio, the protagonist and narrator, walks through the streets of Havana asking questions of himself, and in voice-over we hear him say: 'Cubans always live for the moment, they don't see the relationship between their lives and the bigger picture. They always want someone to think for them.' He considers this a trait of underdevelopment as well, in a sense complementing monoculture and a lack of economic dynamism. Is this an indirect reference to *choteo*? Despite its commitment to planning and building the future, Cuba still seems to be personally, politically, economically always improvising, trying to get by, *inventando*, as the Cubans would say.

Part of this is cultural but part is the disconnect between the government and society at large. This is not a problem unique to Cuba or socialism, although Communist-run governments do have unique characteristics in this regard. (In Brazil, it is called *jeito* – what needs to be done to circumvent the law, bureaucracy or rules that are an obstacle to achieving something, whether through an exchange of favours, bribes or threatening to denounce someone.) In Cuba, the rhetoric of socialist public life is of a life of the common good, building a society that is classless, race-blind and gender-neutral. Transparency in public life is also meant to be matched by transparency in the private realm. However, as historical experience has revealed, public life under state socialism is opaque (and often impenetrably so) and private life becomes the only refuge in a society where leader, government, state, revolution and the people are supposed to be one under the banner of selfless unity.

Another Cuban film that reflects this brilliantly is *Strawberry and Chocolate*, discussed earlier. The film is littered with examples of *doble moral* (a dual morality – one for public consumption, the other more authentic): David tells Diego that in public situations he should not greet him or let on that they are friends; Nancy, Diego's neighbour and head of the local CDR, but who also practises Santería, deals in the black market and presumably turns an occasional trick or two. Diego, despite his friendship with David, doesn't let on that he has been negotiating with a foreign embassy to leave the country, which he eventually does. David's old girlfriend Vivian marries a man she likes but does not love, because he is well situated in the Party structures, allowing them to not only travel – truly rare for 1979 Cuba – but live abroad, working in Italy for two years.

Nancy is the character who best reflects this divide. As the local head of the CDR she is supposed to be supervising (snooping on, if you will) the activities of her neighbours to ensure they uphold revolutionary morality. But in an allegedly atheistic state she keeps a statue of St Barbara (Changó) in her house, procures goods unavailable in Cuban stores, such as Johnny Walker Scotch, and earns extra money through sexual favours. In a dramatic scene she slits her wrists and is rushed to the hospital, where Diego's blood 'saves' her – an ironic scene, to say the least, since it is 'gay counter-revolutionary' blood that cures the local head of the CDR. In fact it is doubly ironic because suicide is frowned upon, viewed as 'counter-revolutionary' by the regime, and what's worse she has already made several attempts. Is it the intolerable living out of *doble moral* that makes her suicidal? The film never makes it clear, but at least she is not treated unsympathetically.

Much has changed since 1979 (and 1993, when the film was made): Cubans have become more outspoken, more critical of the shortcomings of the society they live in. Homophobia is officially criticized by the government, religious expression is openly tolerated, authors previously censored are being published (but not all), concerns over racial discrimination are more openly aired, economic ideas previously viewed as heretical are being discussed or even implemented. But there is still room for considerable improvement.

Raúl Castro has expressed admiration for what China has accomplished in the last thirty years; he has also said, 'Our worst enemy is not imperialism . . . but our own errors.'[4] Some will say this comment is forty years overdue, but at least it is recognition that Cuba can no longer blame everything on the blockade or the 'evil intentions of the U.S.', nor can blame be a substitute for sound economic policy. Earlier, we discussed the Revolutionary Offensive of 1968, when over 58,000 businesses were expropriated by the state; many local economists and the leadership recognize that this was a rash decision that hurt the Cuban economy.

Yet, as others have questioned, who is responsible for these errors, which were the most damaging, and what are the consequences for those responsible? How are these errors still affecting the present? A generic apology of 'mistakes were made' is fine, but does not further a climate of accountability or set a precedent for sanctioning those who made harmful decisions, even if they were made with the best of intentions.

The third option mentioned as a future for Cuba is a transition that would lead to a social democratic system, European or Scandinavian style. This option is usually mentioned in terms of economic policy, but what about the political dimension? It is highly unlikely that Cuba will evolve into a multi-party parliamentary system in the short term. Again, the CCP will most likely retain full political control or perhaps reach a reconciliation agreement where the PCC would retain hegemonic influence, but the latter seems unlikely unless there are guarantees that the Party is not outlawed or persecuted under a multi-party system. The economic advantages of this model would be the coexistence of a private and public sector, strong social benefits (childcare, education, health care, pensions), a solid labour-management contract and strong public support for culture.[5]

But Cuba is not Sweden, some will point out, even if they each can boast an excellent and socially aware novelist of crime fiction (Henning Mankell and Leonardo Padura Fuentes). Sweden has a formidable industrial sector, represented by world-renowned companies like Volvo, Sony Ericsson, Electrolux, IKEA, Scania, a highly educated workforce, a formidable engineering sector, and the thirteenth-highest per capita income in the world, coupled with low income inequality.

Still others have pointed out Brazil as another possible model for Cuba, perhaps since it is closer geographically, and culturally more similar than Russia, China, Vietnam and northern Europe. Brazil has emerged from a dictatorship (1964–85) with major economic problems (high inequality, hyper-inflation, a weak currency) to become the world's sixth-largest economy. It has adopted innovative measures in energy (ethanol production), social services (*Bolsa familia*), agriculture and industry. It has made important strides in crime prevention and corruption, created a vibrant middle class and has made important gains in poverty reduction. All of these make it an attractive model that promotes growth, but without being indifferent to the poor.

But again, Brazil and Cuba are vastly different. Brazil is twenty times larger, population-wise, than its Caribbean cousin, with a huge internal market, a solid industrial base (they make everything from cars to aircraft), with a huge export sector (soybeans, iron ore, ethanol, oil) that totals $350 billion in a $2.5 trillion economy. Its exports alone are six times Cuba's total GDP. Brazil has vast natural resources and is home to the greatest rainforest on the planet. Brazil's recent economic downturn and political volatility since the impeachment of President Rousseff don't inspire much confidence in their model.

So where does that leave Cuba?

Cuba is leaning towards the model of Vietnam, which has made some of the changes more gradually than China, has not shredded the social safety net, and has tried to ensure that market measures don't affect equality in a dramatic way. Politically, the Vietnamese Communist Party has a firm grip on the situation. Cuba is even careful about the language it uses: instead of 'market socialism' they speak of 'socialism with markets', as if to emphasize that socialism is the leading principle of the society, not markets.

The Weekly *Paquete*: Cuba's Window to the World

One of the island's challenges as it tries to propel its economy into the twenty-first century is its telecommunications, particularly the Internet. Given the limited Internet access for Cubans – because of expense as well as tiny bandwidth – and the government monopoly of the media, Cubans have had to find ingenious ways to gain access to foreign films, TV series, news, sporting events and more. It is called El Paquete Semanal (the Weekly Package) and it is a memory stick (or larger) that contains hundreds of hours of films, TV series, animes, soap operas, news programmes, cartoons, video games, music, mobile phone apps, even magazines and advertisements. Up to one terabyte of content can be loaded per week and it costs anywhere from one to three CUCs. It is an offline version of the Internet (some have called it the poor man's Internet). Although presumably the *paquete* is not legal, the government does nothing to prevent it. (Cuba is not alone in this: when I was in Trinidad in late May 2006 *The Da Vinci Code* was still in U.S. cinemas but pirate DVDs were already circulating on the streets of Port of Spain.)

Cuban TV programming is limited in terms of resources and cannot keep up with the staggering quantity, variety or production values of U.S. fare. Even more significant is that *paquete* consumers can have their weekly download tailored to their preferences: some might prefer documentaries and music, others soap operas or cartoons, and that's what they will get, often delivered to their door. Some in the government have criticized the contents of the package, saying that it is filled with mindless entertainment, excessive violence, and extols materialism and consumerism. But the government is also cognizant that ordinary Cubans need a little escapist entertainment under socialism as well. Abel Prieto, the former minister of culture, blames Cuba's own media and cultural institutions for the popularity of the package. He sees the package as a challenge to Cuba's state media: either improve the quality of your programming or face irrelevance.

Satellite dishes are outlawed in Cuba, but many Cubans have found ways to hide or disguise them (for example, in water storage units). So again, here is another kind of grey area where Cubans find that 'Todo está prohibido pero vale todo' (Everything is prohibited, but anything goes). It is in this gap between what is permissible versus what is done that the famous Cuban *invento* intervenes. And the *paquete*, as well as providing entertainment and access to otherwise difficult-to-find material, is also an economic engine providing a series of hackers, programmers, delivery people and so forth with employment. Of course, they are flagrantly defying copyright laws in the materials they distribute, but there is no one in Cuba to go after them. The *paquete* popularity seems to have diminished the need for satellite dishes since it provides much of what a dish was offering.

Final Thoughts on Cuba's Future: A Vignette and a Response

The 20 April 2015 cover of the *New Yorker* by Bruce McCall shows a family – presumably tourists – in a 1950s pink Cadillac on a road up on a hill. There are three signs with directions, one to

Lanskyland, the second to Animatronic Che, the third to the home of Desi Arnaz. To the right of the road are a couple of stands, one for Kiddie Habanos, the other for Soviet Souvenirs (facsimile missiles on sale for $1). To the left of the road a billboard announces Porky's Cove (formerly the Bay of Pigs); there is a pig wearing a beret and smoking a cigar and a greeting (Vets Welcome). In front of the billboard is a beaten-up tow truck hauling a Soviet Lada with a police insignia on the door. On the top of the sign are intertwined U.S. and Cuban flags and, above it, a sign that reads Castro Cola. In the distance you see a highway, with a beach resort to the left, palm trees dotting the landscape and, very far off in the distance, the ever-ubiquitous McDonald's arch. Clearly the cover is meant to be ironic: how the U.S. envisions a future Cuba that is tourist-friendly and 'open for business'. All that is missing are the *jineteras*, the old black women dressed as *santeras* with huge cigars, a musical trio playing 'Chan Chan', and photographers taking shots of ruined buildings. Nonetheless, McCall's cover captures some of the fantasies of 'domesticating' Cuba: missiles that aren't dangerous, but souvenirs; turning anti-imperialism into a bland tourist site devoid of history (Porky's Cove); the desire for commodification (Castro Cola, McDonald's, Kiddie Habanos); and treating the island as a theme park (Lanksyland, Animatronic Che). Can Cuba be turned into a commodity? Is its history fated to become a theme park, another postmodern simulation that would make Baudrillard sigh?

My answer to the *New Yorker* cover would be two songs by *Nueva Trova* singers Silvio Rodríguez and Frank Delgado, and their insights concerning Cuba's future dilemmas. On a 1996 Silvio album there is a song called 'El reino de todavía' (The realm of not yet). Dedicated to singer Amaury Pérez, the song warns of the dangers of globalization and capitalism:

> No one knows what communism is
> and that can be grist for censors.

> No one knows what communism is
> and that can be grist for fortune (joy).[6]

Silvio's title is revealing as well, since 'the realm of not yet' is a reference to Communism. While not everyone will agree with his statement about what Communism really is, we can read it more as a question about a future that is not a blueprint turned straitjacket, but one that is open-ended and negotiable. In that regard the future will not be grist for censors, but for good fortune, possibly joy. The word Silvio uses in Spanish is *ventura*, which conjures up good fortune not only as luck but as material abundance and adventure. What Silvio seems to suggest is that for Cuba (and perhaps other societies that seek to build socialism), new attempts to define and build Communism still lie ahead and that we don't have all the answers. He is cautiously optimistic: another verse has the words, 'One has to grow up dancing to sorrow', a very Cuban sentiment indeed.

Frank Delgado's album *En Directo* has a wonderfully wry song called 'Letter from a Cuban Child to Harry Potter'.

> Harry Potter doesn't have any problems
> a little magic and there's a banquet
> [...]
> Harry Potter you can be entirely sure
> that my *nganga* can face off with your magic wand and win
> [...]
>
> Hey, Harry Potter,
> Come some day to Havana
> Hey, Harry Potter
> And learn a little Cuban magic.[7]

Delgado, with a unique sense of the absurdities of Cuban daily life, has defiantly confronted Harry Potter's magic with a dose of Cuban ingenuity, wit and local magic. The *nganga*, a reference to the

Afro-Cuban Palo tradition, of the cauldron that harbours an ancestral spirit that 'works' for the owner of the *nganga*. The *chibichana* is a makeshift rectangular wooden object with wheels that Cuban children use like a cart. Delgado's local references resonate not only with charm, but with a kind of non-Eurocentric audacity: Third World magic is a kind of resistance to underdevelopment, that of the First World a sort of cutesy wizardry. Cuban magic is not merely luck: you make your own magic; the *nganga* works for you and you have to feed it. It is thoroughly part of Cuban *invento*.

The songs by Silvio Rodríguez and Frank Delgado bring us back to our picaresque 'hero', Juan from *Juan of the Dead*, Marx, Maceo, Martí, Mama Kalunga, *Moyuba areo moyuba Orisa* (with the permission of the orishas) and the ancestral spirits: their presence not only haunts, but asks questions, challenges us to imagine things otherwise. Cuba will continue to surprise us, with or without the blessings of Marx and Babalú-Ayé; both its history and culture are a 'river that never rests'.

References

Introduction

1 Alexei Yurchak, *Everything Was Forever, Until it Was No More: The Last Soviet Generation* (Princeton, NJ, 2005), p. 5.
2 Alan West, *Tropics of History: Cuba Imagined* (Westport, CT, 1997), p. 5.
3 Ibid., p. 2.

1 Building a New Cultural Foundation (1898–1930)

1 Louis A. Pérez Jr, *Cuba between Reform and Revolution* (New York, 2006), p. 146.
2 Rafael Rojas, *Essays in Cuban Intellectual History* (New York, 2008), p. 12.
3 Julián del Casal, *Obra poética* (Havana, 1982), p. 201.
4 Ibid., p. 237.
5 José Lezama Lima, *Analecta del reloj* (Havana, 2010), p. 55.
6 Scholars such as Emilo Bejel, Oscar Montero and Francisco Morán have offered queer readings of Casal. Casal is considered a major poet of Cuba's nineteenth century, even by critics who are not sympathetic to queer readings of his work.
7 Rafael Rojas, *Motivos de Anteo, patria y nación en la historia intelectual de Cuba* (Madrid, 2008), p. 146.
8 Ibid., p. 139.
9 Melissa Blanco Borelli, 'Sexuality: The Mulata Figure in the Cuban Imaginary', in *Cuba*, ed. Alan West-Durán, 2 vols (Farmington Hills, MI, 2012), vol. II, p. 883.
10 Miguel Matamoros, in Tony Évora, *Orígenes de la música cubana* (Madrid, 1997), p. 280.
11 Alan West, *Tropics of History* (Westport, CT, 1997), p. 142.
12 Martí, in Jorge Ibarra, *Un análisis psicosocial del cubano 1898–1925* (Havana, 1985), p. 30.

13 Byrne, in *Poesía cubana del siglo XX*, ed. Jesús Barquet and Norberto Codina (Mexico, 2002), p. 42.

14 Poveda, in Ibarra, *Un análisis psicosocial del cubano*, p. 30.

15 Poveda, in Rojas, *Motivos de Anteo*, p. 147.

16 José Enrique Varona, *Textos escogidos* (Mexico, 1999), p. 144.

17 Ibid., pp. 146, 156.

18 Michael Walzer, *The Company of Critics* (New York, 2002), pp. xiv–xviii.

19 Alan West-Durán, 'Rap's Diasporic Dialogues', *Journal of Popular Music Studies*, XVI/1 (2004), p. 20.

20 Jorge Mañach, *Ensayos* (Havana, 1999), p. 51.

21 Ibid., p. 65.

22 Ibid., p. 83.

23 Edna Rodríguez-Mangual, *Lydia Cabrera and the Construction of Afro-Cuban Identity* (Chapel Hill, NC, 2004), p. 20.

24 Lydia Cabrera, *El Monte* (Miami, FL, 1992), p. 13.

25 Ibid.

26 Juan Mesa Díaz, 'The Religious System of Ocha-Ifá', in *Music in Latin America and the Caribbean: Performing the Caribbean Experience*, vol. II, ed. Malena Kuss (Austin, TX, 2007), p. 58.

27 Ibid., p. 59.

28 Ibid., p. 58.

29 Ocha'ni Lele, *Sacrificial Ceremonies of Santería: A Complete Guide to Rituals and Practices* (Rochester, VT, 2012), p. 13.

30 Alan West-Durán, 'Faith: Regla de Ocha', in *Cuba*, ed. Alan West-Durán, 2 vols (Farmington Hills, MI, 2012), vol. I, p. 298.

31 Ocha'ni Lele, *The Secrets of Afro-Cuban Divination* (Rochester, VT, 2010), p. 91.

32 Natalia Bolívar, 'Faith: Reglas de Palo', ibid., vol. I, p. 304.

33 Cabrera, *El Monte*, p. 131.

34 Stephan Palmié, *Wizards and Scientists: Explorations in Afro-Cuban Modernity and Tradition* (Durham, NC, 2002), p. 171.

35 Ibid., p. 164.

36 Ibid., p. 167.

37 Ibid., p. 179.

38 Ibid., p. 178.

39 Robert Farris Thompson, *Flash of the Spirit* (New York, 1983), p. 229.

40 David Brown, *The Light Inside: Abakuá Society Arts and Culture in Cuban Cultural History* (Washington, DC, 2003), p. 7.

41 Jorge and Isabel Castellanos, *Cultura Afrocubana, las religions y las lenguas*, vol. III (Miami, FL, 1992), p. 212.

42 Brown, *The Light Inside*, pl. 1, after p. 126.

43 Ibid., p. 5.

44 Robert Farris Thompson, *Face of the Gods* (New York, 1993), p. 14.

45 Sosa Rodríguez, cited in Brown, *The Light Inside*, p. 7.

46 See www.ayonbelkis.cult.cu, accessed 15 July 2015.

47 Eloy Machado, in *AfroCuba: An Anthology of Cuban Writing on Race, Politics, and Culture*, ed. Pedro Peréz Sarduy and Jean Stubbs (Melbourne, 1993), p. 158.

48 Ibid.

49 Mercedes Cros Sandoval, *Worldview, the Orichas, and Santería: Africa to Cuba and Beyond* (Gainesville, FL, 2009), p. 199.

50 Los Van Van, *The Legendary Los Van Van: 30 Years of Cuba's Greatest Dance Band* (New York, 1999), p. 94.

51 Adrián de Souza Hernández, *Ifá Santa Palabra: La ética del corazón* (Havana, 2003), p. 21.

2 Curses, Myths and Longing (1930–1959)

1   Robert Whitney, 'The Constitution of 1940', in *Cuba*, ed. Alan West-Durán, 2 vols (Farmington Hills, MI, 2012), vol. I, p. 610.

2   Walker Evans, *Cuba* (Los Angeles, CA, 2001), pp. 21, 24 and pls 15, 23, 25, 32.

3   Alan West, *Tropics of History: Cuba Imagined* (Westport, CT, 1997), p. 110.

4   Alessandra Riccio, cited in Jesús Barquet, *Consagración de La Habana* (Miami, FL, 1992), p. 33.

5   José Lezama Lima, *La expresión Americana* (Mexico City, 1993), p. 49.

6   José Lezama Lima, *Poesías completas, 1* (Madrid, 1988), p. 87; Virgilio Piñera, *La isla en peso* (Barcelona, 2000), p. 37.

7   Piñera, *La isla en peso*, pp. 45, 46.

8   José Rodriguez Feo, ed., *Ciclón*, 5 (1955), p. 1.

9   Witold Gombrowicz, 'Contra los poetas', ibid., p. 14.

10 Dulce María Loynaz, cited in West, *Tropics of History*, p. 97.

11 Ibid., p. 87.

12 Antoni Kapcia, *Havana: The Making of Cuban Culture* (New York, 2005), p. 103.

13 Gustavo Pérez-Firmat, *Life on the Hyphen: The Cuban-American Way* (Austin, TX, 1995), p. 25.

14 Ibid., p. 27.

15 Ibid., p. 52.

16 Nancy Morejón, in *AfroCuba: An Anthology of Cuban Writing on Race, Politics, and Culture*, ed. Perez Sarduy and Jean Stubbs (Melbourne, 1993), p. 229.

17 Velia Cecilia Bobes, *Los Laberintos de la imaginación: repertorio simbólico, identidades y actores del cambio social en Cuba* (Mexico City, 2000), p. 82.

18 Fidel Castro, in *The Fidel Castro Reader*, ed. David Deutschmann and Deborah Shnookal (Melbourne, 2007), p. 105.

19 Nicola Miller, 'The Absolution of History: Uses of the Past in Castro's Cuba', *Journal of Contemporary History*, XXXVIII/1 (2003), p. 147.

20 Hayden White, *Metahistory: The Historical Imagination in Nineteenth-century Europe* (Baltimore, MD, 1994), p. 10.

21 Ibid., p. 9.

22 Ibid., p. 9.

23 Ibid., p. 284.

24 Ibid., p. 316.

25 Leonardo Padura, *Havana Fever* (London, 2010), pp. 158, 159.

26 Ibid., p. 160.

27 Ibid., pp. 160–61.

3 A Revolution in Culture (1959–1980)

1 Lenin, cited in Susan Buck-Morss, *Dreamworld and Catastrophe: The Passing of Mass Utopia in East and West* (Cambridge, MA, 2000), p. 42.

2 William Luis, *Lunes de la Revolución: literatura y cultura en los primeros años de la Revolución Cubana* (Madrid, 2003), pp. 19–55.

3 Boris Groys, *The Total Art of Stalinism, Avant-garde, Aesthetic Dictatorship, and Beyond* (London, 2011), p. 3.

4 José Lezama Lima, cited in Duanel Díaz, *Palabras del trasfondo: intelectuales, literatura e ideología en la Revolución Cubana* (Madrid, 2009), p. 14.

5 Angel Augier, cited ibid., p. 53.

6 Eliseo Diego, cited ibid., p. 90.

7 Kepa Artaraz, *Cuba and Western Intellectuals Since 1959* (New York, 2009), pp. 157–61.

8 Ibid., p. 171.

9 Michel Löwy, *The Marxism of Che Guevara* (Lanham, MD, 2007), p. xxxi.

10 Che Guevara, in *Che Guevara Reader: Writings on Politics and Revolution*, ed. David Deutschmann (Melbourne, 2003), p. 224.

11 Jean-Paul Sartre, *Sartre en Cuba* (Havana, 1961), p. 45.

12 Herbert Marcuse, *The Aesthetic Dimension: A Critique of Marxist Aesthetics* (Boston, MA, 1978), pp. xii–xiii.

13 Fidel Castro, cited in K. S. Karol, *Guerrillas in Power: The Course of the Cuban Revolution* (New York, 1970), p. 394.

14 Fidel Castro, in *The Fidel Castro Reader*, ed. David Deutschmann and Deborah Shnookal (Melbourne, 2007), pp. 220–21.

15 Ibid., p. 239.

16 Casa de las Américas, cited by John Beverley, *Testimonio on the Politics of Truth* (Minneapolis, MN, 2004), p. 98, n. 6.

17 Ibid., p. 32.

18 For a collection of Padilla's poetry see Heberto Padilla, *A Fountain, A House, A Stone* (New York, 1991).

19 Sherrill Grace, ed., *Strange Comfort: Essays on the Work of Malcolm Lowry* (Vancouver, 2009), p. xi.

20 See Lourdes Casal, *El caso Padilla: Literatura y Revolución en Cuba Documentos* (Miami, 1971), for documents, speeches, pen letters and the like.

21 Silvio Rodríguez, *Silvio poeta*, ed. Suyín Morales Alemañy (Havana, 2008), p. 90.

22 Tomás Gutiérrez Alea, in Michael Chanan, ed., *Memories of Underdevelopment* (New Brunswick, NJ, 1990), p. 72.

23 Ibid., p. 73.

24 Ibid., p. 75.

25 Persephone Braham, *Crimes Against the State, Crimes Against Persons: Detective Fiction in Cuba and Mexico* (Minneapolis, MN, 2004), p. 29.

26 Ernest Mandel, 'A Marxist Interpretation of the Crime Story', in *Detective Fiction: A Collection of Critical Essays*, ed. Robin Winks (Woodstock, VT, 1988), p. 215.

27 Braham, *Crimes Against the State, Crimes Against Persons*, p. 29.

28 Ibid., p. 32.

29 Leonardo Padura, ibid., p. 54.

30 Virgilio Piñera as cited in Leonardo Padura, *Havana Red* (London, 2005), p. ix.

31 Ibid., p. 30.

32 Virgilio Piñera, cited by Guillermo Cabrera Infante, *Mea Cuba* (Madrid, 1992), p. 319.

33 Oscar Montero, 'The Queer Theories of Severo Sarduy', in *Severo Sarduy Obra Completa, Tomo II*, ed. Gustavo Guerrero and François Wahl (Madrid, 1999), pp. 1790, 1792.

34 Alan West, *Tropics of History: Cuba Imagined* (Westport, CT, 1997), p. 151.

35 Helen Oakley, *From Revolution to Migration: A Study of Contemporary Cuban and Cuban-American Crime Fiction* (Bern, 2012), p. 84.
36 Carolina García-Aguilera, *Bloody Waters* (New York, 1996), p. 32.
37 Ibid., p. 79.
38 Carolina García-Aguilera, *A Miracle in Paradise* (New York, 1999), p. 98.

4 From Mariel to the Special Period (1980–1990)

1 Radio and TV Martí were funded by the U.S. government and run by anti-Castro exiles. The Cuban government considered them hostile acts of counter-revolutionary propaganda; especially since they used Martí's name for 'anti-Cuban' activities.
2 Reinaldo Arenas, *Before Night Falls* (New York, 1993), p. 90.
3 Reinaldo Arenas, *The Color of Summer* (New York, 2000), p. 254.
4 Ana Mendieta, cited in Jane Blocker, *Where is Ana Mendieta? Identity, Performativity, and Exile* (Durham, NC, 1999), p. 34.
5 José R. Oliver, *Caciques and Cemí Idols* (Tuscaloosa, AL, 2009), p. 59.
6 Gaston Bachelard, *Water and Dreams* (Dallas, TX, 1983), p. 15.
7 Chris Fowler, *The Archeology of Personhood: An Archeological Approach* (London, 2004), p. 8.
8 Ibid.
9 Ibid., p. 9.
10 Blocker, *Where is Ana Mendieta?*, p. 3.
11 Rachel Weiss, 'Visual Arts: The Revolutionary Period', in *Cuba*, ed. Alan West-Durán, 2 vols (Farmington Hills, MI, 2012), vol. II, p. 1037.
12 Flavio Garciandía, in *I Insulted Flavio Garciandía in Havana*, ed. Flavio Garciandía and Cristina Vives (Milan, 2009), pp. 235–51.
13 Milan Kundera, *The Unbearable Lightness of Being* (New York, 1984), p. 257.
14 Ibid., pp. 248–9.
15 Ibid., p. 249.
16 Ibid., p. 251.
17 Matei Calinescu, *Five Faces of Modernity* (Durham, NC, 1987), pp. 228–9.
18 Gillo Dorfles, *Kitsch* (New York, 1968), p. 113.
19 Régis Debray, *Critique of Political Reason* (London, 1983), p. 9.
20 Ibid., pp. 9, 10.
21 For an anthology of Delgado's performances from 1990 to 2011, see www.youtube.com/watch?v=L_GwiFrhwXg, accessed 10 July 2016.

5 From the Special Period to Obama (1990–2014)

1 Caridad Cumaná, ed., *My Havana: The Musical City of Carlos Varela* (Toronto, 2014), p. 211.
2 Archibald Ritter, in Archibald Ritter, ed., *The Cuban Economy* (Pittsburgh, PA, 2004), pp. 7–22.
3 Carlos Varela, in Cumaná, *My Havana*, p. 211.
4 Gema y Pavel, *Art Bembé* (booklet accompanying CD, my translation) (Madrid, 1997), n.p.
5 Pedro Juan Gutiérrez, *Dirty Havana Trilogy* (New York, 2002), pp. 25–6.
6 Ibid., p. 108.
7 Svetlana Boym, *The Future of Nostalgia* (New York, 2002), p. xviii.
8 Antonio José Ponte, in Borchmeyer's film, *Havana: The New Art of Making Ruins*, 85 mins, colour (Munich, 2007).
9 Ibid.
10 Odette Casamayor, cited in Esther Whitfield, *Cuban Currency: The Dollar and Special Period Fiction* (Minneapolis, MN, 2008), p. 129.
11 Boym, *The Future of Nostalgia*, p. xviii.
12 Carlos Garaicoa, *Continuity of Somebody's Architecture* (Kassel, 2002), p. 17.
13 Jean Starobinski, *Jean-Jacques Rousseau: Transparency and Obstruction* (Chicago, IL, 1988), p. xxi. The quote is from Rousseau's *La Nouvelle Héloise*.
14 Byung-Chul Han, *The Transparent Society* (Stanford, CA, 2015), p. 13.
15 Garaicoa, *Continuity of Somebody's Architecture*, p. 9.
16 Michel Foucault, cited in Giorgio Agamben, *What is an Apparatus?* (Stanford, CA, 2009), p. 2.
17 Ibid., p. 14.
18 Carlos Garaicoa, in Enrique Juncosa, *Garaicoa* (Dublin, 2010), p. 207.
19 See Helaine Posner, ed., *Tania Bruguera: On the Political Imaginary* (Milan, 2009).
20 Tania Bruguera, ibid., pp. 64–5.
21 Gerardo Mosquera, ibid., p. 23.
22 Ibid., p. 23.
23 Ibid., p. 24.
24 The event can be viewed at https://vimeo.com/21394727, accessed 10 July 2016.
25 Hannah Ellis Petersen, 'The Woman Trying to Change Cuba's Cultural Landscape – and Stay out of Jail', *The Guardian* (10 April 2016), www.theguardian.com.

26 Richard Curt Kraus, *The Party and the Arty in China* (Lanham, MD, 2004), p. 1.

27 Ibid.

28 Ibid., pp. 1–2.

29 Alan West-Durán, 'Rap's Diasporic Dialogues', *Journal of Popular Music Studies*, XVI/1 (2004), p. 4.

30 Soandry del Río, in *Encuentro de Cultura Cubana*, 53–4 (2009), p. 99 (my translation).

31 Ibid., p. 101.

32 Ibid., p. 103.

33 Gilles Deleuze and Félix Guattari, *Anti-Oedipus, Capitalism and Schizophrenia*, trans. Robert Hurley, Mark Seem and Helen R. Lane (Minneapolis, MN, 1983), p. 335.

34 Todd Ramón Ochoa, *Society of the Dead: Quita Manaquita and Palo Praise in Cuba* (Berkeley, CA, 2010), p. 21.

35 Ibid., p. 15.

36 Carlos Marx, *El 18 Brumario de Luis Bonaparte* (Havana, 1974), pp. 9–10 (my translation).

37 Ibid., p. 9.

38 Erick J. Mota, 'That Zombie is for Fidel', in *Cuba in Splinters: Eleven Stories from the New Cuba*, ed. Pardo Lazo and Orlando Luis (New York, 2014), p. 149.

39 Chris Boehm, 'Apocalyptic Utopia: The Zombie and the (r)Evolution of Subjectivity', in *We're All Infected: Essays on the 'Walking Dead' and the Fate of the Human*, ed. Kettley Dawn (Jefferson, NC, 2014), pp. 133–6.

40 Beisecker, David, 'Afterward: By Gone Days', ibid., p. 209.

41 Alain Badiou, *Ethics: An Essay on the Understanding of Evil* (London, 2002), p. 43.

42 Boehm, 'Apocalyptic Utopia', p. 141.

6 Concluding Remarks (2014–2016)

1 Fidel Castro, in *Granma* (28 March 2016), p. 1.

2 Fidel Castro, in *Granma* (19 April 2016), p. 1.

3 Much of what follows is indebted to Harlan Abrahams and Arturo López-Levy, *Raúl Castro and the New Cuba* (Jefferson, NC, 2011), pp. 177–88. The analysis is mine.

4 Raúl Castro, cited in Carmelo Mesa-Lago, *Cuba en la era de Raúl Castro* (Madrid, 2012), p. 7.

5 For an analysis of the Scandinavian model, see *The Economist*

(2–8 February 2013), where modifications to the welfare-state model have allowed for innovation that is fiscally and socially responsible.

6 Silvio Rodríguez, *Dominguez* (Havana, 1996). Transcribed (my translation).

7 Frank Delgado, *En directo* (2010). Transcribed (my translation).

Bibliography

Abrahams, Harlan, and Arturo López-Levy, *Raúl Castro and the New Cuba* (Jefferson, NC, 2011)

Agamben, Giorgio, *What is an Apparatus?* (Stanford, CA, 2009)

Arenas, Reinaldo, *Before Night Falls* (New York, 1993)

——, *The Color of Summer* (New York, 2000)

——, *Mona and Other Tales* (New York, 2001)

Artaraz, Kepa, *Cuba and Western Intellectuals Since 1959* (New York, 2009)

Bachelard, Gaston, *Water and Dreams* (Dallas, TX, 1983)

Badiou, Alain, *Ethics: An Essay on the Understanding of Evil* (London, 2002)

Barquet, Jesús, *Consagración de La Habana* (Miami, FL, 1992)

——, and Norberto Codina, eds, *Poesía cubana del siglo XX* (Mexico, 2002)

Beisecker, David, 'Afterward: By Gone Days', in *We're All Infected: Essays on the 'Walking Dead' and the Fate of the Human*, ed. Kettley Dawn (Jefferson, NC, 2014)

Beverley, John, *Testimonio on the Politics of Truth* (Minneapolis, MN, 2004)

Blanco Borelli, Melissa, 'Sexuality: The Mulata Figure in the Cuban Imaginary', in *Cuba*, ed. Alan West-Durán, 2 vols (Farmington Hills, MI, 2012), vol. II, pp. 882–4

Blocker, Jane, *Where is Ana Mendieta? Identity, Performativity, and Exile* (Durham, NC, 1999)

Bobes, Velia Cecilia, *Los Laberintos de la imaginación: repertorio simbólico, identidades y actores del cambio social en Cuba* (Mexico, 2000)

Boehm, Chris, 'Apocalyptic Utopia: The Zombie and the (r)Evolution of Subjectivity', in *We're All Infected: Essays on the 'Walking Dead' and the Fate of the Human*, ed. Kettley Dawn (Jefferson, NC, 2014)

Bolívar, Natalia, 'Faiths: Reglas de Palo', in *Cuba*, ed. Alan West-Durán, 2 vols (Farmington Hills, MI, 2012), vol. I, pp. 304–8

Borchmey er, Florian, and Matthias Hentschler, *Havana: The New Art of Making Ruins*, 85 mins, colour (Munich, 2007)

Boym, Svetlana, *The Future of Nostalgia* (New York, 2002)

Braham, Persephone, *Crimes Against the State, Crimes Against Persons: Detective Fiction in Cuba and Mexico* (Minneapolis, MN, 2004)

Brown, David, *The Light Inside: Abakuá Society Arts and Cuban Cultural History* (Washington, DC, 2003)

Buck-Morss, Susan, *Dreamworld and Catastrophe: The Passing of Mass Utopia in East and West* (Cambridge, MA, 2000)

Cabrera, Lydia, *Anaforuana: Ritual y símbolos de la iniciación en la sociedad secreta Abakuá* (Madrid, 1975)

—, *El Monte* [1954] (Miami, FL, 1992)

Cabrera Infante, Guillermo, *Mea Cuba* (Madrid, 1992)

Calinescu, Matei, *Five Faces of Modernity* (Durham, NC, 1987)

Casal, Julián del, *Obra poética* (Havana, 1982)

Casal, Lourdes, *El caso Padilla: Literatura y Revolución en Cuba Documentos* (Miami, FL, 1971)

Castellanos, Jorge and Isabel, *Cultura Afrocubana, las religiones y las lenguas*, vol. III (Miami, FL, 1992)

Chanan, Michael, ed., *Memories of Underdevelopment* (New Brunswick, NJ, 1990)

Cros Sandoval, Mercedes, *Worldview, the Orichas, and Santería: Africa to Cuba and Beyond* (Gainesville, FL, 2009)

Cumaná, Caridad, ed., *My Havana: The Musical City of Carlos Varela* (Toronto, 2014)

Debray, Régis, *Critique of Political Reason* (London, 1983)

Deleuze, Gilles, and Félix Guattari, *Anti-Oedipus, Capitalism and Schizophrenia*, trans. Robert Hurley, Mark Seem and Helen R. Lane (Minneapolis, MN, 1983)

Delgado, Frank, *En directo* (2010)

Deutschmann, David, ed., *Che Guevara Reader: Writings on Politics and Revolution* (Melbourne, 2003)

—, and Deborah Shnookal, eds, *The Fidel Castro Reader* (Melbourne, 2007)

Díaz, Duanel, *Palabras del trasfondo: intelectuales, literatura e ideología en la Revolución Cubana* (Madrid, 2009)

Dorfles, Gillo, *Kitsch* (New York, 1968)

Ducasses Manzano, Karel, *Zona de silencio*, 38 mins, colour (Havana, 2007)

Evans, Walker, *Cuba* [1933] (Los Angeles, CA, 2001)

Évora, Tony, *Orígenes de la música cubana* (Madrid, 1997)

Fernández Olmos, M., and L. Paravisini-Gebert, eds, *Creole Religions of the Caribbean: An Introduction from Vodou and Santería to Obeah and Espiritismo* (New York, 2003)

Fowler, Chris, *The Archeology of Personhood: An Archeological Approach* (London, 2004)

Garaicoa, Carlos, *Continuity of Somebody's Architecture* (Kassel, 2002)

García-Aguilera, Carolina, *Bloody Waters* (New York, 1996)

—, *A Miracle in Paradise* (New York, 1999)

Garciandía, Flavio, and Cristina Vives, eds, *I Insulted Flavio Garciandía in Havana* (Milan, 2009)

Gema y Pavel, *Art Bembé* (booklet accompanying CD) (Madrid, 1997)

Gombrowicz, Witold, 'Contra los poetas', *Ciclón*, 5 (1955)

Grace, Sherrill, ed., *Strange Comfort: Essays on the Work of Malcolm Lowry* (Vancouver, 2009)

Groys, Boris, *The Total Art of Stalinism: Avant-garde, Aesthetic Dictatorship, and Beyond* (London, 2011)

Guerra, Lillian, *The Myth of José Martí: Conflicting Nationalisms in Early Twentieth Century Cuba* (Chapel Hill, NC, 2005)

Gutiérrez Alea, T., and J. C. Tabío, *Strawberry and Chocolate*, 111 mins, colour (Havana, 1993)

Gutiérrez, Pedro Juan, *Dirty Havana Trilogy* (New York, 2002)

Han, Byung-Chul, *The Transparent Society* (Stanford, CA, 2015)

Ibarra, Jorge, *Un análisis psicosocial del cubano 1898–1925* (Havana, 1985)

Juncosa, Enrique, *Garaicoa* (Dublin, 2010)

Kapcia, Antoni, *Havana: The Making of Cuban Culture* (New York, 2005)

Karol, K. S., *Guerrillas in Power: The Course of the Cuban Revolution* (New York, 1970)

Kraus, Richard Curt, *The Party and the Arty in China* (Lanham, MD, 2004)

Kundera, Milan, *The Unbearable Lightness of Being* (New York, 1984)

Lele, Ocha'ni, *Sacrificial Ceremonies of Santería: A Complete Guide to the Rituals and Practices* (Rochester, VT, 2012)

—, *The Secrets of Afro-Cuban Divination* (Rochester, VT, 2010)

Lezama Lima, José, *Analecta del reloj* [1953] (Havana, 2010)

—, *La expresión Americana* [1957] (Mexico, 1993)

—, *Poesías completas, I* (Madrid, 1988)

Löwy, Michel, *The Marxism of Che Guevara*, 2nd edn (Lanham, MD, 2007)

Luis, William, *Lunes de Revolución: literatura y cultura en los primeros años de la Revolución Cubana* (Madrid, 2003)

Mañach, Jorge, *Ensayos* (Havana, 1999)

Mandel, Ernest, 'A Marxist Interpretation of the Crime Story', in *Detective Fiction: A Collection of Critical Essays*, ed. Robin Winks (Woodstock, VT, 1988)

Marcuse, Herbert, *The Aesthetic Dimension: A Critique of Marxist Aesthetics* (Boston, MA, 1978)

Marx, Carlos, *El 18 Brumario de Luis Bonaparte* (Havana, 1974)

Mesa Díaz, Juan, 'The Religious System of Ocha-Ifá', in *Music in Latin America and the Caribbean: Performing the Caribbean Experience*, vol. II, ed. Malena Kuss (Austin, TX, 2007)

Mesa-Lago, Carmelo, *Cuba en la era de Raúl Castro* (Madrid, 2012)

Miller, Nicola, 'The Absolution of History: Uses of the Past in Castro's Cuba', *Journal of Contemporary History*, XXXVIII/1 (2003), pp. 147–62

Montero, Oscar, 'The Queer Theories of Severo Sarduy', in *Severo Sarduy Obra Completa, Tomo II*, ed. Gustavo Guerrero and François Wahl (Madrid, 1999)

Moore, Robin, *Nationalizing Blackness* (Pittsburgh, PN, 1997)

Morán, Francisco, *Julián del Casal o los pliegues del deseo* (Madrid, 2008)

Mota, Erick J., 'That Zombie is for Fidel', in *Cuba in Splinters: Eleven Stories from the New Cuba*, ed. Pardo Lazo and Orlando Luis (New York, 2014)

Oakley, Helen, *From Revolution to Migration: A Study of Contemporary Cuban and Cuban-American Crime Fiction* (Bern, 2012)

Ochoa, Todd Ramón, *Society of the Dead: Quita Manaquita and Palo Praise in Cuba* (Berkeley, CA, 2010)

Oliver, José R., *Caciques and Cemí Idols* (Tuscaloosa, AL, 2009)

Ortiz, Fernando, *Cuban Counterpoint, Tobacco and Sugar* (Durham, NC, 2003)

Padilla, Heberto, *A Fountain, A House, A Stone* (New York, 1991)

Padura, Leonardo, *Havana Fever* (London, 2010)

—, *Havana Red* (London, 2005)

Palmié, Stephan, *Wizards and Scientists: Explorations in Afro-Cuban Modernity and Tradition* (Durham, NC, 2002)

Pérez, Fernando, *La vida es silbar* (Life is to Whistle), 105 mins, colour (Havana, 1998)

Perez, Louis A., Jr, *Cuba between Reform and Revolution* (New York, 2006)

Pérez-Firmat, Gustavo, *Life on the Hyphen: The Cuban-American Way* (Austin, TX, 1995)

Pérez Sarduy, Pedro, and Jean Stubbs, eds, *AfroCuba: An Anthology of Cuban Writing on Race, Politics, and Culture* (Melbourne, 1993)

Piñera, Virgilio, *La isla en peso* (Barcelona, 2000)

—, *Los siervos* (The Serfs), *Ciclón*, 6 (1955), pp. 9–29

—, *René's Flesh* [1952] (Boston, MA, 1989)

Posner, Helaine, ed., *Tania Bruguera: On the Political Imaginary* (Milan, 2009)

Río, Soandry del, 'Tengo' y 'Lágrimas Negras', *Encuentro de la Cultura Cubana*, 53–4 (2009), pp. 99–101

Ritter, Archibald, ed., *The Cuban Economy* (Pittsburgh, PA, 2004)

Rodríguez, Silvio, *Dominguez* (Havana, 1996)

—, *Silvio poeta*, ed. Suyín Morales Alemañy (Havana, 2008)

Rodríguez Feo, José, ed., *Ciclón*, 5 (1955)

Rodríguez-Mangual, Edna, *Lydia Cabrera and the Construction of Afro-Cuban Identity* (Chapel Hill, NC, 2004)

Rojas, Rafael, *Essays in Cuban Intellectual History* (New York, 2008)

—, *Motivos de Anteo: patria y nación en la historia intelectual de Cuba* (Madrid, 2008)

Rosenthal, Stephanie, ed., *Ana Mendieta: Traces* (London, 2013)

Sarduy, Severo, *From Cuba with a Song* (Los Angeles, CA, 1994)

Sartre, Jean-Paul, *Sartre en Cuba* (Havana, 1961)

Solás, Humberto, *Un hombre de éxito* (A Successful Man) (Havana, 1985)

Souza Hernández, Adrián de, *Ifá Santa Palabra: La ética del corazón* (Havana, 2003)

Starobinksi, Jean, *Jean-Jacques Rousseau: Transparency and Obstruction* (Chicago, IL, 1988)

Thompson, Robert Farris, *Face of the Gods* (New York, 1993)

—, *Flash of the Spirit* (New York, 1983)

Van Van, Los, *The Legendary Los Van Van: 30 Years of Cuba's Greatest Dance Band* (106-page booklet with lyrics in Spanish and English) (New York, 1999)

Varona, Enrique José, *Textos escogidos* (Mexico, 1999)

Walzer, Michael, *The Company of Critics* (New York, 2002)

Weiss, Rachel, 'Visual Arts: The Revolutionary Period', in *Cuba*, ed. Alan West-Durán, 2 vols (Farmington Hills, MI, 2012), vol. II, pp. 1033–8

West, Alan, *Tropics of History: Cuba Imagined* (Westport, CT, 1997)

West-Durán, Alan, 'Faith: Regla de Ocha', in *Cuba*, ed. Alan West-Durán, 2 vols (Farmington Hills, MI, 2012), vol. II, pp. 294–304

—, 'Rap's Diasporic Dialogues', *Journal of Popular Music Studies*, XVI/1 (2004), pp. 3–38

White, Hayden, *Metahistory: The Historical Imagination in Nineteenth-century Europe* [1974] (Baltimore, MD, 1994)

Whitfield, Esther, *Cuban Currency: The Dollar and Special Period Fiction* (Minneapolis, MN, 2008)

Whitney, Robert, 'The Constitution of 1940', in *Cuba*, ed. Alan West-Durán, 2 vols (Farmington Hills, MI, 2012), vol. I, pp. 62–6

Yoss (José Miguel Sánchez Gómez), *A Planet for Rent* (New York, 2015)

Yurchak, Alexei, *Everything Was Forever, Until It Was No More: The Last Soviet Generation* (Princeton, NJ, 2005)

Acknowledgements

Thanks to Frank Menchaca, who over many years has supported and had faith in my scholarship, and to Antonio Kapcia who indirectly led me to Reaktion Books.

Many thanks to friends and colleagues over the years for their insight and advice: Víctor Fowler, César Salgado, Juan Mesa and my co-conspirators at Cuba Counterpoints website: Ariana Hernández-Reguant, Jackie Loss and Esther Whitfield, among others.

Thanks to Ben Hayes and Jess Chandler for their patience and hard work on the manuscript.

Greatest of thanks to Ester Shapiro, always my best and most unsparing editor, as well as for being a selfless companion in life. Aché for you all!

Index